INDIA

Economic Resource Base
and
Contemporary Political Patterns

Poverty is the most degrading of human existence—an intensely moral question. Growth by itself does not end poverty, it is the manner in which we plan to grow that matters.... We do still have a long way to go, and the removal of poverty has to be the main plank of all our future planning.

—Indira Gandhi

INDIA
Economic Resource Base and Contemporary Political Patterns

B.L. SUKHWAL

ENVOY PRESS New York

INDIA: Economic Resource Base And
Contemporary Political Patterns

© 1987 B.L. Sukhwal
Library of Congress Catalog Card LC   86-81410
ISBN 0-938719-13-0

First Edition 1987

This edition is copyright under the Berne Convention. All rights are reserved. Apart from any fair dealing for the purpose of private study, research, criticism or review as permitted under the Copyright Act 1956, no part of this publication may be reproduced, stored in a retrieval system, or transmitted in any form or by any means whatsoever, without the prior permission of the copyright owner.

Envoy Press, Inc. 141 East
44th Street, New York. NY 10017, USA.

PRINTED IN INDIA

Preface

THE real political strength of a nation state lies in its natural resource base that forms the physical foundation for its industries and other economic activities. The proper utilization and management of natural resources, as well as conservation, are the cornerstones for the economic and political viability of a nation state. The unequal distribution of economic resources in various regions brings discontent among the masses and disparity among various groups. An elected democratic government has to satisfy every group of the society, based on economic differences, linguistic criterion, cultural heritage, social norms, political affiliations, and regional variations. The elected officials have to be accountable to all sections of the society, not every five years (national elections are held every five years), but constantly. The Opposition parties in India usually act as spoilers, rather than providing constructive criticism of the government. Unnecessary criticism and disruption of government affairs through slogan mongering and rioting by the Opposition make things worse for the general public. The Opposition should extend cooperation and alternative plans for a smooth working of the democracy. The government, on the other hand, should consult the Opposition on important issues rather than stifle the Opposition. India has chosen to solve all her problems through a parliamentary democracy, which might take a longer time to solve all the problems, but may prevent adoption of authoritarian or dictatorial methods of governing.

This book is written on the basic thoughts outlined in the preceding paragraph. Chapter 1 introduces the subject of the economic resource base that affects the political patterns, as well as the political decisions affecting the resource utilization. Chapter 2 discusses the agricultural resource base and its impact on the economy of India. The country's economy is primarily agricultural and political behaviour of the voting public depends upon the quality and quantity of the harvest. If the crop fails, which is quite normal in India, the public blames the government and incumbent politicians lose their elections. Chapter 3 deals with water resources and development strategy which are the keys for agricultural and industrial development. A common saying in India, that water is more important than land, proves valid. Chapter 4 evaluates the planning and development of mineral, fuel and industrial resources. India has built an enormous industrial base through the development of mineral and fuel resources, and through establishing industrial plants in the public and private sectors. The building of this basic infrastructure was essential to raise the standard of living and to bridge the gap between the rich and the poor.

Transportation, communication and trade have been discussed in Chapter 5. Transportation and communications are the arteries to feed raw materials to the industrial plants and finished goods to market. Unfavourable balance of trade has to be dealt with through increasing export of industrial goods and curbing importance of high price technical goods. The foreign aid should be utilized to gain maximum benefit of every dollar acquired through loan or assistance. India's greatest problem is its population explosion, which is dealt with in Chapter 6. The gains attained in the economic sphere were negated by the rapid growth of population. Nearly half of the population is below nineteen years of age, and when this population reaches reproductive age, how a country such as India will cope with this expansion is unknown. India is already overcrowded. Thus, all aspects of the population increase have been analyzed in this chapter. The concluding chapter summarizes the book with prognostications of future emerging patterns. This book will be able to serve university- and college-level students of economics, economic and political geography, and resource management, as well as professionals in these fields. The author would appreciate any creative suggestions extended to him by the readers. Geographers in India and foreign countries have failed to evaluate the resource base and its impacat on the political behaviour of the country as well as the impact of political decisions on economic development. Therefore this book may fill an existing gap in the geographical literature.

University of Wisconsin
Platteville, Wisconsin 53818

B.L. SUKHWAL

The boundaries of all maps in this book are based on *India: A Reference Annual, 1983.* Sterling Publishers Private Limited has obtained permission from the Survey of India to publish these maps while getting approval of my book *Modern Political Geography of India.*

Contents

Preface   v
List of Figures & Tables   viii

Chapter

1. Introduction   1
2. Agricultural Resources   16

    Climatic conditions and agriculture, Land reforms and land legislations, Water supply, irrigation and agriculture, Fertilizers and crop productivity, Crops, crop productions and crop regions, Strategy for self-sufficiency in food production

3. Water Resources and Development Strategy   44

    Physical factors, Cultural factors, International river water disputes, Interstate rivers, Interstate river water disputes

4. Planning and Development of Mineral, Fuel and Industrial Resources   82

    Mineral resources, Fuel and power resources, Atomic power, Solar energy, Other resources, Industrial resources, development and distribution

5. Transport, Communication and Trade   135

    Transportation and communication, Foreign trade

6. Impact of Population Growth on the Economy   155
7. Conclusions   171

Potscript   178
Bibliography   189
Index   193

List of Figures

Number

1. India: Administrative Divisions — 3
2. India: Variability of Rainfall — 19
3. India: Average Annual Rainfall — 21
4. India: Major Crop Regions — 34
5. India: River Systems — 55
6. Cauvery River Basin — 77
7. India: Mineral Resources — 85
8. The Pattern of Future All-India Power Grid — 95
9. India: Oil Exploration Regions — 98
10. Atomic Energy Establishments in India — 106
11. India: Industrialization — 124
12. India: Transportation — 140
13. Imports, Exports and Balance of Trade — 150
14. India: Age Distribution of Population, 1981 — 158

List of Tables

Number

1. Ceiling on Land Holdings — 27
2. Present Regional Production and Future Potentialities of Land Resources in India — 35
3. Agricultural Production — 38
4. Interstate River Water Disputes — 56
5. Present Regional Production and Future Potentialities of Mineral Resources in India — 90
6. Oil Production in India, 1955-1985 — 97
7. Consumption of Various Forms of Energy in India — 114
8. Present Regional Production and Future Potentialities of Industrial Resources in India — 123
9. Large Iron and Steel Plants Established After Independence — 126
10. India: Population Increase, Rural Urban Growth, and Birth and Death Rates, 1901-1981 — 157
11. A—Methodwise Number of Acceptors of Family Planning in India, 1976 — 166
    B—Family Planning—Sterilization Targets and Performance, 1976 — 167

CHAPTER 1

Introduction

POLITICAL geographers are interested in the political significance of a state's economic structure, the areal distribution of resources and their political importance in terms of time and area, and the role of political policies in changing the state's economic structure. East and Prescott examine the economic structure of a nation state in four ways. First, the evaluation of the *industrial structure* focuses on the economic strength and viability of a state, its degree of self-sufficiency and economic stability. Second, the study of the *regional structure* identifies underdeveloped and overdeveloped areas so that planned development may be carried out to achieve economic stability through balanced planning (East and Prescott, 1975, p. 131). Some states in India adopted a secessionist attitude to attract more funds for economic development from the centre: for example, the Dravida Munnetra Kazhagam (D.M.K.) party in Tamil Nadu, at least at the time of elections, repeatedly demanded secession on the basis of poor economic conditions, linguistic differences, and cultural heritage. In the context of developmental planning, a geographer can be an ideal planner for formulating economic policies of a nation state because he is aware of the regional economic inequities, unequal distribution of resources, cultural diversities, and the interrelationship between nation states which could be a source of power for a particular state.

Third, the investigation of *sectional structure* discovers groups which are underprivileged and overprivileged, conditions which are a constant source of political concern. Inequalities of wealth and power are so extreme in India that the rich and powerful have no concept of real poverty and distress, whereas the poor cannot relate themselves to the rich. This inequality has been a constant source of worry for various governments which have been in power in India since Independence. Finally, the *comparative economic structure* of a nation state will allow us to investigate economic alliances and the distribution of foreign aid and to evaluate trade agreements. In essence, by studying the internal economic patterns and external political relationships, a political geographer evaluates the economic viability and political stability of a nation.

Every powerful nation state possesses numerous environmental advantages, demographic features, and the systematic organization of its societies. India, the seventh most extensive and second most populous nation, is the largest democracy in the world occupying a dominant position in the Indian Ocean. Lying in the northern hemisphere between two distinctly different environments, that is, the semi-arid region of southwest Asia and the wet monsoon land of southeast Asia, it encompasses the characteristics of both these regions. Projecting into the Indian Ocean, it extends between latitudes 8° 4' 18" and 37° 17' 53" north and longitudes 68° 7' 33" and 97° 24' 47" east with a land frontier of 15,168 kilometers and coastline of 5,689 kilometers (Fig. 1).

India's central location at the head of the Indian Ocean adds to its significance as a potentially powerful country because its maritime boundary provides spatial exchange of goods and ideas, it has excellent commercial connections with the rest of the world (especially after the opening of the Suez Canal), improvement of economic strength through offshore maritime resources, and a strategic position as a transit zone for global air routes. The geographical situation of India is of great importance in the light of recent developments in the power strategy of the global powers and the place India has in this strategy. These developments are on account of the expanding influence of the Communist ideology in Southeast Asia, the conflict in the Middle East, the rise of new nation states in Africa, the rift between China and the U.S.S.R., the creation of Bangladesh in the subcontinent; and Pakistan's defeat in the 1971 war with India has indirectly added to the importance of India as a strong, viable nation.

India measures about 3,219 kilometers from north to south and 2,977 kilometers from east to west and covers an area of 3,267,053 square kilometers. The compactness of India is a positive factor which helps in its development, in creating economic and political unity, and in increasing cultural homogeneity in the nation.

The real political strength of a country lies in the national resources which form the physical foundation for its industries and other economic activities. The Indian economy commands a position of relative importance in the world in terms of its geographical extent (an area of 3,271,141 sq. km., seventh largest in the world), its population (more than 780 million, second largest in the world), its gross national product (564 trillion rupees, the United States has 23 times more than

Introduction

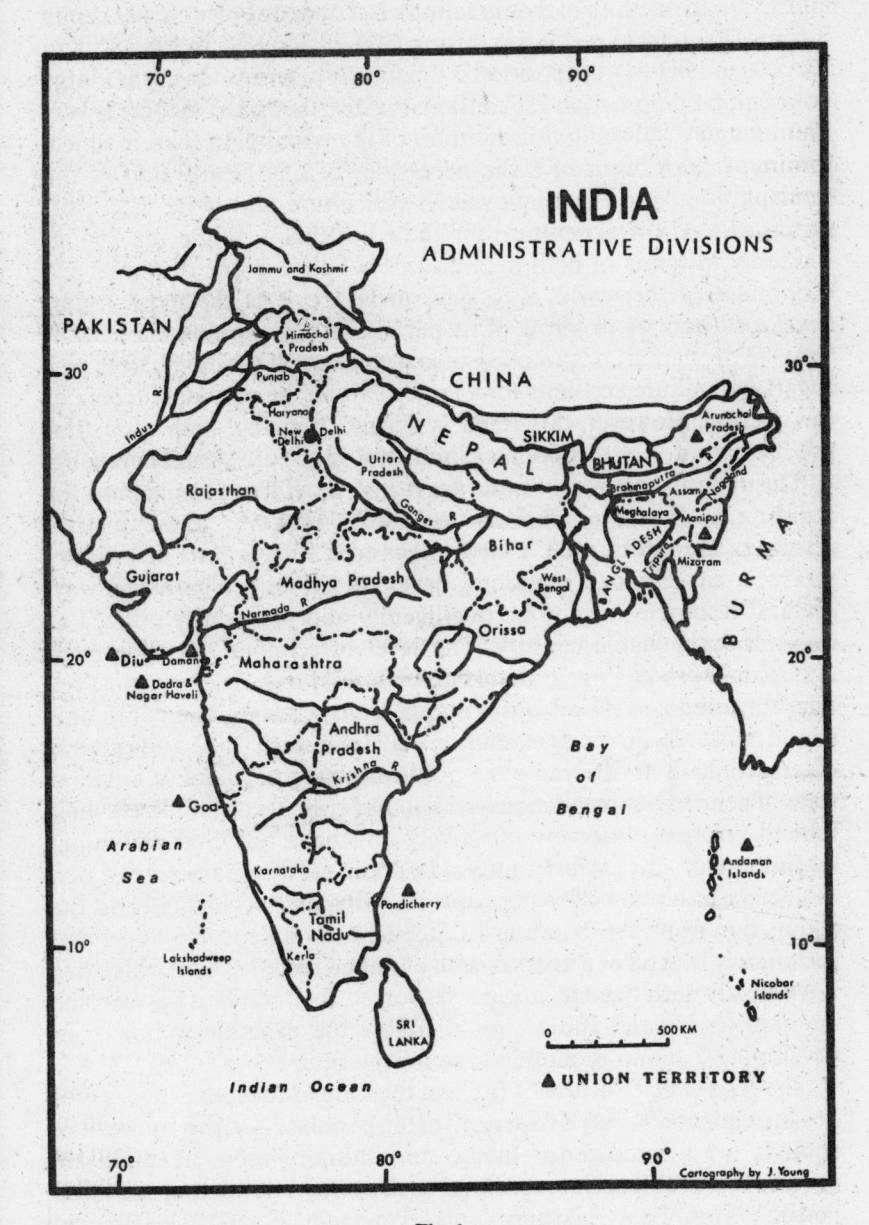

Fig. 1

India), and the size of its manpower engaged in organized manufacturing (5.25 million—less than one-third of that in the United States and less than one-half of that in Japan). But once one turns to per capita income (Rs. 1200 in real terms during 1977-78, Rs. 1890 in 1981-82, and Rs. 2000 in 1983-84), the position is drastically reversed. Owing to a large population of more than 780 million, the distribution of income is very skewed and a substantial proportion of the population lives in abject poverty, in dire want of basic necessities of life. Nearly half of the working population is employed in agriculture and more than two-thirds depend on agriculture for their livelihood. While the Indian economy in terms of both area and population is one of the largest economies of the world, it is, nevertheless, one of the most underdeveloped nations in terms of its per capita national income and in terms of per capita consumption of key items, such as energy, steel, and sugar. Agriculture accounts for a large share in the national income of the country. However, this trend is slowly changing; both industrial production and consumption of industrial goods are steadily growing.

The natural resources of India are varied, providing a sound basis for building a diversified modern economy. However, these natural resources are not of such a large magnitude that exports of primary products can finance economic development in a significant way. Natural resources have to be intelligently and judiciously utilized to make India a viable country. The level of economic development, agricultural production, mineral output, forest products, industrial fuel, manufactured goods, industrial plants, transportation and communication networks, financial institutions, size of foreign trade, and cultural diversities help to determine the political power potential of a nation state. There are some nations which have, in fact, mobilized their limited resource base very effectively and have acquired additional resources from diversified sources; in doing so, they have reaped rich dividends in terms of progress and stability, and accidentally, in the acquisition of power. Japan is an excellent example in the world and specifically in Asia of a country with a limited resource base which has intelligently mobilized its meager resources. As a result, it has become an industrial giant. India should follow the example of Japan in developing a sound economic base for the future.

The economic structure of India at the time of Independence was of no consequence. Barely five percent of the population earned more than enough for a subsistence living, and millions were unemployed. Formidable problems loomed large, such as (i) rehabilitating displaced persons from East Pakistan (now Bangladesh) and Pakistan; (ii) increasing the production of raw jute, cotton and foodgrains to make up

Introduction

for the loss of territory to Pakistan; (iii) establishing communal harmony; and (iv) increasing even slightly the economic level of the people. Partition disrupted trade and commerce, fiscal structure, banking and finance institutions, dislocated transportation and communication networks, and hampered the agricultural system, especially on account of disproportionate loss of area under irrigation to Pakistan. The other problems facing the country were how to provide ample clothing, adequate housing, proper medical and health facilities, better opportunities for education and literacy, and improved conditions for agriculture, mining, industries and transportation for a larger proportion of population as compared to its share in total area. To achieve these objectives was not an easy task in the wake of the newly attained Independence, democratic form of governmental structure, and an economy well exploited by the colonial powers.

The British colonial policy was geared towards the development of Britain as an industrial giant in the world. Colonial policy not only involved the neglect of indigenous needs and interests of the Indians, but also a large-scale decay and destruction of native crafts, skills, and enterprises. The colonialists concentrated on the promotion of British capital, know-how, and enterprise for opening up India. The British developed an extensive network of railways and roads; apart from developing mining through trade, commerce, and finance, they also introduced commercial crops, such as coffee, tea, and jute. However, in spite of this, the British were not interested in developing India economically. As Barbara Ward put it more succinctly—in 1939, after a hundred years of British investment, peace, order and modern commercial law, after nearly a century of modern railways, ports, and export industries, after eighty years of Indian enterprise in a vast internal market of 300 million souls—India still had an industrial establishment of only two million workers, steel output of less than a million tons, and a population which still depended for as much as eighty percent of its livelihood on a static, over-crowded, agrarian economy. Not by any stretch of imagination could this be called a record of dynamic growth. It was simply the first sketch of a first beginning (Ward, 1964, pp. 138-9). The British, however, implanted the seeds of industrialization and introduced the systematic development of transportation in India which after Independence achieved phenomenal progress.

The economic progress made by India since the introduction of the First Five Year Plan (1951-56) has been remarkable. The country is virtually self-sufficient in most of the basic industries. India can be considered a fairly industrialized country on account of a phenomenal growth in infrastructure and basic industries. Another significant achievement has been the improvement and increase in technical manpower which in terms of magnitude is the third largest in the world. This has reduced the dependence on exports, and the country is now supplying technical personnel to many Third World countries as well as to industrialized nations. India's dependence on foreign countries for capital goods has steadily declined and in fact the country is producing sophisticated consumer goods. This was made possible by the adoption of a planned economic programme of a mixed economy. The public sector, which was more organized and planned, accounted for twenty percent of economy. It included government services, part of health and education, many large-scale industries, gas and electricity, and railways (Cole, 1983, p. 188). Although iron and steel and sugar industries have fared poorly, the railways, electrical engineering, defence, and nuclear and space programmes have made impressive gains. The private sector covering most of the agriculture, internal trade, and small household industries also made remarkable progress. India has quadrupled its investments, built dams including the second highest gravity dam (Bhakra in Punjab) in the world, opened new schools for educating and training young people as well as increasing the literacy among older people, and introduced new methods of agriculture including better and improved seeds. It has also added more acreage to the irrigated area, made available better tools and implements to the farmers, and improved the supply of fertilizer, as well as opened hospitals, family planning centres, and better health care facilities. The country has developed sophisticated technology to meet the needs of modern India and is now harnessing nuclear energy as was evident by the successful underground nuclear explosion in 1974 and the construction of three nuclear power plants for generating electricity. However, the progress made was at a very slow pace. The first decade of planning, 1951-60, achieved a rate of growth of only 3.8 percent while the second decade, 1961-70, only 3.7 percent; the accumulated growth rate has been four percent between 1951 and 1984. The four percent average annual growth is two to three times as high as the rate of growth recorded in British India. The rate of growth in the post-Independence era compares favourably with the growth rates of advanced countries during their earlier stages of development, although they were in an advantageous position in that they had much more favourable factor endowments and better socio-economic environments (Uppal, 1984, p. 2). Obviously, with high rates of growth of population, rapid economic growth could not bring about the required improvement in the standard of living of the people. Per capita income increased from Rs. 245.50 in 1951-52 to Rs. 2000 in 1983-84, an eight-fold increase, but even so standards of living are much lower than what they are in industrialized economies. While steel output increased fifteen-fold, agricultural production rose from fifty million tons in 1947 to 160 million tons in 1985-86, a 300 percent increase. The target was set for 156 million tons in 1984-85, on the basis of a four percent annual growth rate. In 1986, there was a surplus of thirty-five million tons of foodgrains and in fact since 1978 India has stopped food-grain imports altogether, except of course for a small amount whenever crops fail as a result of drought or floods.

The First Five Year Plan (1951-56) outlay was Rs. 37,600 million which rose to Rs. 663,351 million in the Fifth Five Year Plan—an eighteen-fold increase. The Fifth Five Year Plan was terminated in 1978 by the erstwhile Janata Government, and the rolling Sixth Five Year Plan was introduced. The Sixth Five Year Plan (1978-79 to 1982-83) was envisaged with an outlay of Rs. 1,161,240 million which was later revised to Rs. 1,413,770 million. The increase in outlay was mainly in the fields of agriculture, rural development, industry, transportation, communication and water supply schemes. The Plan assumed an annual growth rate of 3.8 percent in the agricultural sector as against the past trend of three percent. It was anticipated that with better irrigation and other infrastructural facilities the actual agricultural growth during the five years (1978-79 to 1982-83) would accelerate from about four percent at the beginning of the period to over five percent towards the end. Industrial growth was projected at about seven percent as against the five percent rate experienced. However, during 1978-79 the industrial growth rate was abysmally low at less than two percent. For the five year period (1982-83 to 1987-88), an overall growth rate of 5.5 percent was projected. In the financial year (1979-80), there was a deficit of Rs. 27 billion as against the budgeted figure of 12.82 billion for 1980-81. This deficit was caused by the fall in the earnings from corporate taxes and excise levies, poor performance of the public sector enterprises, higher food and fertilizer subsidies, and a large import bill on account of the import of crude and petroleum products. The central outlay of Rs. 65.73 billion in the year 1980-81 was Rs. 5.58 billion higher than the previous year's allocation. Mrs Gandhi and her government, after the 1980 Lok Sabha elections victory, decided to fold up the rolling Five Year Plan of the Janata Government and introduced in its place a new Sixth Five Year Plan, 1980-81 to 1984-85, prepared to meet the new time schedule. The Sixth Five Year Plan proposed an outlay of Rs. 900 billion in the public sector and Rs. 660 billion in the private sector, a total of Rs. 1,560 billion. The annual growth rate was targeted at five to 5.3 percent; however, the average growth rate for the first four years was 5.4 percent. The per capita income grew at an average rate exceeding three percent per year (Economic Survey, 1984, p. 1). While industrial growth was envisaged at eight to nine percent, actual industrial production rose around five percent. In the key agricultural sector, agricultural production was targeted at four percent with the objective of removing poverty and expanding employment opportunities. The actual production increased from a high of 135.2 million tons in 1980-81 to 160 million tons in 1985-86, a net increase of 11.86 percent in four years despite a severe drought during 1982-83. The 1984-85 budget presented to the Parliament included a total of Rs. 593,640 million with a deficit of Rs. 23,350 million. The budget provided for a large increase of twenty-six percent in central plan expenditure which was higher than the original level. This was done to promote savings and investment, and to strengthen the productive forces in the economy. Some relief was also provided to low and middle income groups. The draft of the Seventh Five Year Plan (1985-86 to 1989-90) has already been prepared with an investment outlay of about Rs. 2000 billion. This would mean the need for enormous investible resources if the Seventh Plan targets are to be met and the growth process speeded up. The growth rate during the Seventh Five Year Plan 1985-86 to 1989-90 is targeted at five percent.

The impressive statistical gains have been partially offset by the rise in wholesale prices for all commodities from an index of 100 in 1970 to over 320 percent in 1984; however, the consumer index declined progressively since August 1975 after the imposition of the Emergency on June 26, 1975. The earlier increase in prices was attributed, at least in part, to three major elements. First, severe droughts during 1965-66 and 1966-67 caused a sharp decline in agricultural and industrial output and, as a result, put an extra strain on the depleted foreign exchange reserves to buy food to feed the people. These successive droughts left the nation stricken by its worst famine since 1943. Surprisingly, millions of people probably had their first really nutritious meal during the famine, since many low caste Hindus who had normally lived under the spectre of starvation benefited from the Government's food distribution programmes undertaken during 1966 and 1967. Second, the cost of wars with Communist China in 1962 and with Pakistan in 1965 and 1971 added extra expenditure on defence. The additional resources devoted to defence efforts reduced the investment in developmental programmes. The war with Pakistan during 1971 also created an additional problem for the Indian economy (when an additional ten million plus refugees from East Bengal had to be fed besides fighting a war and feeding their teeming millions). Finally, foreign aid declined sharply during the 1970s and the oil prices increased tremendously thus putting an extra burden on the shattered economy. Besides, the population

Introduction

increased at an alarming rate of more than thirteen million per year.
The economic progress made since Independence may have reduced to some extent the gap between the very poor and the lower middle class, but a tremendous amount has still to be accomplished. In a country such as India, there are a multitude of problems, and finding solutions to them is a slow and painful process, especially when the problems have to be solved through democratic means. Finding solutions to the various problems becomes even more cumbersome because India is a multifaceted society with different races and cultures, cults and customs, diets and dresses, and faiths and tongues; there is also a wide gap between the rich and the poor and between the educated and the illiterates. Nevertheless, despite this diversity, there is a considerable degree of unity in India, a unity characterized by the love for the country, harmony between materialism and the spiritual aspect of life, devotion to democratic principles, some common historical bonds, at least some elements of cultural similarity, and certain common interests which cement the Indian nation and population together, providing an image of an Indian nation (Sukhwal, 1971, pp. 10-11). During the initial years of Independence, economic progress was slow because the country faced problems such as the integration of princely states, rehabilitation of refugees, stabilization of the governmental structure, as well as keeping pace with a hostile neighbour—Pakistan. These problems were potentially dangerous and were of foremost concern to political leaders. The economic problems of the country did not receive adequate governmental attention during the initial years after Independence with the result that the deterioration of economic conditions was compounded every year. The economic situation remained static until the Government was partially stabilized through the introduction of the Emergency on June 26, 1975; but unfortunately, the Emergency took away the fundamental rights of the people at the root of democracy.

It will be proper to evaluate the economic gains attained by India after the imposition of Emergency in June, 1975. Inflation increased at an annual rate of twenty-three percent in 1973-74 and reached a peak at about 28.6 percent in June, 1975, which could be considered as a world record. There was large-scale unrest among the lower sections of the public, labour strikes were commonplace, low productivity in agriculture and industry was evident, violent riots were frequent, lawlessness was at its height; and thus, under these conditions, Emergency was introduced. There are two major points to be kept in mind while looking at India's problems. First, it should be remembered that in a sprawling federation such as India the composition of federating units on the lines of socio-cultural homogeneity and administrative viability is a sound principle of state organization for effective mass mobilization, based on direct elite-mass linkage and communication (Khan, 1976, pp. 11-12). Second, after four decades of independence, it is possible that India must have compulsory growth and greater democratization at different levels of the republic in this federation. India has to give a second look at the basic problem of rationality restructuring large-sized federal policy in order to satisfy the genuine demands of neglected subregions within the existing large and unwieldy states. Special attention has to be paid to the poorer sections of the population and neglected regions of the country. The ruling Prime Minister Mrs Indira Gandhi announced the following 20-point economic programme on July 1, 1975:

(1) Continuance of steps to bring down prices of essential commodities. Streamlined production, procurement and distribution of essential commodities. Dealers will have to display price lists and statements of stocks. Strict economy in government expenditure.

(2) Implementation of agricultural land ceilings and speedier distribution of surplus land and compilation of land records.

(3) Stepping up of provision of house sites for landless and weaker sections. Special attention paid for providing house sites in rural areas.

(4) Abolition of bonded labour. Bonded labour wherever it exists to be declared illegal. The Parliament has already passed an Act declaring bonded labour illegal.

(5) Plan for liquidation of rural indebtedness. Legislation for moratorium on recovery of debt from landless labourers, small farmers and artisans. An Act of Parliament has already been passed.

(6) Review of laws on minimum agricultural labour and wages.

(7) Expansion of irrigation facilities. Five million more hectares to be brought under irrigation during the Fifth Five Year Plan. National programme for use of underground water and drinking water especially in drought prone areas.

(8) Accelerated power programme. Action under way to generate an additional 2600 Mega Watts. Super thermal stations under the Central Government.

(9) Strengthening of handloom sector. The handloom industry is next only to agriculture in the number of people employed. New development plan for development of handloom industry.

(10) Improvement in controlled cloth scheme, to ensure reasonable price for the common-man for rural and urban areas.

(11) Socialization of urban and urbanizable land. Ceiling on

Introduction 11

ownership and possession of vacant land and on plinth area of new dwelling units.

(12) Measures to deal with tax evasion. Special squads for evaluation of conspicuous construction and prevention of tax evasion. Summary trials and deterrent punishment of economic offenders, especially in tax.

(13) Intensification of campaign against smugglers. Special legislation for confiscation of smugglers' properties.

(14) Improvement of licensing procedures. Liberalization of investment procedures. Action against misuse of import licenses.

(15) Workers participation in industries. Schemes for workers participation in industries particularly at the shop floor level and in production programmes.

(16) Improvement in road transportation. The introduction of a system of national permits with the objective of removing constraints on movement of goods by truck.

(17) Income tax relief. Raising the minimum exemption limit for income tax from Rs. 6000 to Rs. 8000.

(18) Supply of essential commodities at controlled prices. Essential commodities at controlled prices to be supplied to students from poor families in college hostels, and controlled prices in all hostels and approved lodging houses.

(19) Supply of books and stationery at controlled prices. Establishment of book banks.

(20) Increase in employment opportunities for the educated. Particular care taken to ensure a fair deal to the scheduled castes and tribes, minorities and handicapped persons in recruitment of apprenticeship.

The All India Congress Committee (AICC) accepted Mrs Indira Gandhi's recommendation in May 1976 to add four more points to the existing 20-point economic programme. The new four points were (1) Family Planning, (2) National Fitness, (3) Afforestation, and (4) Child Welfare. The 20-point programme was revitalized after the massive victory of Mrs Gandhi's party in the seventh general elections in January, 1980.

These items were not new to the Congress Government but were a part of a continuing programme made by the Planning Commission. The major thrust of this programme was that it was well integrated and special attention was paid to implement it. The Prime Minister had pointed out time and again a sense of national urgency and acute awareness of the fulfilment of targets and goals which were evident all around this programme. The economic progress made since the introduction of this programme was remarkable. As mentioned earlier inflation reached its peak of 28.6 percent during the month of June, 1975. Since then the wholesale prices had fallen by as much as twenty-four percent by April 24, 1976, compared to the prices which ruled in the corresponding week during 1975. The national economy attained a zero rate of inflation by the end of June, 1976. Foodgrain production during 1975-76 reached an all time record of 120.83 million tons. An overall growth rate of 6.5 percent was reached for the year ending on March 31, 1976, as against only 0.2 percent in 1974-75. Coal production increased by thirteen percent, saleable steel twenty percent, nitrogenous fertilizer twenty-nine percent, while the export trade increased by eight percent though world trade generally declined during the same period 1975-76. It was also estimated by the Finance Ministry that an overall growth for 1976-77 was 8.8 percent. The industrial growth during 1976-77 reached a level above ten percent nearly quadrupling 1974's figure. India's GNP doubled from Rs. 218,660 million ($ 24,295.5 million) in 1965-66 to Rs. 615,530 million ($ 76,941 million) in 1976-77 and steadily increased during the last seven years. The production targets were not only fulfilled with speed but also, in a number of cases, there were record-setting achievements. The improvement was mainly the result of a better industrial climate following the declaration of Emergency.

The fall in prices of essential commodities including foodgrains was a sign of relief for the poorer sections of society. The implementation of the programme brought to task smugglers, hoarders, and tax evaders who were breeding for the last thirty years since Independence and even during the British times. Income tax returns increased from 6,270 million rupees in 1974 to 8,100 million rupees in 1975; since then, these have been increasing steadily. It was estimated that the total tax revenue including income tax during 1976-77 would total 78,370 million rupees (approximately 9,086 million dollars) showing an increase of 3,670 million rupees (approximately 424 million dollars) over 1974-75. Wealth tax rose from 268 million rupees to 340 million rupees, recording an increase of nearly twenty-seven percent. However, there continued to exist islands of affluence and privilege in a vast sea of poverty breeding discontent; thus the implementation of this programme was essential. In spite of the continuing high trade deficit, the balance of payments position improved sharply with the accumulation of about $ 2,800 million from December 1975 to September 1976 in reserves.

The improving conditions of the economy raised the hopes of the Finance Ministry to increase the outlay in the third year, 1976-77, of the Fifth Five Year Plan to 78,520 million rupees, an increase of 31.6 percent over 1975-76. This increase was in addition to the increase of 1974-75 of twenty-three percent above the proposed outlay. The main objective of the strategy involved in this increase was full employment of labour and physical resources activating 100 to 120 million people in the 15-59 age group. According to the Finance Minister during the Emergency, around 75 million of those unemployed or underemployed had to be provided jobs in activities other than direct cultivation of land. Production in public sector units increased by fifteen percent. About 5.9 million house sites were distributed to landless rural labourers throughout the country. Agricultural labourers, who had not received adequate attention in the past, were freed from their bonds and a moratorium placed on rural debts. In addition, 20,000 hectares of land were brought under cultivation and a special allocation of Rs. 1000 million was made available for irrigation and power schemes by December, 1975. This was in addition to the total cropped area of about 169 million hectares in 1973-74. The priorities continued to be those enunciated in 1974—agriculture, power, fertilizer, pesticides, oil exploration, steel, and coal with some tentative new starts.

The optimism showed by the World Bank Report and the Secretary of the U.S. Senate, Francis Valeo, towards the economic growth of the country was noteworthy. The report says that India possesses the resources of modernization, such as some of the richest iron and coal deposits in the world, and, increasingly, the equipment and skills to exploit them (Menon, 1976, p. 6). Offshore petroleum has now become a reality for commercial production. India produces and exports railway coaches and locomotives, and a whole range of other machine good products. It can mass produce jet aircrafts and automobiles, while Indian scientists have developed nuclear explosives using original techniques and processes. In fact, India ranks third in the number of scientific trained manpower in the world. Adequate food supplies at reasonable prices were assured for the year 1976 as well as a surplus of eighteen million tons of grain. The World Bank Report listed six favourable points about India. These included: (1) the bumper harvest was expected to be at the record level of 114 million tons in 1975-76 (the actual production was 120.83 million tons); (2) the high rate of inflation was brought under control; (3) deficiencies in the supply of electricity eased significantly; (4) production of petroleum and coal increased by more than ten percent over the previous year as did that of international goods, such as cement and steel; (5) man-hours lost by strikes were considerably reduced and the public sector as a whole, both administrative services and public enterprises, reached high levels of efficiency; and (6) foreign exchange reserves improved with the accumulation of about $ 6.8 billion by the end of December, 1978. The biggest gain of Emergency was the return to discipline in all spheres of activities. Had this discipline and trend of economic progress continued for a few more years, India's major economic problems might have lessened and her power position in the world would have definitely improved. Continued progress, however, largely depends upon a favourable monsoon season together with a cooperative attitude by the people to achieve economic progress.

The then Finance Minister, Venkataraman, projected a gloomy picture of the economy which had been allowed to drift through inaction and mismanagement into stagnation by the Janata and Lok Dal Governments between 1975 and 1979. Because of the mismanagement of the economy, the GNP in 1979-80 declined by over one percent. Agricultural production fell by six percent and industrial production remained stagnant. The output of cement declined by eight percent, steel by 9.5 percent and sugar by thirty-five percent during 1979-80. Prices rose by about twenty percent in one year, particularly of items of common consumption, and continued rising during the late 1970s. The trade deficit climbed to a record level of $ 2,000 million. The economy has been improving since 1980-81 except during 1982-83 when agricultural production dropped on account of severe drought adversely affecting all sections of the economy. Since then Indian economy has been in a stronger position than it had been in the past due to better grain harvest from a good monsoon and an improved balance of payments position. The deficit for the financial year ending on March 31, 1984, was Rs. 16 billion and the projected deficit for the next year was Rs. 18 billion on a revenue of Rs. 407 billion and expenditure of Rs. 425 billion. A tax cut of five percent on personal income and reductions in excise duty on household goods were proposed in the budget. However, a substantial increase in defence spending of sixteen percent over last year's budget with a total Rs. 68.4 billion was also included. The revenue is also keeping pace with the increase in the total budget.

Mrs Indira Gandhi had indicated that the foremost priorities were to increase production and to step up welfare programmes to help half the people who lived below the poverty line. She was interested in reviving her economic policies of the 1975-77 era when the Indian economy was relatively stabilized; however, she proposed doing this through democratic means rather than by imposing another emergency. The economy took an upward swing; as a result, industrial and agricultural production increased, there was a build-up of foodgrains and foreign exchange reserves, and inflation was checked and the trade deficit was brought under control. She revived her 20-point programme initiated during the Emergency period to help the poor directly through public

Introduction

investment and official measures. The massive mandate given to her in the Lok Sabha elections by the voters in January, 1980, and state elections in June, 1980, completely shattered the Opposition; now she could pursue her policies without any obstacle. To improve the economic conditions during the Sixth Five Year Plan, various steps were taken by the government including cuts in government spending, changes in the tax structure and fiscal reforms, curb on imports, promotion of exports in an effort to build up a healthy foreign exchange reserve position, and encouragement of foreign investment in the industrial sector. There is no doubt that there has been a structural change in the economy, transforming it from a stagnant agricultural one to a dynamic industrial one that has incorporated sophisticated technologies. The country is exporting industrial and technological goods to over one hundred countries including the industrialized nations. In addition, Indian technicians, the Indian government and Indian owned companies are building industrial infrastructure in the Third World countries, especially in Africa and Asia through assistance or contracts. The Seventh Five Year Plan places strong emphasis on raising the per capita income and improving the economic conditions of the general public. The stability at the Central and State level may definitely improve the economic situation, and prestige of India as a stable nation will be enhanced.

India is primarily an agricultural country. Consequently, a reasonable success in the development of the agricultural sector is critical both for food supply and for the growth of the industrial and services sectors (Don R. Hoy, 1984, p. 354). Therefore, a detailed discussion on the agricultural sector and its impact on the nation's economy will be analyzed in chapter 2.

NOTES

J.P. Cole, *Geography of World Affairs* sixth ed. (London: Butterworth, 1983), p. 188.

W. Gordon East and J. R. V. Prescott, *Our Fragmented World: An Introduction to Political Geography* (London: The Macmillan Press, Ltd., 1975), p. 131.

Economic Survey, 1983-84 (New Delhi: The Manager, Government of India Press, 1984), p. 1.

Rasheeduddin Khan, "India Polity, 1966-67: Challenges and Development," *Indian and Foreign Review*, Vol. 1, No. 12 (April 1, 1976), pp. 11-12.

N. C. Menon, "India's Progress Impresses U.S.," *The Overseas Hindustan Times*, Vol. 27, No. 20 (May 13, 1976), 6.

B. L. Sukhwal, *India: A Political Geography* (New Delhi: Allied Publishers Private Limited, 1971), pp. 10-11.

J. S. Uppal, "Economy Took a Big Leap After Independence," *India Abroad*, Vol. 25, No. 28 (April 13, 1984), p. 2.

Barbara Ward, *India and the West* (London: W. W. Norton and Co., Inc., 1964), pp. 138-139.

CHAPTER 2

Agricultural Resources

ALMOST all food for human consumption is derived directly from the soil, and as such the volume and quantity of food produced depends directly on the extent and the nature of the soil. Cultivable soil, then, must be regarded as a primary resource in the estimate of national power (Pounds, 1972, p. 157). India is primarily an agricultural country. The agricultural sector is the mainstay of the national economy accounting for nearly forty percent of its gross national production and providing employment to about fifty percent of the work force. Agriculture has traditionally boosted economic growth in India. The share of agriculture in the national economy declined from fifty percent in 1949 to forty percent in 1984 and is expected to decline further to 35.9 percent in 1987-88. Over sixty percent of the population is dependent not only on land for their livelihood but also on agricultural-related industries as compared to a very small percentage in other countries such as forty percent in Japan, six percent in U.K., ten percent in the Federal Republic of Germany, nine percent in U.S.A., nineteen percent in Canada, twenty percent in France and fifty percent in U.S.S.R. Agriculture and agricultural-related products comprise almost eighty percent of the total consumer expenditure. Agriculture is a tradition and a way of life for the people. Fluctuations in agricultural output levels, therefore, play a decisive role in the state of the national economy and the stability of the governmental machinery. Agriculture and land resources form the most important natural wealth of India; their proper utilization and management have been a matter of extreme importance to the Planning Commission and the people. India feeds and clothes its population from two-thirds of an acre per person. There is probably no other country in the world where land is so overworked (Mamoria, 1973, p. 45). Nearly eighty percent of the Indian people live in the rural areas (there are 575,936 villages in India) and until recently food shortages were common. This shortage resulted from several agricultural problems, such as disastrous weather conditions, including floods,

Agricultural Resources

droughts, famine; backward conditions in the agricultural sector; and excessive pressure on land by an ever-increasing population.

Climatic conditions and agriculture

In the past, rulers took appropriate steps to remedy the periodic incidence of famine created by the uncertainties of weather. They built dams, dug wells, constructed canals, and developed a system of famine relief through public work programmes. The British also tried to distribute food to famine victims and set up a network of famine relief operations. These efforts were, however, not well integrated and over 3.5 million people perished through sheer starvation during the 1943 Bengal famine. It is estimated by Wadia and Merchant that 279 famines occurred from 1775 to 1919 and fifteen million people died of famine between 1942 to 1944 (Wadia and Merchant, 1957, p. 100). There is a direct relationship between drought, flood and famine. Indian agriculture is dependent upon the rhythmic cycle of the monsoons. A common proverb among geographers states, "Indian agriculture is a gamble in monsoon rains." The timely arrival of monsoon rains is the biggest single factor which determines the country's prosperity and political stability. Several political problems have arisen over regional shortages of food, floods and drought, conflicts concerning the distribution of waters, location of dam sites, and the preservation of forests, all of which are directly related to the climatic conditions of India. Nowhere else are so many people so intimately dependent upon rainfall rhythms; the whole prosperity of India is tied up with the eccentricities of its seasonal winds (Cressey, 1963, p. 396).

The country receives nearly ninety percent of its rain during the southwest monsoon season, which is concentrated for only four months, that is, from June to September. The winter season creates a water shortage during the rest of the year. The rainfall in India is frequently torrential in character; the rain falls too quickly to be absorbed by the soil, and consequently there is excessive runoff.

The actual amount of rainfall received has an important bearing on the cropping pattern and, hence, on the economic viability of the State. For instance, in India there is the rice and jute economy in West Bengal, the rice and sugarcane economy in the middle Ganges Plain, the wheat economy in western Uttar Pradesh, Punjab and Haryana, and an economy based on millet, acacia trees, and shrubs in Rajasthan. The southern states are mainly rice-producing and rice-consuming ones, though of course they produce several commercial crops as well. Kerala, West Bengal and Bihar are all rice-producing but food-deficit States partly because of climatic uncertainties and partly because of overpopulation. The political instability in some of these areas during the late 1960s, especially in Kerala and West Bengal, was partly caused by food deficits. In Tamil Nadu, the Dravida Munnetra Kazhagam (D.M.K.) government won a majority in the 1967 and 1971 general elections due to the failure in the rice crop and on the basis of the language issue. The reality of a food shortage stared the illiterate masses in the face, and the opposition parties exploited this situation to achieve their goals. Subsistence farmers (most of the Indian farmers come under this category) depend on adequate production for their survival; a failure of crops makes them highly susceptible to joining any faction which promises adequate food to them and their families. In the past, crop failures and poor economic conditions proved to be advantageous to opposition parties, and even Mrs Gandhi won the 1971 general elections on the slogan *Garibi Hatao* (Remove Poverty).

It is the unpredictability of the monsoons rather than fluctuations in temperature which determines the outcome of India's harvest. Too much rain means floods and destruction; too little, famine and death. Wide variations in rainfall seriously affect the life of the people. Similarly, the timely arrival of the monsoons is of major importance. The monsoon rains may be considerably delayed or could come appreciably earlier over the entire country or over certain parts of it. The normal onset of the monsoon is in late May on the southern tip of the Indian peninsula; it reaches Bombay by June 10, and by July 1 the monsoon reaches almost all parts of India. Rains persist until about September 1, when the southwest winds cease to blow and the dry season begins. Whenever the summer monsoon starts late, it frequently retreats early, thus adversely affecting both the summer and winter crops; in fact, winter crops rely largely upon the moisture left in the soil by the summer rains. Frequent droughts cause food shortages, which are often blamed on the government machinery.

There can be one or more breaks or interruptions in the rains during the July and August period. A long break in the monsoon rains or a sudden early cessation of the rains can be very harmful to crops and may lead to famine conditions. Breaks in the rains are longer and more numerous with increasing distance from the coast. Areas on the flanks of the main zone of monsoon rains are particularly liable to such risks (Fig. 2). Gujarat, the southern margins of the Upper Gangetic Valley, and the interior districts of northwest India (Punjab, Haryana and Rajasthan) tend to be especially hard hit.

The government has paid special attention to the development of irrigation. As a result, until recently the State enjoyed political stability. Some of the extremist Sikhs are demanding a separate Sikh nation,

Agricultural Resources 19

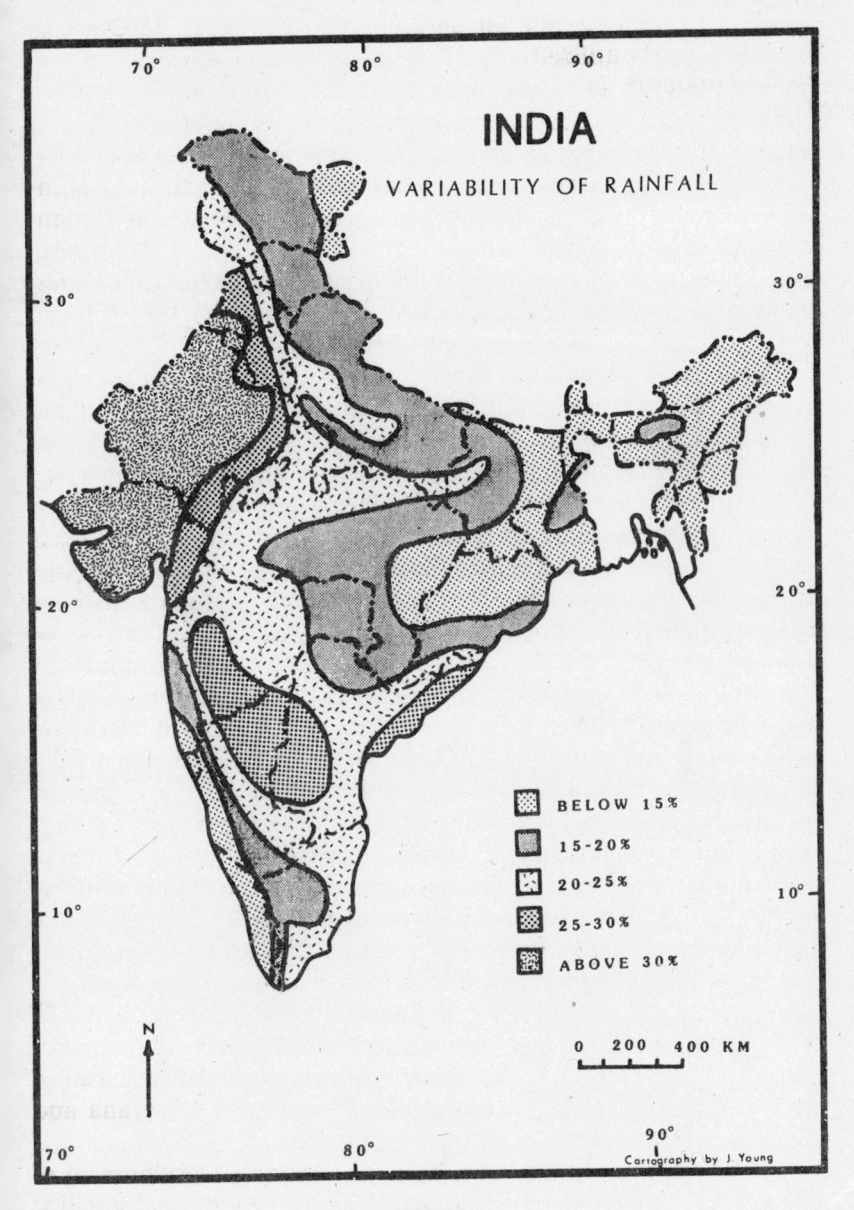

Fig. 2

"Khalistan," and would like all water of the major rivers passing through Punjab to be utilized only by Punjab. The Government of India had to send troops in the Sikh shrine of Golden Temple in Amritsar to weed out a small number of heavily armed Sikh extremists. Altercations do arise, however, over the local distribution of water, especially during the lean years, as was apparent in the "Khalistan" issue.

Insofar as the occurrence and distribution of rainfall affects natural vegetation, agriculture, irrigation, and settlement patterns, it is an important factor in assessing the political problems in India. Areas with 200 centimeters or more of rainfall produce food crops, such as rice and commercial crops, such as tea, jute, coffee, rubber, and spices (Fig. 3). However, these areas with heavy rainfall are always in danger of being flooded. Heavy rainfall encourages the cultivation of commercial crops making these areas suffer from a chronic food deficit.

India's principal famine zones lie in regions with less than 100 centimeters of annual rainfall (Fig. 3). As Stamp has pointed out, the famine areas are not the driest parts of the country but rather those having an intermediate rainfall (Stamp, 1962, p. 198). The most frequent drought-stricken areas suffer markedly during drier-than-normal years. Famines create political unrest and place a great strain on the relief capabilities of the State. The paradox is that during the floods the Kosi River submerged three hundred villages in Bihar and northern West Bengal, while severe drought conditions prevailed in Rajasthan (*Times of India*, October 1968). A drought and a flood condition in the same state can follow in quick succession. A flood hit Rajasthan in the early monsoon period of 1968, and ironically a drought developed later in the same season. Not cyclic in nature, these disasters can strike in any year, and there is no way of predicting in which region these disasters can occur, time of year they can occur, nor the intensity of the occurrence. Such conditions put pressure on the government to incur heavy expenditure on relief measures. When there is a crop failure, which is often in India, the government has to depend on the import of the foodgrains in exchange for precious foreign exchange.

The seasonal and local distribution of rainfall is so uneven and the variation from year to year so marked that in every five years there is said to be one good year, one bad year, and three indifferent years of rainfall; in every ten years there is a scarcity of significant magnitude resulting in famine conditions, and approximately in every half-century the monsoon is abnormal over vast areas causing severe drought (Mamoria, 1973, p. 835). The regions most likely to experience famine due to drought are: (1) Rajasthan—Eastern and Western districts; (2) Maharashtra—Ahmednagar, Satara and Sholapur districts; (3) Andhra

Agricultural Resources

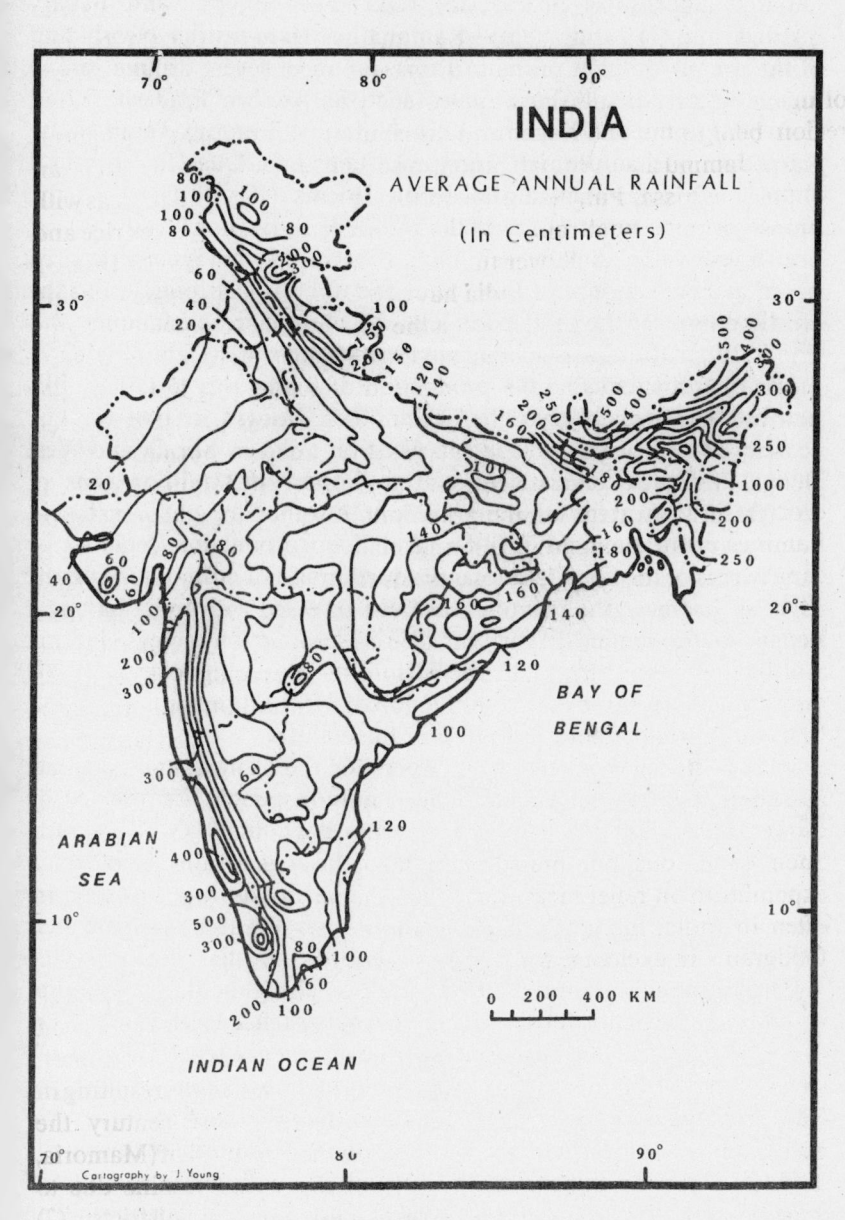

Fig. 3

Pradesh—Anantpur, Kuddapa (Cuddapah), Vishakhapatnam, and Kurnool districts; (4) Haryana—Rohtak and Gurgaon districts; (5) Gujarat—Saurashtra district; (6) Karnataka—Bijapur and Bellary districts, and (7) Tamil Nadu—Ramanathapuram district. Nearly half of the area is drought prone in India, the most severe drought prone region being Maharashtra. States such as Andhra Pradesh, Bihar, Gujarat, Jammu and Kashmir, Kerala, Madhya Pradesh, Tamil Nadu, Karnataka, Orissa, Punjab, Haryana, Rajasthan, Uttar Pradesh and Delhi, have an annual rainfall below 76 cms. (Fig. 3). However, the monsoon rains never fall over the whole of India, nor has there ever been a year when all parts of India have received what is considered to be an average amount of rain. Thus the uneven distribution and the erratic nature of the monsoons leads to the spectres of famines and floods. When the monsoon failed in 1965-66, there was a famine crisis in much of India, causing the production of foodgrains to fall by 19.6 percent; this was followed by yet another drought in 1966-67. The scarcity of food led to riots in places as far apart as Kerala and West Bengal, and the government had to import 10.3 million tons of foodgrains to avert the famine conditions. Another drought prevailed in some parts of India in 1979-80 when food production declined by nearly six percent, that is, a total production of 122 million tons. In the eighties, however, the position has been reversed with India having a surplus in foodgrains. In the year 1983-84, production increased to 151 million tons, the highest in the history of Indian agriculture, a 300 percent increase over 1947's production of fifty million tons, which has stabilized the foodgrain situation in the country.

Floods are another source of worry for the Central and the State governments. On an average, sixteen million people are affected by floods every year. The average cattle loss is about 30,000 (Bhagirath, 1971, p. 54). Nearly 6.3 million hectares of the area are affected of which 2.3 million hectares are under crops. The flood-prone regions are Jammu and Kashmir, Punjab, western Uttar Pradesh, eastern Uttar Pradesh, north Bihar, north Bengal, and Assam; less flood infected areas are peninsular India and the regions along the delta in Orissa.

In the good years, farmers live at the subsistence level, while in the bad years they try to secure loans from government agencies, well-to-do relatives, or through sheer desperation from village money lenders; or they try to find work in famine relief programmes to earn money to feed their families. The purchasing power of the vast majority of the people of India is directly linked with the fluctuating conditions in agriculture. Regional imbalances can be aggravated if areas of deficient rainfall lag behind in agricultural development, eventually leading to political indifference. Droughts and floods cause a decline in national income, recession in industry, violence in streets, and distress in the countryside.

Although India ranks first in the production of peanuts, tea, and jute fibres, and holds virtually a monopoly on lac production and ranks second in the production of rice, sugar, rape, sesame, cotton, castor oil seeds, and sixth in potatoes, its per hectare production is one of the lowest in the world. The average yield of rice is 1.66 metric tons (all figures are in metric tons) per hectare compared to 5.64 tons in Japan; wheat yield is 1.21 tons per hectare compared to 3.44 tons in France and 2.09 tons in the United States; cotton yield is 0.12 tons compared to 0.85 tons in U.S.S.R. and 0.73 tons in Egypt; and the yield of peanuts is 0.80 tons compared to 2.3 tons in the United States and 1.41 tons in Brazil. There are various causes for low productivity in Indian agriculture such as overcrowding in agricultural land and holdings progressively becoming smaller and fragmented with the increase in population. The sub-division of property among all the sons is a result of the common practice prevalent among both Hindu and Muslim laws of inheritance. The passage of the Hindu Code Bill has given the right to daughters to inherit property which may further accentuate the evils of sub-division. In many parts of the country, for instance, "toy holdings", a "miniature farm of 1/160 acres or 31.25 square yards", are not uncommon. The practices of sub-division have reached an intolerable point in the Konkan, Gujarat, West Deccan, Indo-Gangetic plain, and other parts of the country where fields measuring less than half an acre are to be found sub-divided into more than twenty separately-owned plots, many of them less than one-eighth of an acre (Mamoria, 1973, p. 252). Such examples of fragmentation are cited by prominent geographers and economsits time after time. Professor O.H.K. Spate writes that small holdings were made smaller by minute fragmentation; one-sixteenth of an acre has been split among five separate cultivators in one Deccan village in which sixty percent of the holdings were under five acres, 463 of 729 separate plots were under one acre, and 112 under 0.25 acre (East, Spate and Fisher, 1971, p. 149). He further cites that in one Punjab village 5,184 hectares were divided into 63,000 fields; another twenty-eight percent of holdings had each over thirty separate fields. Even if physical division is impossible, partition between heirs has been insisted upon down to a half-share in a tree (Spate and Learmonth, 1967, p. 263). Until 1977 there were 81,596 million holdings in India—71.6 percent of the holdings were marginal and small (below 1 ha.) covering an area of 23.5 percent; semi-medium holdings (2-4 hectares) 14.3 percent of the total number and with 19.9 percent of the area; the medium (4-10 hectares) and large holdings (10 hectares and above) accounted for 57.6 percent of the total holdings. However, about ninety-five percent of the household operational holdings have been below 0.2 hectares and nearly ninety-two percent below 0.15 hectares. Per capita arable land in India is 0.26 hectares. Another important factor is that there are 6.3 million wholly irrigated holdings in the country of a size less than half a hectare. In Uttar Pradesh alone there are 2.5 million such holdings, and another half a million in Bihar, Andhra Pradesh and Tamil Nadu together account for 1.8 million of such holdings. Holdings below four hectares mainly account for the area under rice cultivation in most of the states, whereas the bulk of the wheat area is in holdings which are four hectares and above in most of the states. The rice producing states also have more population and, thus, more demand for food and other necessities. The fragmented holdings are uneconomical and generally generate thousands of law suits among the farmers. The courts have been overcrowded with the law suits between farmers and large landowners and landless labourers. In most cases the landless workers lose the cases because they cannot afford the fees of the lawyers. After the imposition of the Emergency, these law suits were taken out of the purview of the courts and assigned to village councils and government appointed councils. In villages a new ray of hope has been introduced through land reform activities and by transferring land to the landless. However, atrocities against the landless labourers and low caste poor increased, especially in the northern states after the victory of the Janata Party in June, 1977. The reservation formula devised during the Janata rule should have been on an economic basis rather than on the basis of caste; that brought the caste differences in the forefront. There were forty-one police firings in Uttar Pradesh alone where several people died during the period the Janata Party was in power at the Centre in March, 1977. When Mrs Gandhi regained power as the Prime Minister of India, she made a determined effort to carry on the programme of land reforms and to assist the poorer sections of society. Her first act in office was to pass relevant bills on the extension of the constitutional facility guaranteeing a special reservation quota for the members of scheduled castes and scheduled tribes. On the other hand, farmers in the United States holding less than sixty-five hectares (160 acres) have been economically hardpressed to continue farming. More and more farmers are quitting smaller farms and choosing other occupations.

The limited area to which the available cultivated land in India can be extended magnifies the basic organizational problems of land ownership and land tenure. The abuses introduced by the British administration in 1793 by imposing the zamindari system were part of their policy to mobilize support among the feudal elements for their regime. By the middle of the twentieth century the abuses were intensified and thus created fifteen to twenty middlemen receiving rent between the tenant farmer and the absentee land owner. The zamindari system led to agrarian upheavals in different parts of the country, including the famous Telengana revolt and the Tebhaga movement. On the eve of the transfer of power, the Congress Party made land reform an issue of urgent discussion at the highest levels in the government.

Land reforms and land legislations

Ever since Independence, land reform has had a high priority in the government's programme in almost every state in the country. The country is committed under the Constitution to the socialist pattern of society. Land redistribution and agrarian reforms for the protection of the tenants and provision of land to the tillers are part of the scheme to establish a socialistic society. A great deal of land reform has been undertaken by the central government. The age-old system of landlordism has been abolished; however, several loopholes remained in the Zamindari Abolition Act. The abolition of the zamindari system and landlordism aimed at increasing agricultural productivity by granting titles to the landless labourers, reducing high rents, peasant indebtedness, and giving security to the tillers. But the passage of laws and enforcement was left to the State assemblies where landlord interests were strongly represented. The situation of the village poor remained deplorable. The abolition of the system by itself was not enough unless it was reinforced by other measures to break the monopoly of land which was earlier in the hands of the feudal landlords and which recently shifted to capitalist landlords and rich peasants. Many of the laws enacted by the government, including the one on land ceilings, were low in implementation because of prolonged litigation, despite a number of constitutional amendments. Another obstacle was the existence of land owners who had great political influence resulting in slow progress in land reforms. In spite of the handicaps, the major achievement since Independence was the abolition of all intermediary tenures—that is, tenures held by societies or individuals (such as zamindaris, mahalwaris, talukdaris, jagirdaris, and inams) covering about forty percent of the agricultural land. These individuals or societies in turn rented the land to landless labourers or used bonded labour for cultivation. The abolition has affected about 260,000 intermediaries, to whom the government had to make payments of large sums of money as compensation. The majority of these people joined the opposition parties openly opposing the land reform measures adopted by the Congress. The membership of the Swantantra Party is a good example of these absentee landlords and intermediaries during the 1967 general election.

As a result of this reform, more than twenty million peasants were brought into direct contact with the land and became owners of their holdings. About six million hectares of land was distributed to the landless agriculturists including the distribution of land in various states during the Emergency. The beneficiaries have been mainly persons belonging to the scheduled castes, scheduled tribes, and backward castes. Under the 20-point economic programme, land reform has a very high priority, and most of the states have passed legislation to implement the land ceiling and land distribution laws in accordance with the national guidelines issued by the central government. With the passage of the 34th Constitutional Amendment Bill ensuring the implementation of the land reform legislation in the ninth schedule of the Constitution, the land reform laws were taken outside judicial review. Now it will be easier to implement these laws at the state level without lengthy court battles. The rural poor should also benefit from measures enacted as laws such as revision of minimum wages in agriculture, abolition of bonded labour, and a moratorium on rural debts. The zamindari system had also nurtured a barbarous system of bonded labour which has been abolished by the enactment of the Bonded Labour System (Abolition) Ordinance, 1975. With the enactment of the ordinance, a proper rehabilitation of these bonded labourers has been designed by the state and the central governments. Despite the repeal of the 42nd Amendment, the land reform provision remained intact. These freed labourers are again forced by the landlords to work for them or face extinction. However, the landlords cannot force these free labourers to work for them; they are free to work wherever work is available.

A land ceiling of twelve unirrigated hectares (in most of the states) has also been enforced to equalize land distribution (Table 1). It would be no exaggeration to say that never before in the history of land tenure reform has so much legislative action, with such wide social and economic ramifications, been undertaken as in India since Independence (*Swarajya*, 1967, p. 30). Since the conferment of ownership rights in land on the tillers of the soil would not come about everywhere immediately, and even after the realization of this objective there would be a residue of the tenancy system, the planners laid down the ingredients of the security of tenure as follows: (a) the rent payable by the cultivating tenant to the landlord should be so fixed as not to exceed twenty to twenty-five percent of the gross produce; (b) no tenant should be evicted except according to the law which would specify the grounds of eviction. These grounds were nonpayment of rent and abuse of the land in a manner that might impair its productivity and usefulness; and (c) declaration of the rights of tenants in the land as permanent, heritable and transferable.

Table 1
Ceilings on land holdings

State	Level of ceiling (hectares)
Andhra Pradesh	4.05 to 21.85
Assam[1]	6.74
Bihar	6.07 to 18.21
Gujarat	4.05 to 21.85
Haryana	7.25 to 21.85
Himachal Pradesh[2]	4.05 to 12.14
Jammu and Kashmir[3]	3.68 to 7.77
Karnataka	4.05 to 21.85
Kerala	4.86 to 6.07
Madhya Pradesh	4.05 to 21.85
Maharashtra	7.25 to 21.85
Manipur[4]	10.12
Orissa	4.05 to 18.21
Punjab	7.00 to 21.80
Rajasthan[5]	7.25 to 21.85
Tamil Nadu	4.86 to 24.28
Tripura[6]	4.00 to 12.00
Uttar Pradesh	7.25 to 18.20
West Bengal	5.00 to 7.00

[1] Actual area of the orchard, subject to a maximum of 2.02 hectares in excess of the ceiling, can be retained.
[2] In certain specified areas up to 28.33 hectares.
[3] Orchards in excess of the ceiling can be retained subject to an annual tax.
[4] To be revised.
[5] In certain specified areas up to 70.82 hectares.
[6] Standard hectares.

Source: *India 1975: A Reference Annual* (New Delhi: Government of India: 1975), p. 177.

The late Acharya Vinoba Bhave, an elderly leader of the Gandhian principle, launched a nationwide movement for the donation of tracts of land and the gifts of entire villages by large land owners for distribution among landless labourers. His movement solicited "*Bhoomidan* (donation of land), *Gramdan* (village), *Sampattidan* (wealth), *Buddhidan* (knowledge), and *Shramdan* (labour)," to bring about a social change by peaceful means and to help the landless labourers, thereby removing the social evil of the past. The property acquired by donation was to be distributed among the deserving poor and the landless. By these peaceful and democratic methods, the entire agrarian society has been transformed to ensure greater freedom and security to the tiller of the soil. A useful concomitant has been the removing of functionless intermediaries between the state and the cultivators.

The Government of India has adopted a new programme for encouraging cooperative farming, but the Indian peasants, with their profound traditional love of their own little plot of land, are not interested in actively participating in this programme. Besides, legislation has been enacted in several states prohibiting partition, transfer or leasing of a holding or a plot which further fragmented the holding below the specified size. More emphasis has been placed on the consolidation of holdings, and in Haryana, Punjab, and Western Uttar Pradesh where fifty million hectares of land had already been consolidated by 1984 and other states are following suit. The Congress party faced stiff opposition in West Bengal, Uttar Pradesh, Andhra Pradesh, Bihar, and at the central level on the basis of land-tenure and land reform issues even before 1977 general elections. The Congress Ministry had to resign in 1971 earlier than their term of office because they faced strong opposition by various parties opposing land reforms and other issues relating to the agricultural sector as well as to secure more than a two-thirds majority in both the Houses so as to implement various reforms without any unnecessary delay. The Desai and Charan Singh governments lost miserably in the seventh general elections because the rural people were unhappy with the Janata Party's performance in general and in rural areas in particular.

Water supply, irrigation and agriculture

A major factor limiting crop production over most of the Indian Union is water supply. The seasonal climatic regime with its summer monsoon rains and winter drought means that crop growing is very largely confined to the wet season. Two crops per year can be raised in most areas of the country if water is made available during the dry season. Thus, irrigation is clearly the most important ingredient in agricultural production.

The volume of precipitation is estimated to be about 3,700 billion cubic meters of which thirty-three percent is lost due to evaporation, twenty-five percent seeps into the ground, and forty-five percent is run off through various rivers of India. According to the study, in the year 1960 the water resources of the various river basins amounted to 1,888,057 million cubic meters (1,524 million acre feet). The approximate groundwater recharge is 424 billion cubic meters. The utilizable water resources of the country, as assessed by the Irrigation Commission in 1972, was 870 billion cubic meters. Against this, the utilization is about 337 billion cubic meters representing about thirty-eight percent utilization. More than one thousand major and medium irrigation projects have been undertaken by the government since 1951, out of which over nine hundred were completed by March 1984, thereby creating additional irrigation facilities. Out of 157 m.ha. of cultivated land in 1983-84 (through additional land and conservation methods it will be increased to 200 m.ha. at the end of Seventh Five Year Plan), 60.1 m.ha. (38.38 percent of the total cultivated area) have been brought under irrigation and can be said to enjoy an assured perennial supply of water since in many areas minor irrigation works cease to be operational during drought. However, only 9.7 m.ha. were irrigated through major and medium irrigation works in 1951, a six-fold increase. In 1977-78, the area under irrigation went up by 2.6 m.ha., a record for any country in a single year. India accounts for nearly one-fifth of the total irrigated area in the world and the ultimate irrigation potential from both surface and ground water is 112 m.ha. With the introduction of the 20-point programme, 5 m.ha. of extra land was brought under irrigation, and an additional 6.2 m.ha. during the Fifth Five Year Plan through major and medium irrigation projects. The Sixth Five Year Plan (1980-81 to 1985-86), prepared by Mrs Gandhi's government after her election victory in 1980, allocated Rs. 121,000 million for irrigation and flood control to bring 15 m.ha. of additional cultivated land under irrigation.

Notable progress has been achieved in groundwater utilization. The number of dug wells went up from 5.7 million in 1968-69 to 9.7 million in 1984, while energized pumpsets increased substantially from 18,709 before commencement of the First Five Year Plan in 1951 to 5.2 million by the end of 1984. With the increase in irrigation facilities the foodgrain production increased steadily. The point is that increased soil fertility, improved seeds and new tools and implements, and better breeds of livestock and poultry cannot bring about much change in agricultural productivity unless there is a concomitant supply of water. Irrigation has the capacity to create the potential for double or triple cropping in many newly cultivated areas.

The creation and extension of irrigation schemes have many political implications. New areas developed for irrigation frequently face political problems of water distribution, and serious conflicts often arise between farmers and between different villages. Disagreements over the site of dams and the legality of river water use developed between states. Conflicts over the waters of the Narmada River among

Madhya Pradesh-Maharashtra-Gujarat, the Tungabhadra River between Maharashtra and Karnataka, and over the waters of the Cauvery between Karnataka and Tamil Nadu are examples of conflicts over the distribution of waters. Land titles are frequently questioned by neighbours. Land prices have greatly increased. Politicians contest elections on such issues as local water distribution, irrigation, distribution of drinking water in urban areas, and land tenure issues which appeal to the local voters. The Ganganagar district of Rajasthan is one of the many sensitive areas where irrigation improvements have created local political issues. The United Nations team of experts has endorsed the proposal to develop a national water grid in India by joining the northern and southern rivers, especially the Ganges-Cauvery link. The experts mentioned that such a link may avoid the water scarcity problem which may confront India by A.D. 2000, in the wake of substantial growth in economic development. India might in the bargain attain an indirect benefit in the form of national integration and cultural interchange by the link. But before such a link is put into operation, environmental impact statements should be prepared involving public groups and private enterprises.

Although there is tremendous irrigation potential available in India, the land frontier has been more or less exhausted. Unforunately, the average productivity per hectare has gone down by ten percent as a result of reckless deforestation, poor drainage, cultivation of submarginal land, growing salinity, and the lack of artificial fertilizers during the past decade (*Eastern Economist*, 1967, p. 857). A major scheme for reclaiming ravine land in the Chambal river basin adjoining Rajasthan (2.8 million hectares), Madhya Pradesh (2.43 million hectares), and Uttar Pradesh (1.23 million hectares) has been completed. India expected to increase its total cultivated area from 157 million hectares to 171 million hectares by 1984-85 by various reclamation methods. The reclaimed ravine areas were to increase not only the crop production but also to provide safety of life for the local people, since these areas tend to be dominated by dacoits who instil terror in the population. The increased safety of life will build confidence among the people in their government and thereby help to bring stability and peace to the countryside. Under the amnesty programme initiated by the late Acharya Vinoba Bhave, practically all dacoits have surrendered to the government and they are being rehabilitated as productive citizens. But some of them are still at large, creating unrest in various parts of the country.

Fertilizers and crop productivity

The new strategy of agricultural planners is to increase the production of chemical fertilizers and to make proper use of cow manures. The areas of high agricultural yields are precisely those which make the maximum use of fertilizers. Tamil Nadu and Orissa have nearly the same sown area, but the quantity of nitrogenous fertilizers used in Tamil Nadu in 1971-72 was 107,780 tons as against 27,200 tons in Orissa. The corresponding per hectare yields of rice were 2,010 tons in Tamil Nadu as against 825 tons in Orissa. A similar comparison between Punjab and Bihar supports the above generalization. The Government of India has decided to set up fertilizer plants in most of the states and renovate the old plants. During the Fifth Five Year Plan, four fertilizer plants were expanded and a new plant at Talcher was commissioned which will be the largest coal-based plant in the world with a production capacity of 900 tons of ammonia and 1500 tons of urea a day. New plants are being added under successive five year plans to achieve complete self-sufficiency in fertilizer production. The Fertilizer Corporation of India has an abnormally high stock of over 115,000 tons of all types of fertilizers. In 1983-84, there were over seventy factories in operation as against nine in 1950. Owing to special attention being paid to fertilizer production, fertilizer capacity is expected to go up to 6.5 million tons of nitrogenous fertilizer and 1.7 million tons of phosphatic fertilizer at the end of the Sixth Five Year plan, as against the 1975-76 capacity of 2.973 million tons of nitrogenous and 0.069 million tons of phosphatic fertilizers. Under the state sector, rural compost and green manuring, mechanical compost plants, and gobar gas (biogas—preparation of methane gas from cow manure for cooking purposes) plants are increasing at a faster rate than ever before. It was targeted to achieve a production of 500 million tons of rural compost by the end of the Sixth Five Year Plan, out of the potential of 650 million tons. Urban compost, sewage and sludge utilization has been given special attention, and the production during 1983-84 was 9.5 million tons.

The special attention given by the central and state governments towards raising the standard of living of the village population is in tune with the present conditions of India. Several new constitutional amendments were passed by the Parliament benefiting the rural poor. Among these amendments, two significant amendments were the imposition of a moratorium on the repayment of debts and eliminating the traditional, and often unscrupulous moneylenders in the villages. These laws created problems for the rural poor because of the absence of the alternative sources of credit after rural moneylending became illegal. The moneylenders were effective because of their proximity to their clients. After the nationalization of banks, regional rural banks were opened to meet the requirements of the people in need of credit.

Besides, village cooperatives should replace moneylenders, and the membership to these cooperatives should be universal, open to even poor farmers, landless labourers, and rural artisans rather than being controlled by the rich peasantry and vested interests. The villagers need credit when they are hit by a drought, or when there is a crop failure, or they may need credit to dig a new water well, or to purchase a new farm, a pair of oxen, new tools, fertilizers, and bullock carts. They cannot wait for administrative delays, travelling long distances to a bank to procure a loan; therefore, banks should reach the villagers. It has been a common practice that a villager has to bribe officials to sanction a loan from the cooperative bank and at times he has to wait for months. When he receives the loan, he has no need for it; thus the money tends to be spent on some unproductive use, such as some social ceremony. The workers should be advised to process their applications on time, and a tight discipline should be enforced on farmers to utilize the money for the purpose for which it is allotted. Farmers are the backbone of the nation and they should be given all the facilities to raise production.

The production and distribution of crops have a direct impact upon the internal and external patterns of India. Total agricultural production during 1984 was the highest ever harvested by Indian farmers. Irrigation has helped in bringing the traditionally wheat cultivating areas under rice production, for example, areas such as Punjab, Ganga and Rajasthan Canal Projects in Rajasthan and Haryana. Most of this rice is exported to other states as North Indians prefer wheat to rice as their staple food. India is embarked on a plan to export good quality rice to foreign countries. This is exemplary because of a steady increase in demand due to an increase in population in recent years. The production of most food items has increased steadily, and even higher increases were registered during 1984. The output of fruits and vegetables also increased at the same rate. The increase in long staple cotton, tobacco, sugar, vegetable oilseeds, pulses, milk and poultry products, jute goods, cashew kernels, tea, coffee, and mango products also registered a substantial increase.

Crops, crop productions and crop regions

India has about 19.6 percent of its cultivated land under non-food (cash or commercial) crops, and the government has no intention of reducing the area so planted. The land classified as cultivable waste is submarginal and cannot repay the cost involved in bringing it into use. Besides, there are no important reserves of cultivable land awaiting development. The only way to increase production significantly, then, is to increase yields per hectare. Prices received for foodgrains are comparatively lower than those received for so-called cash crops in the international and home markets. Therefore, acreages sown under cash crops have grown at a rate more than twice that of those sown under foodgrains. Indian agricultural policy calls for concentrating on the production of high quality cotton, jute, tea, sugarcane, condiments, and spices; as a result, the production and quality of these crops have improved tremendously during the last few years. Kerala, West Bengal, and in particular Assam concentrate on cash crops of cashew and coir, jute, and tea and coffee, respectively; therefore, these are notable food deficit states (Fig. 4). The government, however, has given special attention to improve the food situation in deficit regions by creating buffer stocks and transportation facilities for distribution; thus acute shortages have been averted. The fall in the prices of foodgrains in recent years except 1982-83 has been felt all over the nation—even in Kerala, which receives half of its foodgrains from other states. The present resources and future developmental possibilities of the various regions are diversified; therefore, planning according to the available and potential resources of the region concerned is clearly indicated (Table 2).

The chronic food shortages in India since Independence and a steady increase in population have had several political implications. In the first place, the need to expend scarce foreign exchange for importing foodgrains places a severe strain on the balance of payments and hence on the overall economy. In 1967, the total quantity of foodgrains imported in India amounted to 8.67 million tons and declined thereafter until 1972 to 445,000 tons. The imports increased again in 1973, 1974, and 1975 to build a buffer stock. The buffer stock has helped to stabilize the prices during periods of shortages, has helped save scarce foreign exchange instead of spending it on food, and has avoided the dependence on foreign nations for food aid. Encouraged by the bumper crop in 1976, the Government of India decided to stop foodgrain imports after June 1976, and now foodgrains are in fact being exported to foreign countries. The government may constantly review the position regarding the need for foodgrain imports and make purchases from abroad to the extent considered necessary after taking into account crop prospects, the gap between internal availability and the requirements of the public distribution system, the need to create a buffer stock of reasonable size, the size of foreign exchange resources, the price trend in international markets, and other related factors. In order to improve the marked availability of foodgrains (particularly in the deficit states), reduce interstate disparity in prices, and relieve the pressure on the public distribution system to some extent, the wheat

INDIA

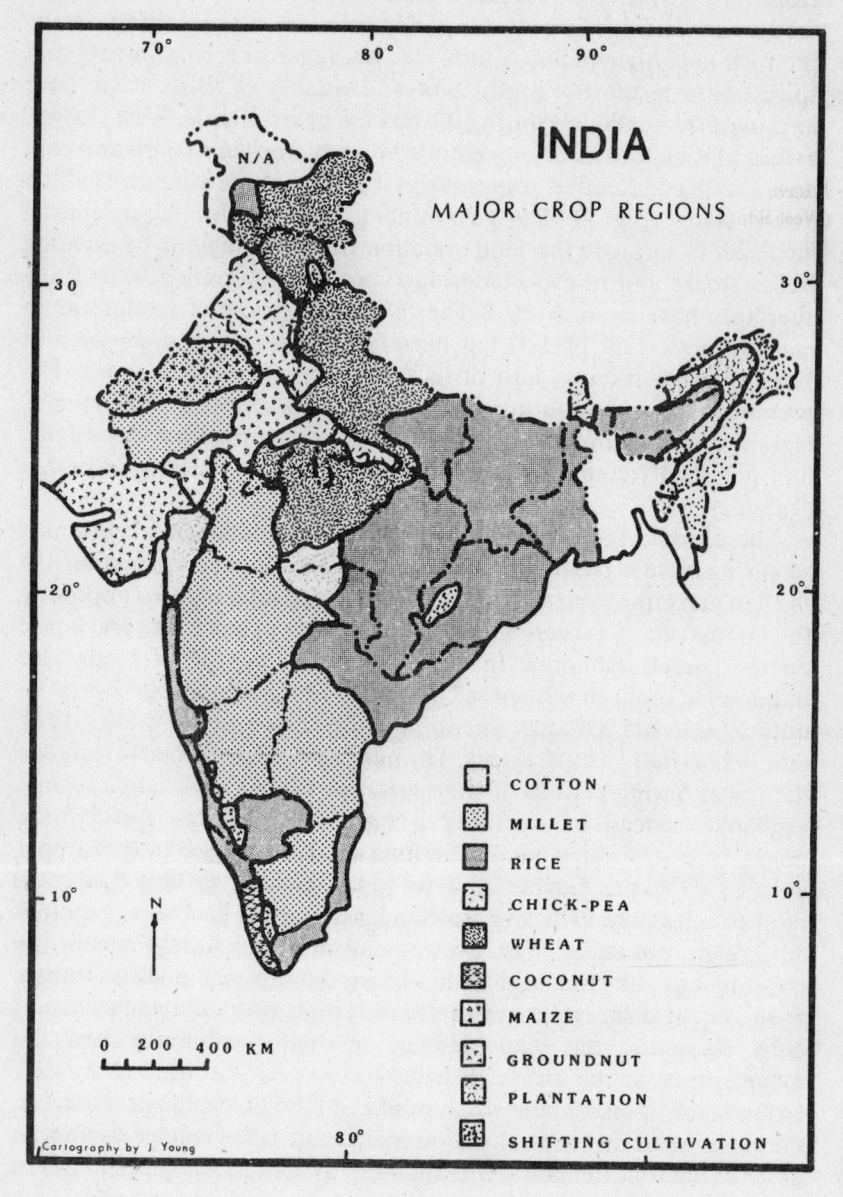

MAJOR CROP REGIONS

- COTTON
- MILLET
- RICE
- CHICK-PEA
- WHEAT
- COCONUT
- MAIZE
- GROUNDNUT
- PLANTATION
- SHIFTING CULTIVATION

Cartography by J. Young

Fig. 4

Table 2
Present regional production and future potentialities of land resources in India

Region (State)	Potentialities for future development	Actual production specialities
Northeastern (Assam, Manipur, Tripura, Nagaland, and Arunachal Pradesh	Horticulture development, self-sufficiency in food, tea, forest resources	Jute and tea
Eastern (West Bengal, Bihar, Orissa)	Forest resources, commercial crops, jute, sugarcane, tea, market-gardening,* dairies*	Jute and tea Sugarcane,* rice*
Southern (Andhra Pradesh, Tamil Nadu, Karnataka, Kerala, Goa, Pondicherry, Mahe, Yanaon, Andaman, and Nicobar Islands, Lakshadweep, Minicoy and Amindivi Islands)	Northern part of the region for livestock farming and irrigation culture, rubber, coconut, cashew nuts, tobacco, spices. Rice,* cotton,* millet*	Diversified commercial crops, coffee, tea, tobacco, coconut, cashew nuts, spices, peanuts, rubber, sericulture, marine-fisheries. Tapioca,* millet,* rice*
Central (Uttar Pradesh and Madhya Pradesh)	Intensive cultivation, forest-resources, rice, wheat, sugarcane, cotton, reclamation of land for future food production, pulses, maize, mustard and rape seeds. Peanuts,* tobacco,* bajra*	Intensive agriculture, sugarcane, rice, wheat, oilseeds, pulses, cotton,* millet,* maize*
Western (Maharashtra, Gujarat, Diu, Daman, Dadra and Nagar Haveli)	Cotton, peanuts, sugarcane, pulses. Millet*	Extensive cotton growing area, livestock, peanuts. Millet,* sugarcane*
Northwestern (Punjab, Rajasthan, Himachal Pradesh, Haryana, Delhi, Jammu and Kashmir, and Chandigarh).	The most promising agricultural zone in the Rajasthan Canal area, reclamation through forests, and irrigation, scientific farming, animal breeding, pasture, wheat, pulses, millet. Sugarcane,* horticulture*	Highly irrigated agricultural, wheat, cotton, fodder crops, highly developed livestock area. Millet,* oilseeds,* sugarcane,* horticulture in hilly areas*

* Indicates minor importance.

policy was modified to allow trade to operate under a system of licensing and control. Steps were also taken to check speculative hoarding and smuggling of foodgrains.

During the poor harvest years, the people in the cities demonstrate for cheaper and larger quantity of grains, while people in rural areas urge the government to provide more jobs to earn money to buy food. With the rise in income, Indians demand better quality of food including milk, poultry, and meat products. The acute problem facing the central and state governments in India is the specific nature of food habits of the people evolved through thousands of years of practice based on climate, geography, and religion; for example, rice-eating regions would not accept any other grain as a substitute for rice, whereas wheat eaters prefer wheat. Unfortunately, the supply of these two commodities in the world is considerably less than the demand. Since rice in particular is a scarce commodity in the world export market, India has to pay higher prices or substitute wheat for rice or align with ideologically unacceptable trade partners. The western press and media usually label India as a poor and starving nation. In the past, import of wheat from the United States, U.S.S.R., Australia, and Canada has been an important factor in relieving acute consumer distress in years of famine; however, according to the agricultural planners, over a period of years these imports are likely to have a depressing effect on incentives for domestic wheat production. Besides, how long these countries will supply foodgrains to India is not certain. In 1975, the debates in the United States Congressional committees emphasized stopping wheat export to India, if India ignored the human rights of all fellow beings according to the United States standards. The United States and the Soviet Union have been willing to provide foodgrains to India because of India's strategic position in world affairs and because India is a very good customer. India paid all her debts to loaning countries with interest on time, but at the same time she has refused to align herself with either of the power blocs in the cold war strategy.

Until 1975, the lack of a national food policy resulted in regional disparities in distribution. In 1966, for example, the regional disparities in food supply increased; while people in Bihar were starving, officials in Tamil Nadu went ahead with a programme to cut the price of rice. In 1964 and 1966, public agitation, rioting, and looting of grain stores broke out in many parts of the country because people in rural and urban areas did not have enough to eat. Predictably, the food shortage was attributed to hoarding by landlords and grain dealers, and even to hoarding by the government and its Congress Party supporters (*The Economic Weekly*, 1964, p. 1187). In 1966 an estimated shortage of

Agricultural Resources

seventeen million tons of food was created with a decrease in production from eighty-nine million tons in 1965 to seventy-two million tons in 1966; this was mainly due to the failure of the monsoon (Table 3). Up to 1965, India was the principal recipient of food aid from the United States and some people argued that India would never be self-sufficient in food production. Contrary to this belief, India has become a classic example of the marvels of continuing agricultural technological revolution and is now self-sufficient in foodgrains. In 1965, however, at the time of the Indo-Pakistan war, President Johnson threatened to stop exporting wheat to India if India did not stop the war. As a consequence, Prime Minister Lal Bahadur Shastri requested the Indian people on an All-India Radio broadcast to observe fast by eating only one meal a day and even to be ready to grow foodgrains in clay pots!

In 1967, at the time of the general elections, the voters rejected almost all the ministers in charge of economic portfolios, including the then central food minister, Mr Subramaniam. In 1974, food riots in Gujarat toppled the state government, resulting in presidential rule. Efforts on the part of the central government authorities to move food from surplus to deficit areas were restricted by states with surpluses. The reluctance of the surplus states to share their bounty and the unwillingness of deficit state governments to take the responsibility for feeding their people showed the weakness of the elected ministers and the all-too-frequent lust for power rather than service. An attempt to nationalize the wholesale trade in foodgrains was frustrated largely because the speculators themselves exerted considerable political power (Myrdal, 1968, p. 283).

The central government and the state governments working in close cooperation evolved a policy of procurement and distribution of foodgrains by creating food zones. With the bumper harvest during the 1976 season, it was suggested that food zones should be abolished; however, the central food minister, Jagjivan Ram, suggested that as long as the Centre had a responsibility for the public distribution system, the zonal restriction should continue. After the imposition of the Emergency, the acute problems of procurement and distribution were easily solved through cooperation between the state and the central government agencies in all fairness through direct pressure on chief ministers. Finally, the food zones were abolished; the result was the creation of a nation-wide market for foodgrains which removed the distortions of supply and prices formerly caused by movement restrictions.

Agricultural experts and scientists predict that India will be able to export wheat in the near future. The country produced 42.50 million tons of wheat in 1982-83, even with a poor harvest season (Table 3) (*Economic Survey*, 1984,

Table 3
Agricultural production

(In million tonnes)

	1975-76	1976-77	1977-78	1978-79	1979-80	1980-81	1981-82	1982-83
Kharif foodgrains	73.89	66.53	77.72	78.08	63.25	77.65	79.38	69.49
Rabi foodgrains	47.15	44.64	48.69	53.83	46.45	51.94	53.92	58.80
Total foodgrains	121.03	111.17	126.41	131.90	109.70	129.59	133.30	128.35
Kharif cereals	69.45	62.64	73.48	74.13	59.90	73.89	75.05	65.58
Rabi cereals	38.54	37.17	40.96	45.59	41.23	45.08	46.74	51.21
Total cereals	108.00	99.81	114.43	119.72	101.13	118.96	121.79	116.78
Kharif pulses	4.44	3.89	4.25	3.95	3.35	3.76	4.33	3.92
Rabi pulses	8.60	7.47	7.73	8.23	5.22	6.87	7.18	7.65
Total pulses	13.04	11.36	11.97	12.18	8.57	10.63	11.51	11.57
Rice (Kharif)	44.75	39.27	48.95	49.34	38.49	50.09	49.25	42.70
Rice (Rabi)	4.00	2.65	3.72	4.44	3.84	3.54	4.00	3.78
Rice (Total)	48.74	41.92	52.67	53.77	42.33	53.63	53.25	46.48
Wheat	28.85	29.01	31.75	35.51	31.83	36.31	37.45	42.50
Jowar (Kharif)	6.99	7.36	8.89	7.93	7.72	7.50	8.77	7.62
Jowar (Rabi)	2.51	3.17	3.17	3.51	3.93	2.93	3.29	3.06

Jowar (Total)	9.50	10.52	12.06	11.44	11.65	10.43	12.06	10.68
Maize	7.26	6.36	5.97	6.20	5.60	6.96	6.90	6.27
Bajra	5.74	5.85	4.73	5.57	3.95	5.34	5.54	5.13
Gram	5.88	5.42	5.41	5.74	3.36	4.33	4.64	5.09
Tur	2.10	1.73	1.93	1.89	1.76	1.96	2.26	1.92
Kharif oilseeds	7.12	5.77	6.38	6.47	5.71	5.00	7.15	5.41
Rabi oilseeds	3.48	2.66	3.28	3.63	3.03	4.37	5.04	5.15
Total oilseeds*	10.61	8.43	9.66	10.10	8.74	9.37	12.19	10.55
Groundnut (Kharif)	6.10	4.83	5.20	5.21	4.73	3.71	5.52	3.81
Groundnut (Rabi)	0.66	0.44	0.88	1.00	1.04	1.29	1.70	1.74
Groundnut (Total)	6.75	5.26	6.09	6.21	5.77	5.01	7.22	5.55
Rapeseed and Mustard	1.94	1.55	1.65	1.86	1.25	2.30	2.38	2.47
Sugarcane	140.60	153.01	176.97	151.66	128.83	154.25	186.36	189.13
Cotton	5.95	5.84	7.24	7.96	7.65	7.01	7.88	7.72
Jute and mesta	5.91	7.10	7.15	8.33	7.96	8.16	8.37	7.17
Jute	4.44	5.35	5.36	6.47	6.07	6.51	6.79	5.95
Mesta	1.47	1.75	1.79	1.86	1.89	1.65	1.58	1.22
Potato	7.31	7.17	8.14	10.13	8.33	9.67	9.91	10.11

*Include groundnuts, rapeseed and mustard, sesamum, linseed, castorseed, nigerseed, safflower, sunflower and soyabean.

p. 85) and an additional 6.6 million tons was expected for 1985 through intensive cultivation, the right selection of seeds, a better breeding system, and the control of diseases and pests, that is, through the green revolution. Rice production reached 51.5 million tons in 1983-84, the highest production in any year. Experts cited the example of Haryana where the production of wheat rose from 860,000 tons in 1965-66 to 4.4 million tons in 1982-83; it was much higher in 1983-84. A study conducted by the Indian Statistical Institute asserted that if the available improved varieties of various crops were to be used and provided with adequate irrigation and fertilizers, it would be possible with the same acreage under cultivation to register a nearly four-fold increase in the output of foodgrains over the level of 160 million tons in 1985-86. Moreover, an unpublished USAID study cites that the annual produce of the alluvial soils of India can be increased by ten times that of the current level even with the help of existing knowledge and proven production technology.

Recent successes in wheat and rice cultivation have shown that a Green Revolution is possible in India. The Green Revolution is a process of technological and structural transformation in agriculture with the goal of maintaining agricultural production at a level well ahead of population growth and making India self-sufficient in foodgrain production. This goal can be attained by introducing technological change in agriculture such as increasing irrigation facilities through building new projects; producing sufficient amounts of fertilizers, insecticides, herbicides; introducing pest control methods; diffusing innovative farming techniques and technology, providing new high-yielding varieties of seeds called "miracle grains" (rice, wheat, corn, etc.) to farmers. Farmers can be encouraged to participate in the Green Revolution programme by offering them price incentives. At the end of 1970, the new miracle wheat contributed to a fifty-two percent increase in grain production and a twenty-eight percent increase in productivity per hectare. The overall wheat yields doubled and in some newly irrigated areas under the Green Revolution wheat fields rose ten-fold. Similarly, rice, cotton, corn and other crops produced the same results. The easy availability of foodgrains in 1977-78 enabled the Government of India to not only return nearly 1.3 million tons of wheat loan to U.S.S.R. but also to supply some quantities of wheat, wheat products, and rice to Vietnam, Afghanistan, Indonesia, Mauritius, and Bangladesh. The excess production will definitely improve India's prestige in the world.

Strategy for self-sufficiency in food

The food problem of India is a very acute one, and the survival of any government in the country depends largely on the supply of foodgrains and

Agricultural Resources

an efficient system of distribution in scarce regions. India has been importing foodgrains since 1961-65 when she became a food deficit country. The largest import was 10.3 million tons in 1966 when drought hit the country. There were various causes for this food deficiency. First, the partition of the country meant giving large food surplus regions of Punjab and east Bengal to Pakistan while a proportionately higher population remained in India. Second, a proportionately higher increase in population growth rate rather than production of foodgrains since 1921 has deteriorated the food situation. The increase in population was 135.58 million during 1971-81. The current increase is also at the same rate as in the previous decade. Third, productivitiy is declining owing to continuous use of land for more than four thousand years without replenishing the soil through rotation, fertilization, and fallow land. Fourth, excessive hoarding and speculation have created artificial shortages. Fifth, drought, floods and other physical calamities have affected food production adversely. Sixth, there is deficiency of food resulting from the lack of a nutritious diet; for example, the average caloric intake for an Indian was only over 200 in 1984. However, in large areas, people have to subsist on around 1,000 calories per day compared to an average of 3,700 in Poland and 3,600 in the United States during the same year. This substandard diet creates problems of malnutrition, low resistance to diseases, and an unhealthy work force. Finally, the government must provide work to the unemployed agricultural workers so that production can be increased. The Janata government introduced a programme called Food-for-Work on a selected basis involving twenty districts in 793 households in eighty villages and ten states. The results of the programme revealed that prices of foodgrains stabilized and there were considerable economic and social benefits accruing to the village community. With proper management, the Food-for-Work programme may prove extremely useful to village communities.

The new strategy of the government is to provide suitable food in ample quantities for a healthy population. The strategy adopted to achieve the highest food production goal was an increase in the area under high-yielding varieties of seeds, an increased and more efficient use of fertilizers, better irrigation facilities, improved cropping systems, better methods of soil conservation, the design and breeding of new crops, the control of pests and diseases, and improved storage to avoid spoilage and storage losses. India has to use her enormous manpower resources in agriculture, rather than completely mechanizing the farms. The title of the land should be transferred to the tillers to enable them to feel that they are real partners in the production process.

The gains of the Emergency (1975-77) seemed to be in the favour of the poorest sections of society and the villagers; however, the goals should have been long term rather than concentrating on the situation under an Emergency era alone. Four favourable monsoon seasons in succession, restrictions on hoarders and speculators, easy credit available in villages through cooperatives, more facilities for fertilizer production and distribution, price stability on the food front, and land to the tillers, have improved the food situation in India. If India wants to maintain a respectable position among the world community, she must feed her population at a respectable level without importing large quantities of food. She must also modernize her farming in accordance with traditions and culture rather than blindly copy the West. Mechanization should be introduced on a smaller scale where manpower can be utilized in addition to machines. For the last several years and especially during the World Food Conference in Rome in 1974 and successive conferences, India reaffirmed a global food policy so that every part of the world is fed well. One suggestion was to build a buffer stock of sixty million tons to be used by various countries which find themselves in a desperate food situation. The Indian delegation pointed out that the economically advanced nations have a more serious responsibility than ever before in supplying the necessary aid to wipe out the prospect of starvation among poor nations.

Mrs Gandhi told a conference of federal government ministers and chief ministers of twenty-two states that the priorities of the Seventh Five Year Plan (1985-90) would be food, work and productivity. A public sector investment of $ 180 billion to achieve five percent annual economic growth rate has been proposed under the plan. The increase in annual foodgrain production is targeted at 190 million tons by the end of 1990 from 160 million during 1985-86. Due to higher productivity per hectare, the surplus of foodgrains in 1986 was thirty-five million tons and the country had food storage difficulties and had to find markets for its surplus foodgrains. The programme for agricultural development will be integrated to remove rural poverty in the less developed areas. The target of five percent growth rate in food production is expected to be ahead of the rate of population growth and will keep pace with the increase in the proportion of income spent on food. If the targets are achieved, this programme may improve the conditions of the rural poor.

NOTES

Bhagirath, Vol. 17, No. 4 (April, 1971), 54.
George B. Cressey, *Asia's Land and Peoples: A Geography of One-Third of the Earth and Two-Thirds of Its people*, 3rd ed. (New York: McGraw-Hill Book Company, 1963), p. 396.
Economic Survey, 1983-84 (New Delhi: The Manager, Government of India Press, 1984).

The Economic Weekly, July, 1964, p. 1187.

"Harnessing the Land Resources," *Eastern Economist*, Vol. 47, No. 17 (April 28, 1967), p. 857.

India, 1975 and 1976: A Reference Annual (New Delhi: The Manager, Government of India Press, 1975), p. 177.

C.B. Mamoria, *Agricultural Problems of India*, 7th ed. (Allahabad: Kitab Mahal, 1973), p. 45.

Gunnar Myrdal, *Asian Drama: An Inquiry Into the Poverty of Nations*, Vol. I (New York: Twentieth Century Fund, Inc., 1968), p. 283.

Norman J.G. Pounds, *Political Geography*, 2nd ed. (New York: McGraw-Hill Book Company, 1972), p. 157.

W.G. East, O.H.K. Spate and Charles A. Fisher, *The Changing Map of Asia: A Political Geography*, 5th ed. (London: Methuen and Company Limited, 1971), p. 149.

O.H.K. Spate and A.T.A. Learmonth, *India and Pakistan: A General and Regional Geography*, 3rd ed. (London: Methuen and Company Limited, 1967).

L. Dudley Stamp, *Asia: A Regional and Economic Geography*, 11th ed. (London: Methuen and Company Limited, 1962), p. 198.

P.A. Wadia and K.T. Merchant, *Our Economic Problems*, 4th ed. (Bombay: New Book Company, 1957), p. 100.

"Who Benefits From Zonal Control," *Swarajya*, Vol. 12, No. 2 (November 25, 1967), 30.

CHAPTER 3

Water Resources and Development Strategy

THE economic prosperity and development strategy of a country depend upon the proper utilization of its water resources, particularly the river waters. Irrigation is vital for the sustained growth of agriculture at a high level, especially in a country like India. Sir Charles Trevelyn pointed out the importance of irrigation in that "irrigation is everything in India; water is more valuable than land, because, when water is applied to land it increases its productiveness at least six-fold and renders great extents of land productive, which otherwise would produce nothing or next to nothing" (Mukherjee, 1939, p. 167). The average rainfall over the Indian subcontinent is about 110 cm. as a whole, and this rainfall over the country's land area of 328 million hectares (m.ha.) gives a total precipitation of 3,700 billion cubic meters (b.cm.m.) of which thirty-three percent is lost due to evaporation, twenty-two percent seeps into the ground and forty-five percent is lost through runoff. According to the Khosla Commission, the water resources of the various river basins amount to 1,888, 057 million cubic meters (m.cu.m.). The approximate groundwater recharge is 424 m.cu.m.

The unequal distribution of water in space and time and a steady increase in the need for water (which is not necessarily limited to areas having adequate water supplies) makes water a scarce resource. The conservation of water and its equitable and rational use is, therefore, a matter of great national importance. Since Independence, an integrated development of water resources has been adopted to meet the requirement of irrigation, drainage, flood control, navigation, recreational facilities, hydroelectric power generation, water supply for industrial and domestic use, land reclamation related to water, control of water pollution from human, animal and industrial waste, and utilization of groundwater. This development has to be pursued in light of the physical and cultural limitations for steady availability and equitable distribution of water. Irrigation has increased the productivity of land, made the value of land soar, increased the revenue derived from agriculture, reduced the grim spectre of famine, brought security of life to the farmers, and has enhanced the standard of living of people in general.

Intensive exploitation and utilization of river waters is most essential in India because of the following physical and cultural factors:

Physical factors
1. Rainfall in India is unequally distributed throughout the year. It is unreliable, with wide variations in different parts of the country as well as from year to year in its quantity, incidence, and duration. In most parts of the country, nearly ninety percent of the rainfall occurs during the four summer monsoon months, June to September; the remainder of the year is practically dry; however, certain regions receive rainfall during the winter monsoon months, November to February, nearly ten percent of the total. Even in a single state, uneven distribution is common during the monsoon season. For example, a newspaper heading may read western Maharashtra is inundated with floods and eastern Maharashtra is facing severe drought conditions where drinking water is in scarcity. The excess water discharged during the four summer months creates undesirable flood hazards, washing away substantial amounts of top soil. The damage caused by cyclones and floods in 1976-77 was of the order of Rs. 7,510 million for the country as a whole, which was the highest for the last twenty-four years. Almost ninety-eight percent of this damage occurred in the states of Andhra Pradesh, Assam, Bihar, Gujarat, Haryana, Punjab, Rajasthan, Tamil Nadu, and West Bengal. Most of these states have unreliable rainfall even during the monsoon season (Fig. 2).

2. Rainfall throughout India is uncertain, erratic, and altogether unpredictable and quite often liable to complete failure. The variation in rainfall is unparalleled in any other country; for example, the average annual precipitation in western Rajasthan is less than 25 cms. and famine occurred several times in the past, whereas Mawsyuran (16 kms, east of Cherrapunji in Meghalaya) receives 1143 cms. of rainfall per year (Fig. 3). Even Mawsyuran, the rainiest spot in the world, experiences water shortages when the monsoon is over. In certain areas with unreliable rainfall, when the rainfall decreases to eighty percent or below, crop failures are common; subsequently, famine results if deficiency reaches forty percent or more. About one-third of the area of India is subjected to drought. Thus, irrigation is the only answer to the catastrophic question of famine.

3. A fast growing population and the spread of education and technological advancement demand higher quantities and better quali-

ties of food for the masses. To attain self-sufficiency and improved quality of food supply, better management of water resources is the key element in meeting the growing demand. While population is growing rapidly, rainfall is not. The use of water domestically, in both agriculture and industry, is steadily increasing while the discharge into the ocean is diminishing. Thus the pollution of the oceans and rivers is increasing rapidly.

4. Many of the Indian rivers are not perennial and carry significant flows during the summer monsoon months. Moreover, there is a wide variation in flows from year to year. The northern rivers are snow-fed and are normally perennial, but the variation between the winter and the summer monsoon flows may be as high as 1:100 in the main rivers traversing the plains and as high as 1:300 or more in small hill streams. For example, the Yamuna river during the summer months retains a width of a few meters in certain areas near Delhi and Agra, whereas during the rainy season, owing to floods, it affects the capital city of Delhi, as it did in 1978. The characteristics of the southern and central rivers is that about eighty to ninety percent of the annual runoff takes place during the four summer monsoon months, whereas during the remaining eight months of the year, they are largely dry. If the excess runoff during the rainy season can be stored and utilized during the drier months when the soil moisture is very low, multiple crops can be grown year round.

5. Prior to the arrival of the first monsoon rain, the evaporation from lakes and rivers is extremely high; as a result, even perennial rivers shrink to a few meters and the land is parched by intense heat. Besides, the drought that follows the first rain is so intense that the surface groundwater is evaporated in a very short period, leaving no residual moisture in the soil. The daily mean evaporation in the country varies from about 2mm. in the winter months in wet areas to as much as 16 mm. in the summer months in dry areas with the annual average for the whole country at about 6 mm.

6. About 19.6 percent of the cropped area is under cash crops which earn nearly sixty percent of foreign exchange earnings; however, only twelve percent of the cash cropped area is irrigated. To attain the maximum benefit of foreign exchange earnings, the irrigation of the area under cash crops must be increased steadily.

7. Irrigation is essential to arid and semi-arid regions for crop production and to increase productivity per hectare in high rainfall regions as well as for producing second and third crops per year.

8. The arrival and departure of the summer monsoon from year to year is uncertain which hinders the sowing and harvesting seasons

resulting in poor harvests.

To combat the adverse effects of uncertain, uneven, and erratic rainfall, artificial irrigation has been resorted to in India from very ancient times. From numerous references available, the use of artificial irrigation in India can be traced to as early as 4000 millenium B.S. In the *Rigveda*, four types of water are mentioned: first, waters that come from sky or rainwater; second, those which flow in rivers and streams; third, those which are obtained by digging; and fourth, those which ooze out from springs. Wells (*Avata*), canals (*Kulya*), dams (*Sursi*), and water courses like *Pranadi, Nala, Naliha, Tilamaha* were mentioned in *Vedas* (four canonical collections of hymns, prayers, and liturgical formulas that comprise the earliest Hindu sacred writings).

Irrigation development received great importance during the Mughal period and canals were built on perennial rivers in north India, in particular the western and eastern Yamuna canals. During the British period, old canals were renovated and new canals were built in north as well as south India. Dam construction was undertaken on some of the south Indian rivers. It is, however, after Independence and with the introduction of the First Fiver Year Plan in 1951 that the problem of irrigation and scientific management of water was taken up. The planned system of irrigation took into account: (a) the supply of necessary water to the crops in season, (b) the drainage and disposal of excess water, (c) prevention of flood damages, (d) conservation or stocking of water for release in the dry season, and (e) conservation of soils in higher elevations.

Since the adoption of the First Five Year Plan, more than one thousand major and minor projects have been taken up to increase the irrigation potential. Of these, more than nine hundred have been fully completed and a number of others partially commissioned and have started yielding benefits. The total water resources of the country have been assessed at 178 m.ha.m. Because of the limitations of physiography, topography, geology, dependability of flow, quality and present state of technology, only a part of this could be utilized. It has been assessed that about 67 m.ha.m. of surface and 26.5 m.ha.m. of groundwater can be tapped and utilized, that is, over fifty-two percent of the total water resources could be put to use; however, the percentage may increase with advancement in technology and better techniques of water utilization.

The total ultimate irrigation potential from both surface and groundwater is estimated to be 112 million hectares, of which 77 m.ha. is from surface and 35 m.ha. from groundwater resources, as against possible gross cropped area of 200 m.ha. on full development of irrigation potential. As a result of major and minor irrigation projects constructed after the First Five Year Plan, the irrigated areas have increased from 9.7 m.ha. in 1951 to 60.1 m.ha. in 1983-84. The irrigation potential from the existing and the new projects has, however, risen from 22.6 m.ha. to 66 m.ha. during the same period from 1951 to 1984, a three-fold increase. The target set for the Sixth Five Year Plan (1980-81 to 1985-86) is 68.1 m.ha. which should be achieved on the completion of the plan.

The environmental factor is responsible for making irrigation a necessary part of agriculture in India. It is also of great significance for the proper management of water resources at the national and international level; for storing water during the rainy season and for distributing it during the dry season; for the proper utilization of the available water potential; and for meeting the ever-growing demand on water resources. The cultural and political factors, however, at times become more important and supersede environmental limitations, especially in the case of India. For example, some important political implications of Indian rivers may be suggested.

Cultural factors

1. For one thing, political boundaries of the states in India are not drawn along drainage basins or along existing streams; rather the boundaries have been drawn on a linguistic basis and do not coincide with the river basins and channels. Most of the rivers, along with their tributaries in India, originate in one state, flow through another, and empty out into the coastline of a third state. In the case of some of the rivers, there are four to five states involved in the development of the river basin, such as in the case of the rivers Narmada, Godavari, Krishna, and Sutlej and their tributaries. Therefore, the exclusive control of the water of any river by one state may create tension among the neighbouring states. As a result, political differences arise particularly when the distribution of water is uneven and when the availability of irrigation water is of crucial importance. International law holds, like common law, that a state "is not only forbidden to stop or divert the flow of a river which runs from its own to a neighbouring state, but likewise to make such use of the water of the river as either causes danger to the neighbouring state or prevents it from making proper use of the flow of the river on its part" (Pounds, 1972, p. 320). The Farakka Barrage issue between India and Bangladesh has been under negotiations on the basis of mutual benefit and most of the tribunals on international rivers base their judgement on the principle of equitable sharing of waters and benefits. A number of rivers in different parts of the world form international or interstate boundaries; thus equitable sharing of water

between the states becomes easier. The interstate rivers of the United States, Canada, and Australia are of this category.

2. Since Independence, it has been proven through seven national elections that India can successfully run the largest democracy in the world; however, there are numerous regional parties with narrow parochial, regional, linguistic, and economic interests. This creates a desire on the part of state governments to avoid settlements on river disputes with neighbouring states so as to gain voters' confidence. In several cases, water was extensively utilized by the upper riparian states while ignoring the necessities of the neighbouring state. Many of India's river water disputes stem from the decisions of the regional parties who adopt an uncompromising attitude towards their neighbours. For example, Tamil Nadu's Dravida Munnetra Kazhagam (D.M.K.) and later on Anna D.M.K. showed uncompromising attitudes towards its neighbours, Karnataka and Kerala.

3. The states of India have been formed along linguistic lines representing anthropogeographic boundaries: people are loyal to their states because of linguistic affiliations. When such a linguistic, social or regional group gives preference to local disputes, the national interest is sacrificed and progress is hampered. This is true in cases of interstate water disputes where local disputes overshadow the national interest.

4. If the party ruling the states involved in an interstate dispute is the same as the one at the Centre, the central leadership may be more successful in settling the dispute, than if the states are ruled by different political parties. It is also evident that most of the river water disputes were amicably settled among various states when most of the state governments belonged to the same party and had a strong central leadership. A large number of disputes arose after the 1967 general elections when the strength of the Congress Party was reduced at the Centre and eight of the state governments were formed by the opposition parties or a coalition of political parties. Numerous disputes were settled after the 1971 general elections and during 1975 and 1976 when the central government became more powerful—in 1971, owing to the massive support of the voters and in 1975 and 1976 owing to constitutional changes and the imposition of Emergency when the Prime Minister became more powerful.

5. India has chosen parliamentary democracy form of government, and thus all interstate disputes have to be settled through democratic means. This creates an additional problem where disputing parties have to be satisfied and local as well as minority interests have to be considered important, whereas in a dictatorship or in an authoritarian regime, states are asked to follow the settlement dictated by the

ruling authority. In this case, local and regional interests have to be sacrificed in the national interest.

All interstate development projects should solve the economic problems faced by the people living in the river basin region; projects should be constructed with this intention. In spite of the often expressed hope that the execution of river basin projects would result in significant economic advantages to all contestant "parties" and would pave the way for political reconciliation, political issues have maintained their priority as a separating factor (Weigert, 1957, p. 100), and have overshadowed economic advantages.

The construction of new projects and the functioning of existing ones depend on the cordial relations between the neighbouring states. The creation and extension of irrigation schemes have many political implications. New areas brought under irrigation are frequently faced with the political problems of water distribution, and serious conflicts often arise between farmers and different villages. Disagreement over the site of a dam and legality of river water use between states is a common phenomenon in newly developed democracies. The Punjab crisis in 1984 has been a prime example of such disagreement. Land titles have frequently been questioned by neighbours and the value of land has soared to an unprecedented level, especially in newly irrigated areas. Politicians contest elections on the basis of local water distribution, development of new irrigation schemes, distribution of drinking water in urban areas, and land tenure issues that appeal to the voters.

International river water disputes

To evaluate the interstate water disputes, it is important to examine a few examples of international as well as interstate disputes in different parts of the world so as to apply some of the principles to the conditions in India. International river water disputes originate because a river may pass through several nation states while flowing its natural course. Most international rivers were used for navigation, fishing, domestic and sanitary purposes, small irrigation projects, and recreational purposes. The minor uses mentioned above did not affect the flow of the river. However, modern technological advancement in the construction of large dams, diversion canals, and linking the rivers by building canals have altered the situation dramatically.

There have been a few international examples of disputes, the settlement of which was brought about by mutual agreement, by the auspices of the United Nations, the International Bank of Reconstruction and Development (World Bank), or by a third party mediation at the international level. The examples include: the United States and Mexico agreed in 1906 to share the waters of the Rio Grande; the United States and Canada agreed on sharing the waters and the boundary treaty on the Columbia River in 1909 and again in 1964; the United States and Mexico agreed on sharing the waters of the Colorado in 1944-45; the United States and Mexico again agreed on sharing the waters of the Rio Grande and Colorado in 1948; the Paris Peace Conference in 1919-20 appointed a Commission which met at Barcelona in 1921 and drew up a list of basic principles governing navigation on international rivers; Egypt and Sudan agreed to share the waters of the Nile in 1959; India and Pakistan agreed to share the waters of the Indus system through the mediation of the World Bank in 1960 (Garretson, Hayton, Olmstead, 1967, pp. 167-607); and India and Bangladesh conditionally agreed to share the waters of the Ganga and build a dam at Farakka in 1978.

International and inter-regional conferences were held at different places to discuss possible answers to solve international water disputes, such as the Peace Conference of Paris Commission (1919-20) which met in Barcelona in 1921; Conference held in Montevideo in 1933; Buenos Aires in 1957; New York in 1958; Hamburg in 1960; Salzburg in 1961; and Helsinki in 1966. The Helsinki Conference was the most elaborate one which set definite rules governing the distribution of water and utilization of international rivers. Besides, the United Nations and its specialized agencies also helped in settling international disputes. Disputes have been settled through the international joint commission, the permanent engineering board, the international boundary and water commissions, and mutual agreement between the disputing nations. The Helsinki Rules adopted on August 20, 1966, by the International Law Association with six chapters and thirty-seven articles gave first preference to settling the dispute through mutual agreement and through the application of the equitable apportionment theory.

The dispute can be referred to a third party adjudication under established international law; it can be sent to an arbitral tribunal or to a permanent tribunal or to the International Court of Justice. In the case of the Indus Water Treaty, it was settled through the arbitration of the International Bank of Reconstruction and Development which has set up a Permanent Indus Commission to look after any disagreement arising between India and Pakistan. To maintain good neighbourly relations, India accepted the principle of equitable apportionment of the Indus system waters between Upper (India) and Lower (Pakistan) riparian states. India could have insisted on following the Harmon Doctrine (1895). Contrary to the settlement of the Indus dispute through arbitration, the Farakka Barrage issue is being settled through mutual agreement between India and Bangladesh which has also set up a permanent commission for advising both the nations, if and when the necessity arises. Mutual agreement has also been reached between India and Nepal as well as between India and Bhutan for development of international rivers affecting these countries.

Interstate rivers

Problems more acute and pressing than international disputes are the interstate water disputes among various states or provinces in a country, because all projects related to developing and utilizing the water resources beneficially depend upon the successful harnessing of interstate rivers. Besides, when control of water resources lies in the hands of the state government rather than the federal government, the interstate disputes become more complicated. In most countries, however, federal laws are stronger than the state laws. For example, if a state project is not in the best interest of the nation, it should be abandoned. Such cases have been settled in most federal countries such as the United States, Australia, Canada, Nigeria and India by the highest court in the land. In the case of Arizona vs. California (U.S. Supreme Court Judgement, 1963 and 1964), the Supreme Court of the United States has stated that the power to build a dam and store the water of a navigable stream by the federal government gives the power to apportion the water to states in such shares as Congress or its delegate may decide. Further, the war and treaty powers (U.S. Constitution) of the United States give added authority to the federal government to build projects to strengthen the national defence or comply with a treaty obligation. The federal government is also given power to allocate funds to develop and regulate water resources for the purpose of (a) flood control, (b) irrigation, (c) navigation, (d) power, (e) water supply, (f) water quality control, (g) fish and wildlife enhancement, and (h) recreation.

The state powers are the residuum of sovereignty left to the states after the grant of specific powers to the United States, such as the power to create property rights and the police power to regulate property rights. Water was considered as property during the early settlement, especially in the western United States. In certain cases, Congress has opted to waive federal powers and has given more powers to states for water distribution. Most of the interstate disputes in the United States were settled through "equitable apportionment" by the Supreme Court or by forming an interstate compact with the consent of Congress or by appointing a commission or study groups by the federal government. In other federal structures, too, most of the interstate disputes have been resolved through the appointment of commissions by the federal government, the Supreme Court rulings, and by interstate water compacts or boards.

Interstate river water disputes

In India, during the British rule, the interstate or inter-province water disputes were settled by the central government because the irrigation projects were virtually under the control of the central government. However, in 1937 under the Government of India Act of 1935, irrigation was transferred to the sole legislative jurisdiction of the provinces (The Government of India Act, 1935). The central government was not responsible for irrigation and water development in various states. The concern of the centre was to settle interstate water disputes through mutual negotiations leading to agreement. The matter was kept out of the federal courts and was to be settled by the Governor General with the assistance of an expert commission. Under this rule, the Governor General of India appointed the Indus Commission in 1941 to settle the dispute between Punjab and Sind over sharing the Indus waters (Rau, 1941). The Commission applied the principle of equitable apportionment to settle the dispute. The Republic of India upon adopting a Constitution made irrigation a state subject (The Constitution of India, 1951). State governments, at present, virtually exercise full control on planning, development, regulation, distribution, and control of water flowing through their territories. For the settlement of interstate water disputes, the Draft Constitution of India contained virtually identical provisions as the Government of India Act, 1935. But Article 262 was adopted with a view to increasing irrigation and power potential in independent India and exploiting the interstate river waters to their full potential. The article empowers the Parliament to provide for the adjudication of any dispute or complaint with respect to the use, distribution or control of the waters of, or in any interstate river or river valley and to bar the jurisdiction of the Supreme Court or any other court in respect of such disputes (The Constitution of India, 1951). In accordance with this provision, the Parliament has enacted the Interstate Water Dispute Act, 1956. The Act provides for the constitution of a tribunal by the central government for the settlement of an interstate water dispute when a request is received from a state government and when the central government is of the opinion that the dispute cannot be settled by negotiations. It provided for a one-man tribunal appointed from among judges of the Supreme Court or a High Court, sitting or retired, nominated by the Chief Justice of India (The Interstate Water Dispute Act, 1956). The provision was amended to increase membership of the tribunal to three sitting judges of the Supreme Court or High

Court (The Interstate Water Dispute Act, 1968). The central government has also been given the responsibility of:

regulation and development of interstate rivers and river valleys to the extent to which such regulation and development under the control of the Union is declared by Parliament by law to be expedient in the public interest (The Constitution of India, 1951).

The Parliament has also enacted the River Board Act, 1956, which authorizes the central government to constitute river boards in consultation with the state governments for regulation and development of interstate rivers (The River Board Act, 1956). Three river water disputes were referred to be settled. These disputes were on the rivers Krishna, Godavari, and Narmada. The Government of India formed rules on June 30, 1959, to settle interstate water disputes. It is laid down that where the government of a state desires to refer any water dispute to a tribunal for adjudication, it should address itself to the Secretary to the Government of India, Ministry of Irrigation and Power, giving particulars of the dispute.

The tribunal for such a dispute would require the parties to nominate representatives to present their case before it within a specific period of time in a prescribed form. If one of the parties fails to nominate a representative or the representative does not appear before the tribunal, a decision might be given in his absence by the tribunal. On March 22, 1962, the central government announced the establishment of nine river boards for the Mahanadi, Tapti, Mahi, Krishna-Godavari, Sutlej, Beas-Ravi, Yamuna, Cauvery, and Ajoy basins. The boards were designed to help control and regulate the supply of waters of the interstate rivers for optimum utilization and deal effectively with the problems of irrigation, hydroelectric power generation, flood control, soil conservation, drainage and navigation.

Interstate rivers in India are for the general welfare of all the states through which they flow irrespective of political boundaries. The Harmon Doctrine has never held sway in India. Under the Constitution of India, a co-riparian state is not free to develop an interstate river regardless of the inquiry to other co-riparian states. Besides, Parliament is empowered by Article 262 of the Constitution of India to adjudicate any interstate dispute or complaint. A number of disputes in India have been settled on the basis of equitable apportionment which is the universally accepted principle (Fig. 5 and Table 4). These settlements include (a) the three states of Haryana, Rajasthan, and Uttar Pradesh reached an agreement on draining the flood waters which inundated vast stretches of land in the three states besides sharing waters; (b)

Water Resources and Development Strategy

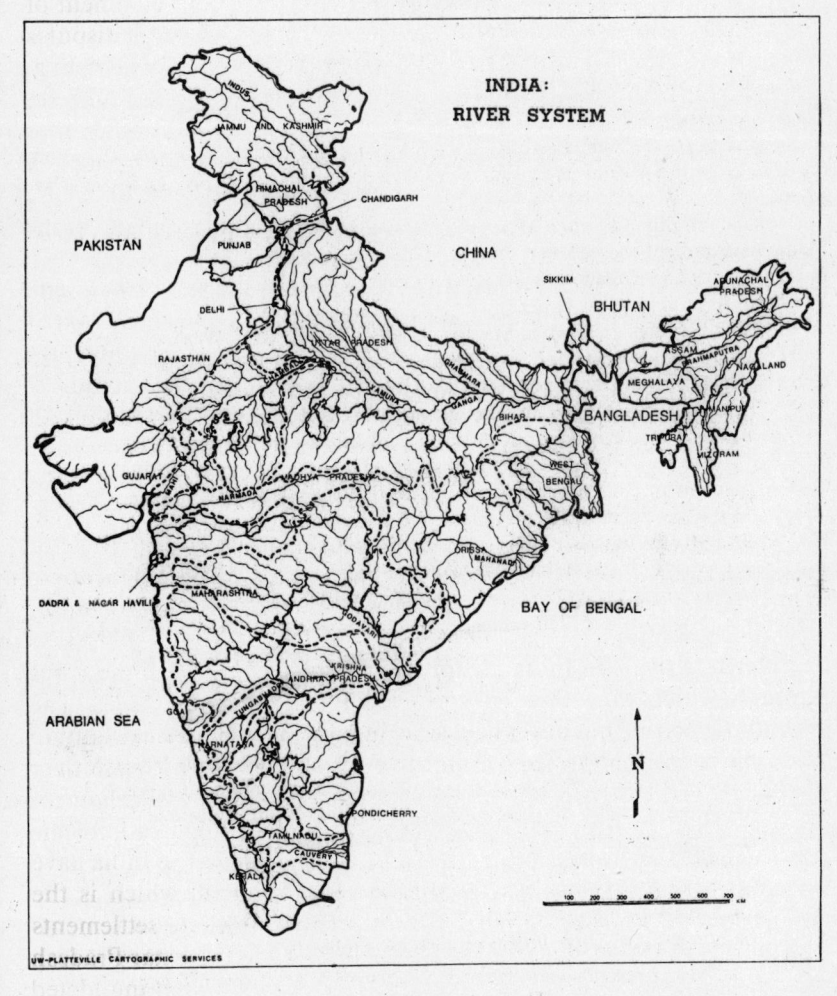

Fig. 5

Table 4
Interstate river water disputes

Case 1

States involved: Karnataka, Kerala, Tamil Nadu
River: Cauvery. The Cauvery rises in Coorg in Northeast Karnataka, enters Tamil Nadu where Coimbatore and Salem districts meet, and ends up as a vast spreading delta in Thanjavur district and enters in the Bay of Bengal. It is considered as the Dakshina Ganga or "The Ganga of the South." The major tributaries flowing through Karnataka are the Hemavati, Lakshmanatirtha, Kabini, Suvarnavati, and Yagachi. The tributaries originating and flowing through Tamil Nadu are Bhavani, Amravati, and Noyil. Nearly seventy-five percent of the water is contributed by Karnataka.

Causes of dispute

A dispute arose between the Princely States of Mysore and Madras for building dams on the Hemavati and Kabini at the upper reaches of the River Cauvery by the state of Mysore.

Trouble arose in 1909 when Mysore began to construct the Krishnaraja Sagar Dam. Madras Government feared that its construction would affect the Tanjore delta and disturb the existing irrigation facilities. Madras itself was planning to build the Mettur Reservoir. After long talks, an agreement was reached in 1925.

In 1950 difficulties arose when Madras planned three projects: (1) Mettur high level canal, (2) Kattalai Bed Regulator, and (3) Pullambady Scheme. The last two schemes were below the Mettur High Dam on the Cauvery River. The Mysore Government objected to Madras for taking up these projects. The agreement allowed certain fixed flows to Madras.

Mysore complains that Madras has been permitted by the Central Government to build the Mettur high level canal, the Kattalai regulator, the Pullambedi Canal, and the Coleroom anicut and that Madras would appropriate the surplus waters in the Cauvery which would have otherwise been available for diversion in 1974 after the expiry of the 1924 Treaty. Mysore has also objected to the proposal of Madras for improving and remodelling the Cauvery delta canal system to provide for irrigation to 141,640 hectares. Mysore felt that construction of reservoirs by Madras at lower Bhavani and Amaravati would affect it. Madras has been complaining that construction of reservoirs by Mysore on the Hemavati, Lakshmanatirtha, Kabini and Suvarnavati are intended to take away the supplies that are legitimate to Madras. Kerala has also filed its objection to the Kabini Project.

Mysore and Kerala wanted to repudiate the 1924 agreement for their own benefit. Mysore stand was that the 1924 agreement between Mysore and Madras (Tamil Nadu), although was valid up to 1974, had worked to its disadvantage and needed to be revised through negotiations. The Mysore Government felt that the agreement had been operating harshly on account of the fact that whereas seventy-five perent of the catchement area of the Cauvery Basin lies within its territory, its utilization is much less.

On March 5, 1970 the Central Government proposed that Mysore (Karnataka) should stop its Hemavati, Lakshmanatirtha, Kabini, and Suvarnavati irrigation projects under implementation in the Cauvery Basin. Tamil Nadu wanted to refer the matter to tribunal in 1971. Karnataka contended that referring the dispute to a tribunal will delay the work on various projects. Kerala firmly stood by the position that Karnataka should utilize the Cauvery waters for its schemes only after there had been an understanding on water apportionment among Karnataka, Tamil Nadu and Kerala.

Water Resources and Development Strategy

In 1971 Karnataka was under Presidential rule, therefore the Prime Minister wanted to delay the matter of setting up for a tribunal. Tamil Nadu filed a suit on August 4, 1971, against the Central Government for not referring the Cauvery waters dispute to a tribunal. The suit was filed under Article 131 of the Constitution dealing with Centre-State and interstate disputes. On August 12, 1971, the Constitution Bench of the Supreme Court declined to grant to the State of Tamil Nadu *ex parte* stay restraining the State of Karnataka from proceeding with reservoir projects across the Cauvery River and its tributaries. On September 7, the Supreme Court dismissed the Kerala Government's application for impleading it as a party in Tamil Nadu's suit against the Central Government on the Cauvery waters issue.

Again on October 3, the Supreme Court rejected a plea by Tamil Nadu to restrain Mysore from proceeding with the construction of certain projects across the River Cauvery and its tributaries. The Court decided that there did not appear to be any infringement of rights on the part of Karnataka because the works in dispute were in progress within its own territory. There was, further, no diminution of water at present.

In September 1978, again dispute arose among Tamil Nadu, Kerala and Karnataka concerning the 1976 agreement and sharing the Cauvery waters. Kerala and Karnataka contended that seepage of water should be stopped through conservation methods so that more water will be available to their utilization whereas Tamil Nadu declined to spare any waters to Kerala and Karnataka.

Method and year of settlement	Agreement
Mutual Agreement 1892	An agreement between the then princely states of Mysore and Madras over the sharing of the Cauvery water was reached in 1892. The agreement imposed restrictions on both the states to construct new irrigation reservoirs. The Mysore Government shall not without the previous consent of the Madras Government build any new irrigation reservoirs across any part of the fifteen main rivers. The Madras Government should not refuse consent except for the protection of prescriptive rights already acquired and existing....
Mutual Agreement 1924	The agreement of 1925 allowed Mysore to irrigate 44,515 hectares by means of reservoirs constructed on the Cauvery and its five tributaries up to the Belmur bridge with reservoir capacity of 1.274 million cubic meters (MCM). Madras was to limit the area of irrigation under their Cauvery Mettur Project to 121,810 hectares with the reservoir capacity of 2.647 billion cubic meters (BCM). Should Madras construct any new storage reservoirs on the Bhavani, Amaravati or Noyali rivers, Mysore was at liberty to construct storage reservoir on a tributary as an offset with a capacity not exceeding sixty percent of the new reservoir in Madras. There was no mention in the agreement about building new reservoirs on the main rivers. The agreement stipulated that if any disagreement arises, it should be referred to an arbitration or the Government of India.
	The Central Minister for Agriculture and Irrigation had convened meetings of the three chief ministers in November 1974 followed by another meeting in February, 1975. Mutually acceptable settlement could not be reached at these meetings. The matter was further discussed with the officers of the three states where frank discussion took place.

Mutual Agreement with the assistance of the Union Minister of Agriculture and Irrigation Aug. 27, 1976

According to a mutual agreement reached on August 27, 1976, among the chief ministers of Kerala, Tamil Nadu, and Karnataka with the assistance of the Central Minister of Agriculture and Irrigation, a Committee of representatives of the three states and the Central Government shall be constituted immediately to work out the manner of sharing the available waters in lean years. The existing utilization of the Cauvery waters is 19 BCM comprising 13,847 BCM by Tamil Nadu, 3.313 BCM by Karnataka, and 141.585 MCM by Kerala. Under the agreement the Cauvery Valley Authority will be formed to administer the existing projects and sanction new ones to the concerned states.

Case 2

States involved: Maharashtra, Karnataka, Andhra Pradesh

River: Krishna. The River Krishna is the second largest of the east flowing rivers of the Peninsular India. It rises in the Western Ghats in Maharashtra and flows east through the states of Maharashtra, Karnataka, and Andhra Pradesh. Its total length is about 1,400 km and the total area of its catchment basin is about 259,000 sq. km, out of which 26.81 percent is in Maharashtra, 43.74 percent in Karnataka, and 29.45 percent in Andhra Pradesh. The tributaries are Konya, Sangli (also receives waters of the Verna), Panchganga, Ghat Prabha, Malprabha, Bhima, Tungabhadra and Musi. The main irrigation canals on the Krishna are navigable and connect the Krishna District with its northern neighbours Godavari and, by means of the Buckingham Canal, with the City of Madras in the south. The Buckingham Canal is dry because Andhra Pradesh refused to supply navigation waters for the canal. The Krishna and Godavari basins include most of Andhra Pradesh, Maharashtra and Karnataka and parts of Madhya Pradesh and Orissa.

Causes of dispute

Prior to 1951 Andhra Pradesh was diverting 8.215 BCM of waters, Maharashtra 1.218 BCM and Karnataka 2.217 BCM, respectively. The Krishna Delta Canal was constructed in 1855 which has been the major irrigation work on the river.

Irrigation projects existed prior to 1951 on the Krishna River

State	Name of canal	Year of construction	Irrigation in hectares	Diversion of waters by states
Andhra Pradesh	Kurnool-Cuddapah Canal	1886	40,468	8.215 BCM
Andhra Pradesh	Krishna Delta Canal	1855	60,703	—
Maharashtra	Nira Canal	1885	60,703	1.218 BCM
Mysore (Karnataka)	—	—	—	2.217 BCM

About 449,201 hectares of irrigated areas lay outside the basin of the Krishna River. The total water being diverted from the Krishna was 11.650 BCM that irrigated 931,739 hectares before the commencement of the First Five Plan in 1951. The states were not satisfied by the distribution formula.

The States Reorganization Act, 1956, forming the states on the basis of languages altered situation through shifting the boundaries and readjusting the areas in **Karnataka** (Mysore), Andhra Pradesh, and Maharashtra, the riparian states. In view of the territorial changes, demands were made to re-evaluate the allocations made in 1951. Maharashtra and Karnataka questioned the validity of the 1951 agreement because of territorial changes, but Andhra Pradesh objected to any revision until the stipulated time of 1976. Even an interstate conference convened under the auspices of the Union Minister of Irrigation and Power in September, 1960, could not solve the dispute. The Government of India appointed a three-man commission headed by N.D. Gulhati. The discharge data, evaporation rates and underground seepage for Krishna and Godavari were insufficient to measure the dependable flow even at seventy-five percent dependability and, thus, the Commission gathered sub-basin data, upstream diversion and evaporation loss from reservoirs. This on the Krishna as worked out was 53.069 BCM.

Andhra Pradesh insisted that the 1951 agreement could be reopened only after twenty-five years since it is valid up to 1976. Andhra also protested to the Central Government on November 23, 1968, for clearing some of the projects to be constructed by Maharashtra and Karnataka on the River Krishna. It stated that the three governments agreed to abide by the 1951 agreement and now Maharashtra and Karnataka are diverting excess waters for utilization ignoring the limits as agreed in 1951. Karnataka, however, did not ratify the 1951 agreement.

Method and year of settlement	Agreement
Planning Commission, Government of India July, 1951	The Planning Commission convened an interstate conference in July, 1951 to discuss various projects on the river Krishna. After discussion and consultation, a formula was devised depending upon the annual dependable flow at 48.567 BCM. The existing utilization was 21.068 BCM. The remaining 27.482 was rounded off to 28.317 BCM to be divided among the states. The agreement provided for a review of the allocations after twenty-five years. According to 1951 agreement Andhra Pradesh was allocated 27.807 BCM. Maharashtra-8.070 BCM, and Karnataka-13.450 BCM. Maharashtra was permitted to divert waters for Konya hydel power project for which Karnataka and Andhra Pradesh complained that Maharashtra was diverting excess water than the permissible limit.
Minister of Irrigation Government of India 1963	In 1963 under the Hafiz Mohammed Ibrahim (Minister of Irrigation and Power at New Delhi) award the following ad hoc allotments were made to ensure continuity of work by the various states. Andhra Pradesh-22.654 BCM, Karnataka-16.990 BCM, and Maharashtra-11.327 BCM.
The Krishna Waters Dispute Tribunal April 10, 1969	The Krishna Waters Dispute Tribunal which was constituted by the Government of India on April 10, 1969, held that Maharashtra will not use more than 16 BCM, in any water year (June to July), Karnataka not more than 19.680 BCM, and Andhra Pradesh can use the remaining 22.654 BCM but will not acquire any right to use water

beyond this limit. This may be reviewed at any time after May 31, A.D. 2000 as directed by the tribunal. The tribunal giving its first report on December 24, 1973, determined that seventy-five percent of dependable flow of the Krishna River up to Vijayawada is 58.333 and this entire flow is available for distribution. The tribunal has placed restrictions on the use to be made by certain states in Ghataprabha, Tungabhadra, and Vedavati sub-basins as well as from the main stream of the Bhima River and from the catchment area of the Kanga River. It has also laid down regulations regarding gauging and gauging sites in the Krishna System and other strict restrictions were imposed on the concerned states.

Tribunal March 27, 1976

The final report submitted on March 27, 1976, by the tribunal was binding upon all three states. According to the award, Maharashtra would get not more than 15.857 BCM, in any water year, Karnataka not more than 19.822 BCM, and Andhra Pradesh not more than 22.654 BCM, making a total of 56.643 BCM. This representing seventy-five percent dependable flow of the river up to the Krishna barrage site at Vijaywada, which was the terminal point of diversion of the Krishna River. Andhra Pradesh shall not acquire any right whatsoever to use nor be deemed to have allocated in excess of 22.654 BCM.

Maharashtra would not be permitted to divert any waters from the Krishna basin except for the Konya hydel project and the Tata hydel works. The return flow from various projects in these three states was estimated at about 707.925 MCM, 962.279 MCM and 311.487 MCM in Maharashtra, Karnataka, and Andhra Pradesh, respectively and the states were also permitted to use for their own benefit.

The tribunal suggested to form an administrative authority called "the Krishna Valley Authority" consisting of representatives of the three states and the Centre.

Mutual Agreement October 28, 1977

A mutual agreement reached between the three states on October 28, 1977, allowed Madras City to get up to 424.755 MCM of the Krishna waters to supplement the metropolitan water supply system. The agreement was signed incorporating the decision of the chief ministers and the irrigation ministers of the states concerned. It was agreed that between July 1 and October 21 Tamil Nadu will be permitted to draw water from the Srisailam reservoir through an open-lined channel from Srisailam to Pennar.

Case 3

States involved: Andhra Pradesh, Karnataka
River: The Tungabhadra.

The River Tungabhadra is a tributary of the Krishna. It is formed north of Shimoga by the union of twin rivers Tunga and Bhadra which rise together in the Western Ghats at Gangamula. It flows through Karnataka and Andhra Pradesh and joins the Krishna beyond Kurnool. Tungabhadra's tributaries include the Varada and the Vicavati. It has a drainage area of 71,417 square miles.

Water Resources and Development Strategy

Causes of dispute
The Tungabhadra project was undertaken between the erstwhile State of Hyderabad and the State of Mysore through an agreement in 1944. The complication arose after the reorganization of Andhra Pradesh and subsequently on the reorganization of the States in 1956. The States Reorganization Act left the whole dam area in the states of Andhra Pradesh and Mysore. The central government appointed a four-member board with Chairman and one member appointed by the Centre as well as one member from Mysore and Andhra each.

Method and year of settlement	Agreement
Planning Commission of India 1956.	In 1956, with the assistance of the Planning Commission, the Government of India agreed to share the waters in the ratio of 35:65 between Mysore and Andhra Pradesh.

Case 4
States involved: Tamil Nadu, Kerala
Rivers: The Parambikulam, Aliyar and Bhivani
Causes of dispute: Sharing of cost and power generated

Method and year of settlement	Agreement
Mutual agreement May 29, 1970	Tamil Nadu will construct two dams—the Neerad Weir and the Peruvari Pallam at a cost of 36 million rupees. Kerala agreed to allow Tamil Nadu to generate hydro-electric power at the Periyar Plant just across the border in Kerala. It will generate 300 million units of power per year.

States involved: Tamil Nadu, Kerala
Rivers: The Pandiar, Punnapuzha, Nihar
Causes of dispute: Dam site and sharing of waters.

Method and year of settlement	Agreement
Mutual agreement March 11, 1974	Tamil Nadu will construct storage dam in the Pandiar-Punnapuzha system in its territory. Kerala is entitled to the use of regulated discharge of water from the Tamil Nadu power station.
	Kerala agreed to the location sugested by Tamil Nadu for a dam site on the Nihar River.

Case 5

States involved: Maharashtra, Andhra Pradesh, Madhya Pradesh, Karnataka, and Orissa.
River: Godavari. The Godavari is the largest of the east flowing rivers of the Peninsular

India. It rises in the Nasik district of Maharashtra and flows in a southeasterly direction through Maharashtra and Andhra Pradesh, covering a distance of 1,465 kms. The tributaries joining the Godavari in Maharashtra are Darna, Kadam and the combined waters of Pravara and Mula. The tributaries, Purna, Manjra, Maner, Kinarsari, Pranhita, Wardha and Wainganga originate in Madhya Pradesh. The tributaries Indravati and Sabari rise in Orissa. Some portion of Karnataka also falls in the drainage basin of the river. The drainage basin covers an area of 313,390 sq. kms. The total waters being diverted from the Godavari was 13.326 BCM that irrigated 1,106,760 hectares before the commencement of the First Five Year Plan in 1951.

Maharashtra occupies nearly 48.65 percent of the total catchment area of 315,000 sq. kms. in the Godavari basin, Andhra Pradesh, 23.41; Madhya Pradesh, 20.86; Orissa, 5.67; and Karnataka, 1.41. Although endowed with considerable surface water potential, the water distribution within the Godavari basin is highly uneven. The basin above Pochampad is drought-affected and that below it receives more rainfall. The area up to Pochampad is about thirty percent of the total catchment area whereas the surface water run-off at this site is roughly twenty percent of the total run-off in the basin.

Irrigation projects which existed prior to 1951 on the river Godavari

State	Name of canal	Year of construction	Irrigation in hectares
Andhra Pradesh	Nizamsagar	1914	52,069
Maharashtra	Godavari Canal	1915	20,234
Maharashtra	Pravara	1926	24,281
Madhya Pradesh	Wainganga	1926	20,234
Karnataka	—	—	—
Orissa	—	—	—

Diversion of waters by States

Andhra Pradesh	11.123 BCM
Maharashtra	1.568 BCM
Maharashtra	—
Madhya Pradesh	572.003 MCM
Karnataka	1,333 cubic meters
Orissa	39,644 cubic meters

There were nearly 32,000 tanks and diversions on the river and 319,702 hectares outside its basin were irrigated by the river. According to states, the water was not equitably distributed.

Causes of dispute

The States Reorganization Act of 1956 has affected the agreement because of changes through boundary making and readjustment of areas in Maharashtra, Karnataka, Madhya Pradesh, Andhra Pradesh, and Orissa, the riparian states.

In view of the territorial changes, demands were made to re-evaluate the allocations made in 1951. Karnataka and Maharashtra questioned the validity of 1951 agreement. Madhya Pradesh and Orissa asked for a fresh consideration of the whole issue, while Andhra Pradesh insisted to continue the allocation till 1976, the stipulated date. Even an interstate conference convened under the auspices of the Union Minister of Irrigation and Power in September 1960 could not solve the dispute. The Government of India appointed a three-man commission on May 3, 1961, to investigate the availability of waters at seventy-five percent dependability of the Godavari and Krishna and submit its report by the end of November, 1961: however, the report was submitted in August 1962. The commission recommended to set up a board or commission immediately to coordinate the development projects on these river basins. Maharashtra and Karnataka governments expressed disappointment about the finding of the commission and Andhra Pradesh had mixed feelings. The flow of the Godavari according to this commission chaired by N.D. Gulhati was 117.997 BCM.

Method and year of settlement	*Agreement*
Decision taken by the Planning Commission, Government of India July 1951	The Planning Commission convened an inter-state conference in July 1951 to discuss various projects on the river Godavari. Orissa although a riparian state, was not invited. After discussion and consultation a formula was devised depending upon the annual dependable flow at 70.729 BCM. The existing utilization was 27.043 BCM and remaining balance of 53.944 BCM was rounded off to 53,900 BCM to be divided among the states as follows: Maharashtra—1.614 BCM, Andhra Pradesh—13.988 BCM, Madhya Pradesh—12.912 BCM, and Tamil Nadu—25.287 BCM, respectively. The agreement provided for a review of the allocation after twenty-five years.
The Godavari waters dispute tribunal April 10, 1969	No concrete development programmes were carried out due to continuing disputes over the sharing of waters of the river. The Gulhati commission could not make specific allocations: therefore, the Union Minister of Irrigation and Power, Hafiz Mohammed Ibrahim, made tentative allocation which would not exceed the limit of dependable flow of the river. To solve the existing dispute, the Government of India constituted the Godavari Waters Dispute Tribunal on April 10, 1969, to go into the details and settle the dispute among the contesting states. Before the submission of the final report by the tribunal, some mutual agreements were arrived at between the contesting states.

States involved: Andhra Pradesh, Karnataka
River: The Godavari

Method and year of settlement	Agreement
Mutual agreement September 18, 1975	Andhra Pradesh and Karnataka arrived at a stop-gap arrangement for the sharing of the Godavari River waters. Andhra Pradesh will allow Karnataka to build the Karanja 370.953 MCM and Chilkanala 33.131 MCM projects utilizing 396.483 MCM of water. Karnataka in return had agreed to allow Singur project utilizing 111.268 MCM of water and the construction of balancing reservoir with a capacity of 849.510 MCM to meet the needs of the twin cities of Hyderabad and Secunderabad. The arrangement would have to be ratified by the Godavari waters tribunal, because the dispute was with the tribunal. Karnataka, Andhra Pradesh, Madhya Pradesh, Maharashtra and Orissa were interested in the Godavari waters.

States involved: Andhra Pradesh, Maharashtra
River: The Godavari

Method and year of settlement	Agreement
Mutual Agreement October 6, 1975	Maharashtra would be free to use all waters up to the Pajthan Dam site on the Godavari and up to the Siddheshwar Dam site on the Manjira, and up to Pochampad Dam site.

Below the Pochampad Dam site, Maharashtra and Andhra Pradesh would be free to use an additional quantity of 8.495 BCM each for new projects. Several minor projects were also settled during the negotiations. Andhra Pradesh can withdraw 111.268 MCM for drinking water supply to Hyderabad site from its proposed Singur on the Manjira. Andhra Pradesh can also use 1.642 under Nizamsagar project. Maharashtra and Andhra Pradesh have agreed jointly to take up Landi, Lower Panganga and Pranhita projects. |

States involved: Madhya Pradesh, Orissa
River: The Godavari

Method and year of settlement	Agreement
Mutual Agreement December 9, 1975	An agreement has been reached between Madhya Pradesh and Orissa to develop a joint project on the Saveri (Kolab) River.

Orissa would be free to use the water of the Saveri above the common boundary as it deemed fit. According to the agreement, Orissa and Madhya Pradesh would be free to use for their new projects 8.495 BCM and 5.663 BCM, respectively, over their committed utilization. |

Orissa assured a supply of 1.274 BCM of flow in the Indravati River and its tributaries at its border with Madhya Pradesh on the basis of seventy-five percent dependability. Madhya Pradesh conceded to Orissa the right to execute the Indravati power-cum-irrigation project in the manner suggested by it to the Central Government.

States involved: Maharashtra, Andhra Pradesh, Madhya Pradesh, Karnataka, Orissa
River: The Godavari

Method and year of settlement

Agreement

Mediation by the Central Agriculture and Irrigation Minister December 19, 1975

The agreement related to sharing of as much as 66.129 BCM of waters of a total of 84.951 BCM in the Godavari basin. The agreement will be filed before the Godavari waters dispute tribunal. The tribunal would be free to discuss claims in regard to the remaining quantity of waters, 19.822 BCM below the Pochampad Dam site. The mutual agreement reached between Andhra Pradesh and Karnataka; Andhra Pradesh and Maharashtra, Madhya Pradesh and Orissa mentioned above will be incorporated in the settlement.

Andhra Pradesh and Madhya Pradesh will be free to use an additional quantity of 8.495 BCM out of the water in the Godavari and its tributaries below Pochampad Dam site for new projects. The quantity of 8.495 BCM will not be in addition to the 8.495 BCM agreed between Andhra Pradesh and Maharashtra.

Madhya Pradesh and Andhra Pradesh will consider the feasibility of taking up the Inchampalli Project as a joint project with costs and benefits equitably shared amongst the three interested states in accordance with an agreement.

This was the major agreement involving five different states and major south Indian river.

Case 6

States involved: a. Gujarat, Madhya Pradesh, Maharashtra, Rajasthan
b. Madhya Pradesh and Maharashtra
c. Gujarat, Madhya Pradesh, Maharashtra and Rajasthan

River: The Narmada

The Narmada rises in the Amarkantak Plateau at the northeast apex of the Satpura Range in Madhya Pradesh and flows through Madhya Pradesh, Maharashtra and Gujarat for a length of 1,311 kms. Of the total length of 1,311 kms, 1,076 kms of the river length lies in Madhya Pradesh, 161 kms in Gujarat, and 74 kms in Maharashtra. The total catchment area of 98,796 sq. kms is divided among the three states as follows: Madhya Pradesh, 85,858 sq. kms; Maharashtra, 1,538 sq. kms; and Gujarat, 11,399 sq. kms, respectively. It is the least utilized river in India. The total quantity of water available from the Narmada for nine months of the year is 3.454 million hectare meters. Its tributaries are the Hiran, the Barna, the Kolar, the Osrange, the Tawa, the Chota Tawa and the Kundi.

Causes of dispute

a. The disputes among the states existed prior to independence. The right of lower riparian state of Gujarat to build a high dam at Navagam so as to reach the river water towards the Rann of Kutch and Rajasthan on the Indo-Pakistan border. This will submerge 70,415 hectares of Madhya Pradesh territory, upper riparian states to river basins of the Sabarmati and Banas and other rivers to irrigate additional hectares at the cost of Madhya Pradesh.

The right of Madhya Pradesh to build three dams at Maheshwar, Hiranpal, and Jalsindhi (jointly with Maharashtra for hydroelectric power). If these projects are allowed, it will restrict the height of the Navagam Dam.

The disputes date back to 1946 when the then Government of Central Provinces and Berar as well as Government of Bombay requested the Central Water, Irrigation and Navigation Commission to investigate the possibility of development of the Narmada river.

The suggestion of the Central Water and Power Commission of 1955 to build dams across the Narmada in Madhya Pradesh and Gujarat did not solve the dispute.

On May 1, 1960, the State of Bombay was reorganized into Maharashtra and Gujarat through the Bombay Reorganization Act of 1960. The reorganization of former Bombay state caused readjusting the borders and exchange of areas between two states. In 1961, differences arose between Madhya Pradesh and Gujarat for the utilization of the Narmada waters.

With an idea to have an expert study of the maximum utilization of the Narmada waters, which would be agreeable to the states of Madhya Pradesh and Gujarat, the Government of India appointed a commission headed by Dr. A.N. Khosla in 1965.

b. A new project to be developed at Jalsindhi for mutual benefit.

c. Since 1966 many attempts were made by the Union Minister of Irrigation and Power to settle the dispute and profitably utilize the waters of the Narmada but without any success. The Government of India made it clear that if the dispute was not settled by mutual agreement, the matter will be referred to a tribunal.

Madhya Pradesh objected to the construction of Navagam Dam with a height of 152.4 meters that might submerge vast areas of Madhya Pradesh. Besides, Madhya Pradesh preferred the dispute to be referred to a tribunal.

The Government of India appointed a three-man tribunal in July 1969 under the Inter-State Water Dispute Act of 1956. Madhya Pradesh went to court for stay order against the Central Government for appointing a tribunal which was rejected by the Court because the suit was considered premature.

Water Resources and Development Strategy

Method and year of settlement	Agreement
Ad hoc committee appointed by the Government of India	The 1948, *ad hoc* committee recommended four projects to begin with, i.e., Bargi, Tawa, Punasa, and Broach. In 1955, the Central Water and Power Commission suggested to build three dams below Punasa, namely, Barwaha in Madhya Pradesh, Hiranpal in Madhya Pradesh, and Keli in erstwhile State of Bombay (now on the border of Bombay and Gujarat.
The Union Minister of Irrigation and Power along with M.P. and Gujarat reached an agreement November 17, 1963	The Union Minister of Irrigation and Power along with the chief ministers of M.P. and Gujarat came to an agreement on November 17, 1963, keeping in view the best interest of the nation. The agreement provided the building of Navagam Dam in Gujarat, and Punasa and Bargi Dams in Madhya Pradesh with cost shared by Gujarat, Maharashtra, and Gujarat according to an agreed formula. The Government of Madhya Pradesh did not ratify the agreement.
	Madhya Pradesh urged the Central Government to reduce the height of Navagam Dam proposed to 152.4 meters and expressed its willingness to restrict withdrawal to eighty percent of the net utilization supply (2.763 million hectare meters) because of the consideration of building a dam at Navagam by Gujarat which may utilize twenty percent of the potential utilization of 690,750 hectare meters.
	The State of Gujarat, on the other hand, agreed to restrict its use to 2.048 MHM leaving 1.046 MHM to be used by Madhya Pradesh. The State of Maharashtra avoided any comments in the dispute because it may jeopardize their Jalsindhi Hydel Project.
The Khosla Commission appointed by the Government of India September 1965	The Commission submitted its report in September, 1965, and suggested twelve projects in Madhya Pradesh and one project, namely Navagam with a height of 152.4 meters. The Khosla Commission estimated the irrigation potential of the river at 4,451.542 hectares and power potential at nearly 2000 mw. The Committee prepared a master plan for Narmada Valley Development giving irrigation benefits of 2,630,500 hectares to Madhya Pradesh, 4,047 hectares to Maharashtra, 1,853,865 hectares to Gujarat, and 40,468 hectares to Rajasthan. The states of Madhya Pradesh and Rajasthan rejected the Khosla Report entirely and the State of Gujarat accepted it in principle.
Mutual Agreement April 21, 1965	Both states agreed to build a trans-boundary hydel project at Jalsindhi on the Narmada River. This will be only a hydroelectric plant and no irrigation will be involved.
Mediation by the Prime Minister, Government of India July 22, 1972	The chief ministers of Gujarat, Madhya Pradesh, Rajasthan and Maharashtra signed on July 22, 1972, a six-point agreement for the rapid development of the Narmada whose potential for irrigation, navigation, and power generation had hitherto remained unutilized.
	The total quantity of water available from the Narmada for nine

months of the year is 3.454 million hectare meters. Of this, Rajasthan's requirement is a mere 30,837 hectare meters and of Maharashtra 61,674 hectare meters. The remaining 3.361 million hectare meters is to be apportioned between Madhya Pradesh and Gujarat by the Prime Minister. The height of Navagam Dam in Gujarat will also be fixed by the P.M., taking into account the relevant factors. The four chief ministers decided to withdraw the Narmada water dispute from the tribunal before which it had been languishing for the past few years.

Appointement of Tribunal 1974	The dispute was sent to a tribunal again in 1974.
Mutual agreement among all four states March 8, 1975	Without prejudice to 1974 tribunal, an agreement was signed by the four chief ministers in New Delhi. The agreement allows projects utilizing the waters of the Narmada. Gujarat and Madhya Pradesh will go ahead with the construction of four projects. Gujarat projects are Karjan, Heran, Rami and Sukhi and that of Madhya Pradesh are Kolar, Bichia, Sukta, and Bichhualatia. The height of Navagam Dam has been fixed at 138.7 meters instead of 152.4 meters as desired by Gujarat.

Case 7

States involved: Gujarat, Rajasthan, and Madhya Pradesh
River: The Mahi The Mahi river rises in the northern slopes of the Vindhyan ranges in Madhya Pradesh, flows through Rajasthan, finally enters the Gulf of Cambay in the State of Gujarat. The catchment area in the three states of M.P., Rajasthan and Gujarat is 4,634 sq. kms., 16,086 sq. kms., and 12,959 sq. kms., respectively.

Cause of dispute
The Mahi Stage I—Construction of a diversion weir with a canal system at Wanakbori in Gujarat with an irrigation of about 186,000 hectares.

The Mahi Stage II—Construction of dam at Kadana in Gujarat. The Government of Rajasthan objected to the height of the dam because large areas of the state will be submerged. To compensate the loss of storage by lowering the dam, Rajasthan agreed to build a dam at Bajajsagar.

The Mahi Stage III—Rajasthan to build a dam at Bajajsagar at Banswara. The dispute relates to the sharing of the cost of Bajajsagar between Rajasthan and Gujarat.

The power generated on the Bajajsagar dam was to be exclusively utilized by Rajasthan. Rajasthan wanted that the cost of the project should be shared in proportion to the amount of water utilized by each state. Rajasthan will also not pay any charges for power utilization. Gujarat wanted that Rajasthan should pay for power utilization.

Water Resources and Development Strategy

Method and year of settlement	Agreement
Union Minister of Irrigation and Power March 1966	The entire cost and benefits will be borne by Gujarat. Out of the total cost of Banswara dam in Rajasthan, a portion will be allocated for power which Rajasthan will develop from the waters of this reservoir. This will be at the rate of Rs. 1,250 per KW firm power. At a later date when Narmada development takes place and when Mahi areas are fed by the waters of Narmada and the Mahi waters at Banswara are released for use in Rajasthan. Rajasthan should reimburse the cost of the Banswara project paid to Gujarat.

States involved: Gujarat, Rajasthan
River: The Mahi
Causes of dispute: Existing dispute between Gujarat and Rajasthan.

Method and year of settlement	Agreement
Mutual agreement providing compensation to Rajasthan May 29, 1975	Gujarat and Rajasthan reached an agreement on the compensation to be given to the people affected by the construction of Kadana dam on the Mahi. Gujarat, which will get 113,312 hectares of land irrigated by the dam will pay.

States involved: Gujarat, Rajasthan
River: The Mahi
Causes of dispute: Dispute about compensation and sharing of cost and benefit.

Method and year of settlement	Agreement
Mutual agreement with the assistance of the Union Minister of Agriculture and Irrigation, New Delhi April 5, 1978	Rs. 81 million to Rajasthan as compensation for the 9,172 hectares including 4,109 hectares of agricultural land likely to get submerged by the dam. The amount will also include the expenditure for rehabilitation of the displaced persons. Union Minister of Agriculture and Irrigation mediated to settle the claim by Rajasthan to pay twenty-eight million rupees for the acquisition of structures and rehabilitation involved under the agreement. Gujarat will construct Kadana Dam and another dam will be constructed at Bajajsagar near Banswara in Rajasthan as a joint project. Both these projects will ensure an additional irrigation facility of 71,000 hectares in Rajasthan and 280,000 hectares in Gujarat.

Case 8

States involved: a. Punjab, Haryana, Rajasthan, Delhi, Jammu and Kashmir
 b. Punjab, Jammu and Kashmir
 c. Punjab, Haryana, Delhi and Rajasthan

Rivers: a. The Ravi and the Beas. Ravi known as the Indravati rises near Kulu and emerges into the plains near Madhopur, the headworks of the Upper Bari Doab Canal. It flows on the boundary between India and Pakistan for some distance and then enters Pakistan near Lahore.

The Beas is the shortest of the Punjab rivers. It rises near the Rohtang Pass at the southeastern end of the Pir Panjal Range. It flows into the Sutlej at Harike.

Ravi along with Beas joins the Sutlej and their catchment area is 8,030 sq. kms., 16,835 sq. kms. and 48,045 sq. kms., respectively.

Under the Indus Water Treaty of 1960, Pakistan has no claim on the waters of these rivers after March 31, 1970, as in the meanwhile it is supposed to have built an alternate source of water supply.
 b. The Ravi
 c. The Beas

Causes of dispute
a. After the reorganization of the States of Punjab and Haryana as separate states a dispute arose between the two states for their respective shares in the water allocated to the composite state of Punjab.

Punjab wanted the entire quantity of water on two grounds, (1) that the river flows through Punjab, and (2) that all canals for which water is utilized lie in Punjab. Haryana demanded 592.071 hectare meters of water.

Haryana wanted equitable distribution and contends that Punjab has no right on the waters of the Ravi and Beas because the Government of India has acquired the surplus water from Pakistan through payment of compensation.

Two projects were proposed to be constructed, the Beas Dam at Pong for storing water for the Rajasthan Canal, and the Beas-Sutlej-Link Project was power-cum-irrigation project. The purpose was to divert 468,723 hectare meters of water from the Beas to the Sutlej for onward flow into the Bhakra Lake.

In September 1978 Punjab and Haryana again started an argument on sharing of the Ravi-Beas waters. The Punjab chief minister contended the March 1976 decision was taken on the basis of wrong facts and figures. Punjab was not ready to release additional water on the basis of 60:40 basis or in proportion to the cultivatable land in the two states. On the other hand, Haryana objected to this because of losing some water. Haryana filed a suit in April 1978 in the Supreme Court against Punjab.

b. Pre-existing dispute between states.

c. A long-standing dispute between the states.

Water Resources and Development Strategy

Method and year of settlement	Agreement
Decision of the central government on the basis of interstate conference 1955	a. The central government decided to distribute 1.955 m.h.m. of available water for utilization as follows: Rajasthan, 986,785 hectare meters; Punjab (composite), 888,107 hectare meters; Jammu and Kashmir, 80,176 hectare meters. b. Punjab and Kashmir governments reached an agreement to construct a multi-purpose dam project across the Ravi in Punjab which will generate 480 mw of power and irrigate about 404,686 hectares of land. The central and Himachal Pradesh governments will be consulted in the very near future for the project.
Mutual agreement between Punjab and Kashmir January 17, 1976 The Central Government by a notification of Punjab, Haryana, Delhi and Rajasthan March 25, 1976	c. The central government had fixed the sharing of the waters of the Beas by a notification. The central government directed that out of the 897,975 hectare meters of water which would become available to the erstwhile State of Punjab (now Haryana and Punjab) on completion of Beas Project, 24,670 was earmarked for Delhi water supply and Haryana and Punjab would get 431,791 hectare meters each. The remaining of 9,867 hectare meters was recommended as additional quantum for **Delhi Water Supply for acceptance by both the governments of** Haryana and Punjab. The object of the Beas Project included integrated use of the waters of the Ravi, Beas and Sutlej rivers and extension of irrigation to arid lands in Rajasthan and Haryana as well as to meet the water supply demands of Delhi.

Case 9

States involved: Uttar Pradesh, Haryana, Himachal Pradesh, Punjab, Rajasthan, Madhya Pradesh and Delhi

Haryana, U.P.
River: The Yamuna and other tributaries
   The River Yamuna

Causes of dispute
Disputes about sharing the waters, cost of construction and maintenance, and benefits.

Building new barrages at Tejawala and Iklha and two canals on the Yamuna.

Method and year of settlement	Agreement
Mutually and with the central help 1963 to 1972	Settlement arrived at on different dates between different states involving the Yamuna and its tributaries and other basin rivers.
Mutual agreement March 8, 1970	A barrage at Tejawala and two separate canals one from the western and the other from the eastern Yamuna canal will be constructed. Another barrage will be constructed at Okhla. Tejawala barrage will irrigate 48,562 hectares and generate 750 mw of electricity and will be constructed by Haryana. Haryana will pay two-thirds of the cost and U.P. one-third.

States involved: Haryana, Uttar Pradesh
River: The Yamuna

Causes of dispute
To construct Kishau Dam and two barrages at Tejawala and Okhla. Haryana also proposed to augment the Western Yamuna Canal.

Method and year of settlement	Agreement
Mediated by the central Minister of Irrigation and Power, and the Central Deputy Minister of Irrigation and Power September 11, 1972	The construction cost of barrages at Okhla and Tejawala, Kishau Dam, and western Yamuna canal will be shared in proportion to the water drawn by both the states.

States involved: Himachal Pradesh, Uttar Pradesh
Rivers: The Tons and the Yamuna

Cause of dispute:
Dispute existed since the reorganization of the States in 1956.

Method and year of settlement	Agreement
With the assistance of the Central Minister of Irrigation and Power November 7, 1963	A dam to be constructed on the Tons River about 16 km upstream of its junction with the Yamuna on the U.P.-Himachal Pradesh border. It will irrigate 115,740 hectares of land and generate 287,000 kw of power. Its height will be 222.50 meters. The investigation of the project was entrusted mainly to U.P., however, the cost will be shared by all—U.P., Haryana, Himachal Pradesh, Punjab and Rajasthan.

Water Resources and Development Strategy

States involved: Himachal Pradesh, Uttar Pradesh
River: The Yamuna Hydel Scheme

Causes of dispute: Dispute over sharing the power between the two states.

Method and year of settlement	Agreement
Mutual Agreement between Himachal Pradesh and U.P November 21, 1972	An agreement was reached to make available twenty-five percent of the power generated by the Yamuna Hydel Scheme Stage I and II to Himachal Pradesh at generation cost. Himachal Pradesh would make available to U.P. power from the Giri Bata Hydel Project on a preferential basis.

States involved: Uttar Pradesh, Madhya Pradesh
Rivers: The Betwa, the Urmil, the Ken and the Banne

Causes of dispute: Disagreement over sharing the water and the construction cost.

Method and year of settlement	Agreement
Mutual Agreement by both the chief ministers September 24, 1972	Uttar Pradesh and Madhya Pradesh agreed to share waters by building the Rajghat Dam on the Betwa River, the Urmil River, the Greater Gangu Dam on the Ken, the Rangwar Dam on the Banne, and the Lalitpur Dam. All these are in Bundelkhand area.

Case 10

States involved: Uttar Pradesh, Bihar
River: River Karamnasa. Catchment area of 1,474 sq. kms. out of which 425 sq. kms. being in the State of Bihar.

Causes of dispute
U.P. planned to build a dam at Musakhand 203 meters high and 3.2 kms. long with equal cost sharing basis with Bihar. U.P. contended to share cost and benefits in proportion to the total catchment area in the two states. Bihar had doubted whether its benefit would come to one-third of the total storage capacity of the dam. Bihar wanted 93.446 MCM of water whereas U.P. would share only 42.475 MCM. Besides, U.P. wanted Bihar to bear the cost at sixty-six percent, and Bihar was ready only at fifty percent basis.

India: Economic Base And Political Patterns

Method and year of settlement	Agreement
Agreement under the auspices of the Minister of Irrigation and Power, Government of India 1965	The agreement provided 63.713 MCM of water to Bihar and 84.951 MCM to U.P. out of the total 148.664 MCM dependable flow. The cost and maintenance will be equally shared by both the states. The cost of the canals would be shared by both the states. Further, the Bihar Government was to bear the entire cost of canals from the U.P. border towards Bihar.

Case 11

States involved: Assam, Manipur

River: Barak River

Cause of dispute: Sharing of water for irrigation and power generation.

Method and year of settlement	Agreement
Central Minister of Irrigation and Power with Mutual Agreement December 27, 1975	Flood control and power generation on the Barak River to sites. One at Bhubander and the other at Tipaimukh.

Case 12

States involved: Bihar-Orissa
River: Subarnarekha

Causes of dispute: Sharing of water for irrigation and power generation and building a dam on the Subarnarekha.

Method and year of settlement	Agreement
Mutual Agreement January 17, 1976	Bihar and Orissa have reached an agreement on sharing of the waters of the Subarnarekha ending the decade-old interstate dispute. Under the agreement, of the total 555,067 hectare meters of the Subarnarekha river basin, Bihar will get a share of 394,714 hectare

meters; Orissa, 148,019 hectare meters; and West Bengal, 12,335 hectare meters.

The proposed Chandil Dam will have a flood water storage capacity of 49,339 hectare meters. The proposed dam at Icha will have storage of 83,877 hectare meters, of which Bihar and Orissa will be entitled to 61,674 hectare meters and 22,207 hectare meters acre-feet, respectively. The cost of the dam will be shared by Bihar and Orissa in the ratio of 5:18.

Orissa will draw its share of water from the Kharkai dam at Icha and also from the flow of the river from the Galudhih barrage through a common canal on the right bank.

Punjab and Kashmir reached an accord on January 17, 1976. Similarly, Punjab, Rajasthan, Haryana and Delhi have been sharing waters of the three northern rivers. The Rajasthan Canal Project (the longest lined canal in the world) was initiated in 1958 based on the first guidelines issued by the Government of India for the use of the river waters. The water was to be shared by the benficiary states of Rajasthan, undivided Punjab, (Punjab, Haryana and Himachal Pradesh), and Jammu and Kashmir in the ratio of 9 MAF; 7.2 MAF:0.65 MAF (Sukhwal, 1974, p. 302). The share of Punjab and Haryana would be allotted according to the mutually agreed formula. In accordance with the Indo-Pakistan Indus Water Treaty of 1960, India acquired exclusive rights over the waters of the rivers Sutlej (average flow of 13.5 MAF), Beas (average flow of 13 MAF) and Ravi (average flow of 1.9 MAF) on March 31, 1970. The government followed the previously established formula for the division of waters among the states, with an exception made to allot 0.2 MAF of water to the Delhi drinking water scheme. Another agreement was reached between Punjab and Haryana on February 20, 1976, to share the waters of three rivers in which Punjab was awarded 3.5 MAF of water. Punjab, however, did not accept this agreement. When Mrs Gandhi regained the prime ministership in 1980, a new agreement was signed in 1981 whereby the share of the Punjab water was increased to a higher level than it was according to the 1976 agreement. Punjab is still not satisfied with the agreement as is evident by recent troubles created by the Akalis. In 1983 and 1984, a small group of extremist Sikhs disputed that Punjab was not getting its proper share of river waters and further extended numerous demands including a separate sovereign Sikh nation "Khalistan". The waters from the Pong reservoir have been brought into the Rajasthan Canal by constructing three reservoirs, namely, the Pong on the Beas, the Thein on the Ravi, and the Bhakra on the Sutlej with three link canals so as to utilize ninety-two percent of the average flow of these three rivers. The irrigation facilities will be extended to about 1,457,000 hectares of cultivated land at 110 percent intensity in the canal command area (Sukhwal, 1982, p. 110). At present, Punjab being a surplus electric power producing state due to the Bhakra Nagal Dam, the state is selling 1.5 million units of power daily to Madhya Pradesh, Uttar Pradesh, Himachal Pradesh, Jammu and Kashmir, Haryana, and Rajasthan through various agreements.

Third, the long-standing Godavari river dispute was resolved on December 19, 1975, by the signing of an agreement among five concerned states of Andhra Pradesh, Karnataka, Madhya Pradesh, Maharashtra and Orissa. Fourth, the Krishna water tribunal gave a binding award to Maharashtra, Karnataka, and Andhra Pradesh on May 31, 1976. Fifth, the Idukki Project on the Periyar river which was developed with the financial and technical assistance from Canada was scheduled to be completed by 1974 but was delayed, was finally completed in February, 1976. The government of Kerala is expected to net Rs. 180 million annually from the sale of Idukki power to its power-starved neighbours, especially Tamil Nadu and Karnataka, if the project comes through. Sixth, a long-standing and complicated dispute over the sharing of water and power of the Cauvery River among Tamil Nadu, Karnataka, and Kerala ended on August 14, 1976. This agreement was considered a landmark in the settlement of some of the most complex issues relating to the use of the Cauvery waters and the development of the river basin (Fig. 6). A Cauvery Valley Authority will be constituted under the agreement. Seventh, Andhra Pradesh and Orissa agreed in December 1976 to share the waters of the Jhanjavati River, and finally, a long-standing dispute between Assam and Manipur to share the waters of the Barak River was resolved on January 1, 1976 (Table 4). An active cooperation between two southern states for sharing river waters was initiated by the chief ministers of Andhra Pradesh and Tamil Nadu to take the waters of the Krishna River for a distance of 550 kms. to Madras city for drinking purposes. It was also meant to irrigate 225 hectares of land in Rayaleseema and Nellore districts of Andhra Pradesh. The cost of the project will be $ 637 million and the central government will finance part of the cost. The project is expected to be completed by 1990. The agreement was signed on April 19, 1983, by both the chief ministers to supply fifteen billion cubic feet of water to Tamil Nadu. The water is to be tapped from Srisailam reservoir and carried through the Srisailam left branch canal passing through Karnool and Cuddapah districts. It will be emptied into the Pennar river at Chennumukapali village also in the Cuddapah district. The downward flow of the Pennar will be picked up at the Somasila dam then to the Kandaleru reservoir on its way to

Water Resources and Development Strategy

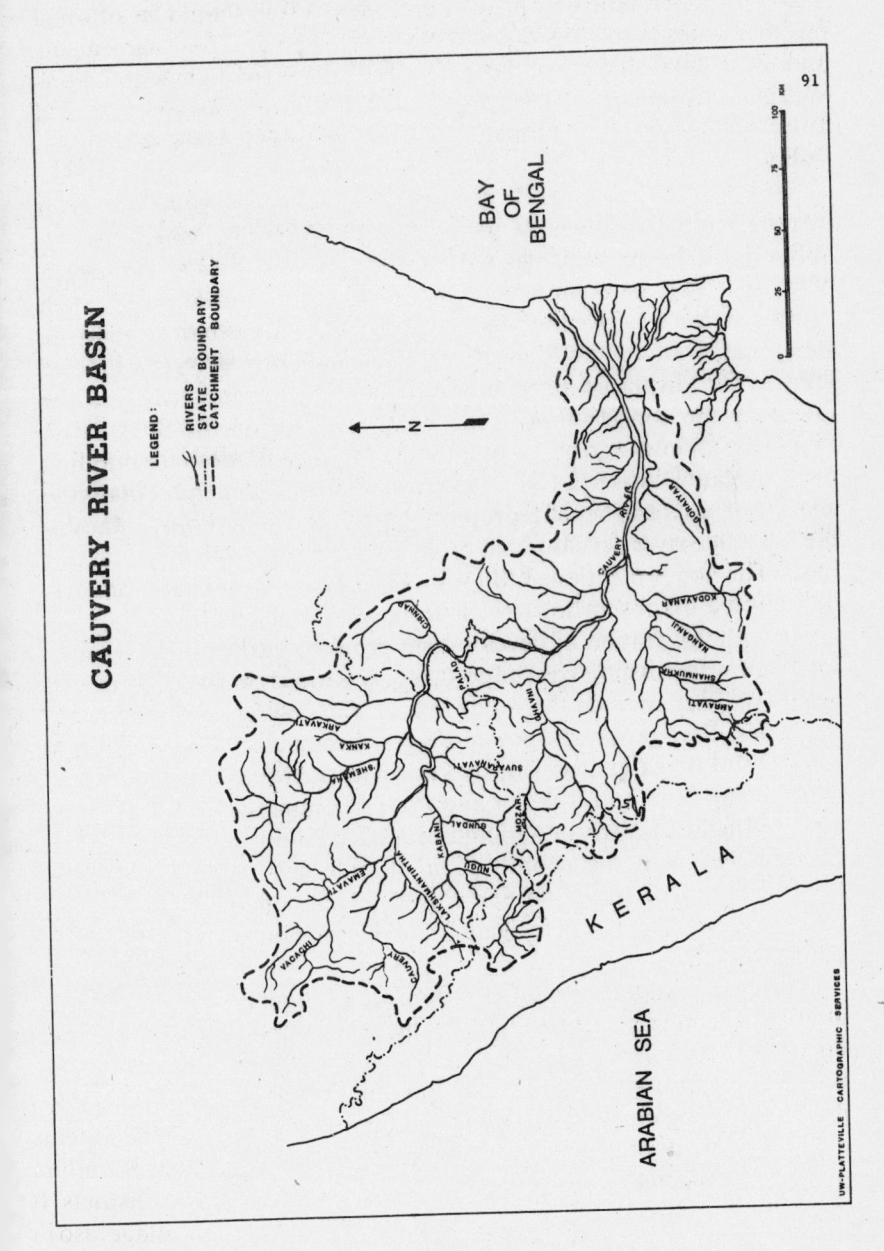

Fig. 6

Madras. Such ambitious projects through mutual agreement and regional cooperation are a healthy precedent which should be followed by other states in solving difficult interstate disputes. These agreements and the mutual sharing of the waters and power through negotiations and peaceful means is an example of stability of a nation state and reflects that unity and national integration are in fact being achieved in India.

The principle of equitable distribution may not be applicable to all interstate water disputes in India. Another principle which may be applied is in the payment of compensation for areas of states submerged when another state builds a dam over an interstate river. Such compensation was given to Madhya Pradesh by Rajasthan to build the Bajajsagar Dam on the Mahi River. Rajasthan also agreed to allocate land to the displaced persons whose land was inundated by water following the construction of the Pong reservoir on the Beas River. Similarly, Gujarat agreed to compensate Madhya Pradesh for building the Navagam Dam on the Narmada river. The third principle entails the sharing of costs and benefits proportionately for a joint project. Many of the interstate river development projects have been undertaken on this basis. The above mentioned Mahi waters and the Musakhand projects were settled on proportionately sharing costs and benefits.

The administration of development projects and considerations of interstate water disputes are undertaken by various central government agencies. They include the following: 1) The central government coordinates all irrigation and power projects through the Ministry of Agriculture and Irrigation (previously known as the Ministry of Irrigation and Power); the Central Water and Power Commission (Water Wing) attached to the Ministry of Agriculture and Irrigation; the Central Water Commission with the coordination of state governments; and the Central Board of Irrigation and Power which conducts research on various subjects related to irrigation and has stations in different parts of the country.

2) The central government also indirectly influences the settlement of dispsutes among various states by means of controlling the federal funds. In theory, the Constitution has listed irrigation as a state subject; yet it is the centre which exercises a dominant role through its financial power in settling interstate water disputes and allowing the construction of development projects through its budget allocations. States are practically dependent on the Centre for the financing of irrigation projects.

3) The central government has developed a systematic functioning of development projects through control boards. These boards design,

Water Resources and Development Strategy

construct, implement, and supervise various river valley projects and even have a say in the day-to-day functioning of these projects. The Bhakra-Nangal Management Board (involving the states of Punjab, Haryana, Rajasthan, Delhi, and Himachal Pradesh), Tungabhadra Control Board (Andhra Pradesh and Karnataka), Rajasthan Canal Board (Rajasthan and Punjab), Chambal Control Board (Rajasthan and Madhya Pradesh), Gandak Control Board (Bihar and Uttar Pradesh, and Parabikulam Aliya [Tamil Nadu and Kerala]). Besides, there are single state boards controlling one river or a project, such as Nagarjunasagar and Pochampad (Andhra Pradesh); Kosi (Bihar); Kakapara, Ukai, and Mahi (Gujarat); Bhadra, Upper Krishna, Chataprabha, and Malaprabha (Karnataka); Tawa (Madhya Pradesh); Bhima and Jayakwadi (Maharashtra); Hirakud and Mahanadi Delta Scheme (Orissa); Sarda Sahayak and Ramganga (Uttar Pradesh); and Farakka, Mayurakshi, and Gangsabati (West Bengal). There are also river valley authorities established, such as the Damodar Valley Authority (West Bengal and Bihar), and Cauvery Valley Authority. These authorities are established on the same pattern as the Tennessee Valley Authority in the United States.

Some of the disputes were referred to the Supreme Court of India; however, according to the Constitution, the Supreme Court had no jurisdiction and did not interfere with the decision of the central government. In the final analysis, interstate disputes are being settled through the mediation of the central government; as a result, the prospect of utilization of interstate water has improved significantly. This is reflected in respect of numerous disputes which have been settled during the last five years as well as through the increase in irrigation acreages and power development projects constructed by way of mutually agreed formulae. In a developing nation like India, interstate disputes must be resolved quickly so that natural resources can be utilized beneficially on a national scale, thereby reducing the dependence on foreign countries. The reduced dependence on foreign nations may allow India to follow its nonaligned position and lead the Third World nations as a symbol of independent-minded nation. The peaceful settlement of interstate disputes in India may pave the way for other nations to follow India's examples to resolve their interstate disputes.

It is essential to enlarge the spatial limits of the development of irrigation water beyond state boundaries and extend them to various regions, the main reason being non-availability of water in many states during times of acute need. The state autonomy creates a hindrance in the rational distribution of available water on an interstate or regional basis, until all regions attain a comfortable position in acquiring irrigation water the year around. In the first place, no state will want to transfer water without a steady supply to meet its own growing demand, especially during periods of shortage. Moreover, even if the political willingness is there among the states to share irrigation water with other states, they would still find it difficult, for technical reasons, to effect smooth interstate exchange due to a lack of a transfer mechanism. The initiative can be taken by the central government through proper planning and additional utilization of water to remove the fear of shortages, thereby increasing the possibilities of easy exchange across interstate boundaries.

International cooperation in the field of water resources has been phenomenal. India and Pakistan signed the Indus Water Treaty on September 19, 1960, thereby agreeing to peacefully use the river water resources. The agreement between India and Pakistan on the Salal Dam is an excellent example of cooperation between two countries. India and Bangladesh are also working together to finally settle the issue of Farakka Barrage permanently. The issue has already been settled and the details are being worked out by a Joint Commission. India is also assisting developing countries such as Afghanistan, Sri Lanka, Nepal, Bhutan, Kenya, and the Middle Eastern countries to set up irrigation and power projects. Besides, in cooperation with various U.N. agencies, India is participating in the development of the Lower Mekong River basin to benefit Kampuchea, Laos, Thailand, and Vietnam. Such cooperation, especially with neighbouring countries, should definitely bring about goodwill and eventually stability in the South Asian region.

NOTES

The Constitution of India, Article 262 (New Delhi: The Manager, Government of India Press, 1951).

The Constitution of India, Seventh Schedule, Entry 17, List II (New Delhi: The Manager, Government of India Press, 1951).

Albert H. Garretson, R.D. Haton, and C.J. Olmstead, eds. *The Law of International Drainage Basins* (Dobbs Ferry, New York: Oceana Publications, Inc., 1967), pp. 167-225.

The Government of India Act, 1935, Entry 19, List II (London: H.M. Stationery Office, 1935).

According to the Attorney General Harmon of the United States in 1895, who alleged while replying to the Government of Mexico on sharing of the Rio Grande waters that the fundamental principle of international law is the absolute sovereignty of every nation, as against all others, within its own territory. In his opinion, the rules, principles and precedents of international law impose no liability or obligations upon the United States in its relationship with Mexico over the waters of the Rio Grande. In practice, however, the United States Government and the Supreme Court expounded the policy of equitable apportionment rather than following the principle of absolute sovereignty.

Water Resources and Development Strategy

The theory is that the riparian states have exclusive and sovereign rights over the waters flowing through their territory. According to U.S. Attorney General Harmon (1895), "the fundamental principle of international law is the absolute sovereignty of every nation, as against all others, within its own territory."

The Interstate Water Disputes Act, 1956 (New Delhi: The Manager, Government of India Press, 1968).

R.K. Mukerjee, *Economic Problems of Modern India*, Vol. 1 (London: Longmans, Green and Co., Ltd., 1939), p. 167.

Norman J.G. Pounds, *Political Geography*, 2nd ed. (New York: McGraw-Hill Book Company, 1972), p. 320.

B.N. Rau, *The Indus Commission, 1942* (London: H.M. Stationery Office, 1942).

The River Boards Act, 1956, S. 13 (New Delhi: The Manager, Government of India Press, 1956).

B.L. Sukhwal, "Preliminary Survey of the Development of Irrigational Facilities in the Thar Desert Area: A Case Study of the Rajasthan Canal Project, India," *Problems of the Management of Irrigated Land in Areas of Traditional and Modern Cultivation; I.G.U. Working Group on Resource Management in Drylands*. Edited by Horst G. Mensching. Hamburg, FRG: UNESCO/MAB Programme, 1982, pp. 107-114.

B.L. Sukhwal, "Politicogeographic Analysis of Bifurcation: A Case Study of Punjab and Haryana, India," *Geographical Review of India*, Vol. 36, No. 4 (December, 1974), pp. 291-308.

The United States Constitution, Article I, S. 8(ii); Article II, S. 2(2).

The United States Supreme Court Judgment, 373 U.S. 546 (1963), U.S. 340 (1964).

CHAPTER 4

Planning and Development of Mineral, Fuel and Industrial Resources

WITH the introduction of the First Five Year Plan (1951-56) in India, economic planning became the crucial instrument for achieving such objectives as: rapid growth of agricultural and industrial output, capital formation, survey and identification of mineral resources, population control, improvement in the quality of life through the promotion of literacy and education, improvement in health, development of transportation and communication networks, generation of employment, and the creation of a more equitable and egalitarian society. In formulating the planning process, Indian planners learned from the shortcomings of the Soviet planners, who gave undue emphasis to heavy industrial plants, while neglecting agricultural production in the formative years of planning. Conversely, China placed importance on agricultural productivity and neglected heavy industries in their earlier decades of planning. The Indian planners had to develop a development stragegy according to the principles of a democratic framework in which they had to face many obstacles in achieving their stated goals. On the other hand, Soviet and Chinese planners worked through an authoritarian system in which planned targets were easy to attain without outside interference. The Indian planners started with the dual objectives of self-sufficiency in foodgrain production and the development of an industrial infrastructure. It was a balanced approach to attain progress through indigenous means.

The development of agriculture and heavy industries led to immense diversification and self-reliance, which in turn led to a wider production base. The result of balanced planning has been a change in the composition of exports from agro-based primary commodities such as tea, jute, cotton textiles, and limited quantities of ores, to manufactured goods and capital goods, as well as engineering goods. Engineering goods account for fifteen percent of the exports signifying a diversification of exports. Economic transformation in India has been slow,

Planning and Development of Resources

enabling India to preserve its cultural heritage and indigenous value system. Even though about forty percent of the population of the country is still below the poverty line, more than 200 million additional people have risen above the poverty line since 1951—a major achievement for a developing country. The progress on all fronts has been impressive. The employment in the organized sector has increased by 110 percent between 1961 and 1984; the number of children enrolled in primary schools has increased by 290 percent, middle and high school enrolment by 580 percent, university attendance by 1000 percent, engineering and technical college enrolment by 1270 percent, and medical school attendance by 300 percent; the number of hospital beds has risen by 170 percent; the number of doctors has increased by 200 percent and the number of nurses has risen by 525 percent; industrial production increased by 700 percent. Such phenomenal progress in just thirty-three years of planning (1951-1984) could only have been achieved through a successful planning process and careful utilization of mineral, fuel, industrial and agricultural resources of the country.

Mineral resources

Mineral resources are as important as land and water resources for the development of a country and the stability of its political system. Likewise, they are important for human development and are essential for national defence, especially when one is measuring the national power of a nation state. A deficiency of food can be overcome by importing it or through careful management of land under agriculture, but the extraction or importation of minerals is not so easy because mineral resources are more narrowly localized than are crops. With careful management, soil can produce food indefinitely, whereas minerals are exhaustible and non-renewable and are therefore considered an unstable factor in national power. Mineral resources, on the other hand, do not deteriorate in quality if left in the open, but food resources can only be preserved for a short time with scientific storage facilities. China and India, the two largest countries in Asia, possess the largest potential volumes of industrial power by virtue of their mineral resources. Although India is not as fortunate as her neighbour China, she is, nevertheless, better placed than Pakistan and her other immediate neighbours.

Iron ore and steel, along with copper, aluminium, lead, zinc, tin, uranium, manganese, nickel and a number of other necessary metals, are considered basic strategic metals. The importance of these minerals cannot be questioned, especially at the time of war. If a country lacks these minerals, it must possess two basic ingredients in order to be a viable nation: first, the capacity to use sub-marginal resources through a high level of technology; and second, the economic ability and ideological influence to form partnerships with the producing nations to purchase these metals. India has vast reserves of high grade iron ore, manganese, mica, thorium, titanium, and bauxite, along with ample quantities of dolomite, magnesite, and coking coal to support both ferrous and non-ferrous metal industries. It is equally rich in other minerals, including those needed for cement, ceramics and refractory industries. The relations of India with the neighbouring countries are steadily improving. India can always import those minerals which it lacks from these countries; for example, tin, lead and petroleum from Indonesia, copper from Central Africa, petroleum from the Middle East, and tin from Malaysia.

Before Independence, India was not an important mineral producing country, and in fact minerals were worked in an unscientific manner. Interest was shown only in the high grade, easily accessible and minable minerals and ores which could serve as basic raw materials for foreign industries (especially British) without any consideration for the conservation or proper utilization of the mineral wealth of the country (Chopra, 1975, p. 410). The minerals were exported as raw materials to Great Britain, and highly priced finished industrial goods were sold in Indian markets in return. Professor H.R. Dewan made an interesting observation about mineral development in India during the British period. He maintained that there was no attempt to develop a self-reliant and self-sustained economy for minerals which could hold out a promise of starting mineral-based industries in the country, and provide a continually rising standard of living to the people, more opportunities for gainful employment, and a sense of security and self-sufficiency both in peace and war (Chopra, 1975, p. 411). Minerals vary in importance from region to region over the country. While the Chota Nagpur Plateau, the states of Bihar, Orissa, West Bengal, and the Deccan Plateau hold a significant position in mineral production, Jammu and Kashmir, Punjab, Himachal Pradesh, Haryana and Uttar Pradesh are relatively unimportant (Fig. 7). In India, since 1948 when the Bureau of Mines was established, mineral exploration has experienced revolutionary changes. New exploration methods, such as photo-geology, geo-chemical and geo-physical methods, ground mapping, aerial photography and remote sensing, and more sophisticated computerized programmes are utilized. The geo-physical surveys employ seismic, gravimetric, magnetic, and electrical methods. The estimated reserves of iron ore in the country are twenty-one billion tons, which is

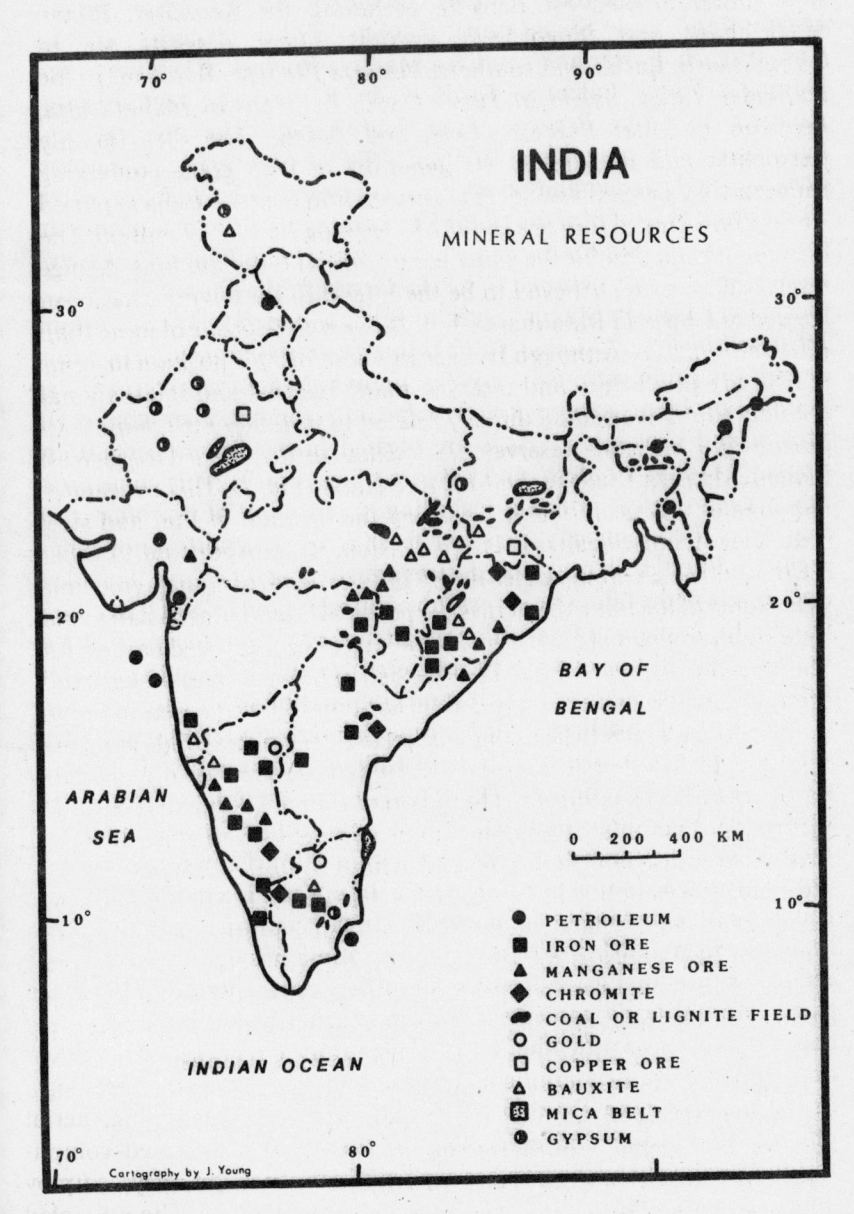

Fig. 7

more than twenty-five percent of the estimated reserves of the world—about eighty-three billion tons. The largest deposits are in the tri-state area (Bihar-Orissa-West Bengal), including the Keonjhar, Bonai, Mayurbhanj and Singhbhum districts. Other deposits are in Chhattisgarh, Bastar and southern Madhya Pradesh, Raniganj in the Damodar Valley, Salem in Tamil Nadu, Ratnagiri in Maharashtra, Kumaon in Uttar Pradesh, Goa, and Assam. The ores (mainly haematites and magnitites) are generally of high grade containing between sixty percent and seventy percent iron content. India exported 20.7 million tons of iron ore in 1982-83 earning Rs. 3,737.9 million. The iron ore production for the same period was 41.6 million tons. A huge reserve of iron ore, believed to be the largest in the country, has been located at Chiria in Manohargarh in Bihar with deposits of more than 1,970 million tons. Although India is in a comfortable position in terms of iron ore production and reserves, many internal and international political problems can be directly related to iron ore. First, almost all proven and probable reserves are located in the Bihar-Orissa-West Bengal, Madhya Pradesh, and Mysore states (Fig. 7). This concentration creates a great problem regarding the location of iron and steel industries. Economically, it is not feasible to transport ore to other regions, although all the states desire industry and, of course, consume steel. Some of the mines lie across the political boundaries of states, and legal rights to them are sometimes challenged by interested parties; for example, the dispute over the Purulia district between West Bengal and Bihar before the states reorganization commission was a case in point.

Second, India has to face competition in international trade as an ore exporter. The principal importers of Indian ore are Japan and some countries of Eastern Europe. The export of iron ore to Japan is steadily increasing year after year. The main competitors in the Japanese markets are Australia, Malaysia, and certain countries of South Africa, especially the Republic of South Africa. In the east European markets, India's main competitors are the West African countries. Since signing the treaty of friendship with the U.S.S.R., India has developed a good relationship with East European countries, especially in spheres of trade. Mutual trade agreements are increasing with East European countries as well as with other European nations. To compete with other ore exporting countries, India must either export ore at a cheaper price or lower costs by integrating the various processes involved in production, processing, and marketing. In 1975 and 1976, a new united forum was created by the iron ore exporting countries. On April 3, 1975, an Association of Iron Ore Exporting Countries was formed in Geneva comprising eleven countries from four continents. The countries are

Planning and Development of Resources

Algeria, Australia, Chile, India, Mauritania, Peru, Sierra Leone, Sweden, Venezuela, Brazil, and Tunisia. The Association calls for close interdependence among different nations, whether they are producers or consumers, exporters or importers, if a lasting solution is to be found for the present economic problems in the world. While producers of raw materials, renewable or otherwise, must get reasonable and fair returns for their products, this should not be viewed in isolation from its overall implications for the world economy. Like world peace, world economy is also indivisible. Total world production of iron ore in 1983 was 794 million tons. The production of signatory countries was 243 million tons, that is, thirty percent of total world production. World export of iron ore in 1982 was 246.5 million tons, and the share of signatory countries was 189 million tons (that is, seventy-six percent of total world export). Many of the members felt that they were not getting the proper price for their ores and were paying very high prices for importing technology and finished products from the industrialized nations or so-called developed nations. Several countries newly independent from the colonial rulers do not want to be exploited by the developed and industrialized nations; rather, they like to fulfil the needs of their citizens through industrial development.

Manganese is another important mineral resource of India. India is the fifth largest producer of manganese in the world, other countries being Soviet Union, South Africa, Australia, and Gabon. The estimated reserves of high grade ore are about 200 million tons to twenty-five billion tons, with an additional fifty to sixty million tons of low grade ore. The manganese mines are concentrated in the Chota Nagpur Plateau. The important manganese producing states are Orissa, Madhya Pradesh, Andhra Pradesh, Maharashtra, Gujarat, Goa, and Rajasthan. The production was 1.468 million tons in 1981-82, a decline of 373,000 tons from 1970-71. India earned Rs. 150 million in 1982-83 through the export of manganese. On the international market, the Soviet Union supplies manganese at a rate which is $ 2.00 to $ 3.00 cheaper per ton, which makes that country a serious competitor in the export markets in Japan (Japan has reduced her dependence on the Soviets for industrial raw material including manganese in recent years) and East European countries. The other countries which import manganese are the United States, Great Britain, and West Germany, and these are markets where India holds a better chance.

Mica is another very important mineral product from the point of view of foreign exchange. India is the world's largest producer and exporter of mica. It produces nearly three-fourths of the world's supply, earning Rs. 185.5 million in foreign exchange in 1982-83 from exports.

The United States alone imports forty percent of India's mica. The three important mica producing states in India are Bihar, Rajasthan, and Andhra Pradesh. Bihar alone accounts for eighty percent of the total mica production in India.

India's production of gold is insignificant, accounting for only one percent of the world's production. Even so, this gold has considerable political significance. The production of gold is confined to the Kolar gold mines in Karnataka. India's gold prices have been well above world prices. The rising price level of commodities and the low official interest rate help to encourage the hoarding of gold in the form of traditional ornaments or jewellery serving as an excellent hedge against inflation. Attempts by the Indian government to reduce the drain on foreign exchange by placing tighter controls on gold smuggling and by encouraging people to invest their hoarded gold in the industrial establishments have been largely unsuccessful for political reasons. Most of the hoarded gold is controlled by rich industrialists or the business communities who wield considerable influence in the legislatures by illegal means. In recent years, gold prices have increased tremendously and touched $ 900 per ounce in early 1980. Imposing control on jewellery manufacturing and lowering the carat content from 24 carats to 22 carats has been resisted by all sections of the population, especially the rich and middle class families. In 1982, the other important minerals which were produced were bauxite 1.847 million tons, chromite 323,000 tons, copper 2.007 million tons, gypsum 931,000 tons, lead 17,800 tons, zinc 48,000 tons and limestone 32,900 tons.

The production of non-ferrous metals and other minerals is also increasing steadily. Three different organizations are working in cooperation for mineral exploration. These are: the Indian Bureau of Mines, the Mineral Exploration Corporation and the Mineral Division of the Atomic Energy. Since nuclear energy plants are increasing at a fast rate in India, the production and exploration of uranium is becoming very important. Canada has refused to supply fuel to the nuclear plants in India and other western countries will follow suit as the United States Nuclear Regulatory Agency refused to supply enriched uranium for the Tarapur Plant, and President Carter had to overrule the agency during 1978. The Reagan administration has not cooperated with India in supplying the needed uranium but France is supplying the enriched uranium to India now. Mrs Gandhi had expressed the feeling in the Lok Sabha and Rajya Sabha that India would follow the policy of national security and develop its own nuclear policy for future tests. To avoid stagnation in the field of nuclear energy, India had to be self-sufficient in its uranium requirement. Three different deposits of high grade uranium have been discovered by the recent exploration. These regions are: Beleswar Kemtrassaur and Ingedinala localities in Tehri district and Lalitpur of Uttar Pradesh; Mardeora-Hirapur area of Chhatarpur and Sagar districts of Madhya Pradesh; and in the vicinity of Kalasapura and Devagondanahalli village of Chikmagalur districts of Karnataka.

Several consequences of the unequal distribution of minerals are reflected in Indian politics. First, approximately sixty-three percent of the mineral production is concentrated in the three states of Bihar, Orissa and West Bengal (Table 5). This concentration of minerals was responsible for the early establishment of the iron and steel industries in these states. However, other states of the Indian Union have opposed the establishment of more industrial plants in this region. Officials of Andhra Pradesh, Assam, Tamil Nadu, Punjab, and Haryana, for instance, have agitated for more manufacturing establishments in their respective states. On the national level, opposition party members always accuse the ruling party of neglecting certain regions in the planning of industrial development.

Second, mine union members are always agitating for better housing, higher pay, more medical facilities, and a higher share of the profits. The decisions about these matters are taken by the central government with the help of state planning departments; however, labour has not been equitably represented in negotiations in the past. Agitations have been particularly strong in West Bengal, Orissa, and Bihar (where most of the mine workers have settled) because the working conditions of the mine workers have been deplorable in this region. Besides, both the Communist Parties of India have a strong hold on the workers of this region. Bonus for workers was an important issue in the 1977 general elections when the Janata Party won overwhelmingly.

Third, India has had to develop good relations with other mineral-rich countries like the United States, the Soviet Union, West Germany, and Great Britain to supplement the shortages in mineral resources and to export iron, manganese, mica, and ilmenite. Walking the neutralistic tight rope requires a most astute political balancing act, and pleasing different ideological blocs is politically difficult. India should also be aware that she has joined various raw material exporting associations including the Association of Iron Ore Exporting Countries; therefore, she should follow the guidelines established by these associations. Competition among these countries has been curtailed, and prices have been stabilized to some extent. It is possible that India may continue to aid the developing nations in their quest for progress by transferring her technological know-how and mineral resources at a cheaper rate. This

Table 5

Present regional production and future potentialities of mineral resources in India

Region (State)	Potentialities for future development	Actual production specialities
Northeastern (Assam, Manipur, Tripura, Nagaland, and Arunachal Pradesh) 1.2%**	Natural gas and petroleum. Coal*	Oil and sillimanite-graphite. Coal*
Eastern (West Bengal, Bihar, Orissa) 63%	Coal, iron, manganese, mica, bauxite, chromite, copper. Limestone*	Coal, iron, mica, manganese, copper. Bauxite*
Southern (Andhra Pradesh, Tamil Nadu, Karnataka, Kerala, Goa, Pondicherry, Mahe, Yanaon, Andaman and Nicobar Islands, Lakshadweep Islands) 12%	Lignite, gold, ilmenite, thorium, Iron ore*, mica*, limestone*, manganese*, and copper*	Lignite, gold. Coal*, iron*
Central (U.P. and Madhya Pradesh) 11%	Mining, manganese, bauxite, limestone, diamond. Coal*, and iron*	Manganese, bauxite, Coal*, iron*, limestone*
Western (Maharashtra, Gujarat Diu, Daman, Dadra and Nagar Haveli) 7%	Petroleum, bauxite. Manganese*	Petroleum*, manganese*
Northwestern (Punjab, Rajasthan, Himachal Pradesh, Haryana, Delhi, Jammu and Kashmir, and Chandigarh) 4%	Uranium, rocksalt, copper, zinc, gypsum, mica. Lignite*	Uranium, thorium, copper, zinc, gypsum. Lignite*, mica*

* Indicates minor importance.
** Percentages are calculated from the actual production figures.

may improve the Indian economy and also help her to make new ideological friends. The western world has always been critical of India's performance; thus India needs friends among the developing nations so as to form a new coalition of the developing world. India will face lesser competition in these developing nations for her finished goods and technological assistance when the United States and the Soviet Union are engaged in larger pursuits of development and ideological supremacy. The United States and the Soviet Union are independently preoccupied in bringing China within their respective fold and ignoring, to a large extent, the developing nations of the Third World. Thus, India has a better chance to make friends among these new nations.

Fuel and power resources

Fuel resources are more widely distributed than are most mineral resources; even so, only fifteen countries produce about ninety-five percent of the world's coal and ten produce eighty-five percent of the petroleum. This imbalance necessarily creates grave problems for the states lacking fuel resources. Rich coal fields, perennial rivers, and more than two decades of experience with atomic energy offered India's power planners exceptional opportunities for self-sufficiency in power. Economic growth in India depends critically on the development of the power sector. As the rest of the Indian economy expands, demand for power grows roughly twice as fast and, because power is relatively capital intensive, its share in the total fixed asset formation is increasing rapidly (Taylore, White and Gullerson, 1983, p. i). At present, India is fairly self-sufficient in coal and water power resources, and the production of petroleum is increasing with the discovery of new oil fields; however, the country is deficient in natural gas. The atomic power resources are increasing steadily, and the scientists are investigating the possibilities of harnessing solar and wind power, as well as resources from recycled material, gas from cow dung, and geothermal energy sources. India with about fifteen percent of the world population consumes only 1.5 percent of the world energy—a very low level of consumption; however, the per capita consumption is increasing at a fast pace, and to meet the increasing demand, planning should be based on anticipated consumption rather than on present levels. Electricity consumption has increased by about ten percent per year since 1950; nearly two-thirds of this consumption is by industry, nearly fifteen percent by agriculture, ten percent by the service industry and the rest by private households. The generation of energy depends upon the availability of various sources of energy.

The total proven, estimated, and inferred reserves of coal are placed at 123 billion tons (coking and non-coking combined). Recent exploration has shown that the overall quantity of coal resources in the country is considerably larger than estimated earlier. The Talcher coal-fields alone may contain coal reserves of the order of ninety million tons, and a new 153 meter coal seam, the thickest in the world, was discovered in Jhinguda colliery in Madhya Pradesh in early 1976. The reserves of coking coal suitable for metallurgical purposes have been assessed at 28.5 billion tons up to a depth of sixty meters and are restricted to the Jharia coal-fields in Bihar. The major fields are in the Damodar Valley including Jharia, Raniganj, Burdwan, Bokaro, Ramgarh, Daltonganj, and Karanpura. This region accounts for over fifty percent of the total Indian production. Other fields are in the Pench Valley, Korba, Talcher, Singareni and Chanda, all in or around the Chota Nagpur Plateau, in the south, and in Rajasthan. Coal production reached a record figure of 128 million tons in 1983-84, and ranked sixth in the world. If the production increases from its present level to about 500 million tons per annum in the next thirty years, and then levels off, the known reserves should last for over a century. Besides, lignite reserves at Neyvelli are estimated at about two billion tons in the South Arcot district of Tamil Nadu, considered to be the largest so far discovered in India.

The Government of India nationalized the coking coal mines in 1972 and the non-coking mines in 1973. As a result, the production of coal in the country is now completely in the public sector except for two captive coking coal mines of the two private sector steel companies. Before the nationalization, over eighty percent of the coal fields were owned or leased by small producers in the private sector. The private producers employed tribesmen from the forested hills of Chota Nagpur as miners who joined labour unions and entered upon several labour strikes during the 1960s. The production of coal in the public sector is organized through three companies; namely, Coal Mines Authority Limited, which includes its subsidiary, the National Coal Development Corporation; the Bharat Coking Coal Limited; and the Singareni Collieries Company Limited. Recently, two important factors came into consideration in planning the future energy policy of India: first, the recent discovery of new coal mining areas which made the prospects for coal production brighter, and second, a high rise in crude oil prices by OPEC (the Organization of Oil Producing and Exporting Countries) countries in 1973-74. India has undertaken a phased substitution of furnace oil by coal in a number of industries, consistent with the availability of coal and transport capacity. In addition, the government adopted the policy of substituting coal and electricity for petroleum products wherever feasible in public sector enterprises. Powerhouses are switching from oil to coal without major modification in plant designs. This switchover may save four million tons of furnace oil every year. India and the United States have planned to collaborate in energy development projects aimed at substituting oil with gas and gasified agricultural waste. The first project includes a village-level gasifier that will use charred agricultural waste to produce fuel gas to replace diesel oil in irrigation pumps. The second project is the development of a small wood-based gasifier for operating five horse power to thirty horse power engines in rural areas. Another project is intended to develop fluidized bed technology that will allow efficient use of high-ash Indian coal.

The uneven distribution of coal producing regions has major political implications for internal stability and peace. For example, the coal deficiency is acute in the heavily populated areas of southern India; and lack of coal in Maharashtra, Gujarat, Haryana, and Punjab in the west and north creates a serious hindrance in these regions. The transportation of coal is difficult and costly. Coal-deficient states are also deficient in heavy industrial establishments, especially steel and heavy manufacturing. These states have always pressed hard for equal consideration in locating new industrial plants.

Mines across the political boundaries of the states create tension between adjoining states. For example, when the States Reorganization Commission decided to transfer 1,250 square kilometers of the Purnea subdivision of Bihar to West Bengal, the Bihar Government protested against the transfer. Apparently, the central government chose to support Bihar in the dispute on the grounds that the coal reserves and water works belonging to the Tata Iron and Steel Company in Jamshedpur should not, for reasons of political-economic convenience, extend beyond the state boundaries.

In the wake of the oil embargo in 1973 and the increasing prices of petroleum, India had to depend more on coal and thermal energy. With the localization of high grade coal in the Chota Nagpur Plateau, the production and transmission of energy may create a high percentage loss of energy (about thirty percent) as well as result in a high cost of erecting sub-transmission stations. The distribution of energy, and the high cost involved, may create political frictions among various groups and segments of the country, including industries, railways, farming, and poor household consumers. The total installed electric capacity increased from 2,300 million in 1950 to 40,000 million in 1983-84. The number of electrified villages increased from 3,060 in 1951 to 333,878 by March 1, 1984, fifty-eight percent of total villages. The central government has formulated a plan to set up one super thermal power station each in the coal belts of the northern, western, southern, and northeastern regions during the Sixth Five Year Plan period, and the establishment of extra high voltage transmission systems at 400 kv and 220 kv interconnecting these stations with the state grid systems. This will tie up the regions with high capacity transmission lines and a computer-based load dispatch system which has also been considered for installation. The 400 kv lines are under cosntruction in the northern part of the northern region including part of Uttar Pradesh, and the western part of the northern region including part of Maharashtra. In addition, 220 kv lines have been connected in different parts of the country (Fig. 8). This national grid, which might ease the tension between various regions was completed at the end of 1983-84. The Planning Commission has targeted that nearly 590 MW of generating capacity will be added in the northeastern region, 871 MW in the western, 748 MW in the southern, 350 MW in the eastern and 82.5 MW in the northern region during the Sixth Five Year Plan. Several super-thermal power stations near pit-heads are also planned to be established and large hydrostations located at favourable points. To meet the growing demand for power, the national power policy should aim at a minimum of 150 million KW by A.D. 2000 and fifty super-thermal power stations during the next twenty years.

Currently, there is a good possibility of an export market for Indian coal because of increased production resulting from the coordinated efforts of the various agencies of government. India signed a contract in February 1976 to export 48,000 tons of washed non-coking coal to Taiwan; 400,000 tons to European countries; and 200,000 tons to Japan. Australia, Pakistan, Sri Lanka, and other countries of Southern Asia are deficient in coal resources and largely depend upon imports. India's chief rival for these markets is currently the Republic of South Africa, but China is a possible future competitor. Conservationists feel that India should retain its high grade coal instead of aspiring to export it. At present, they admit, India has sufficient coal resources for her home demand, but they argue that there is an imperative need for conserving coal, since reserves of coking-quality and other high grade coal are limited. Should India increase per capita consumption of energy to three tons of coal—Europe consumes 2.72 tons per capita at present—by A.D. 2000, its known resources would be exhausted in less than fifteen years (Sethna, 1967, p. 16). However, even with such a large number of people, India is not likely to consume as much coal as the European nations have been consuming.

The Fuel Policy Committee made the following recommendations in respect of the coal sector in 1974: (a) coal should be considered a prime source of energy in the country for the next two decades and the energy policy of the country has to be evolved on this basic premise; (b) a perspective plan should be prepared for coal production and project

Planning and Development of Resources 95

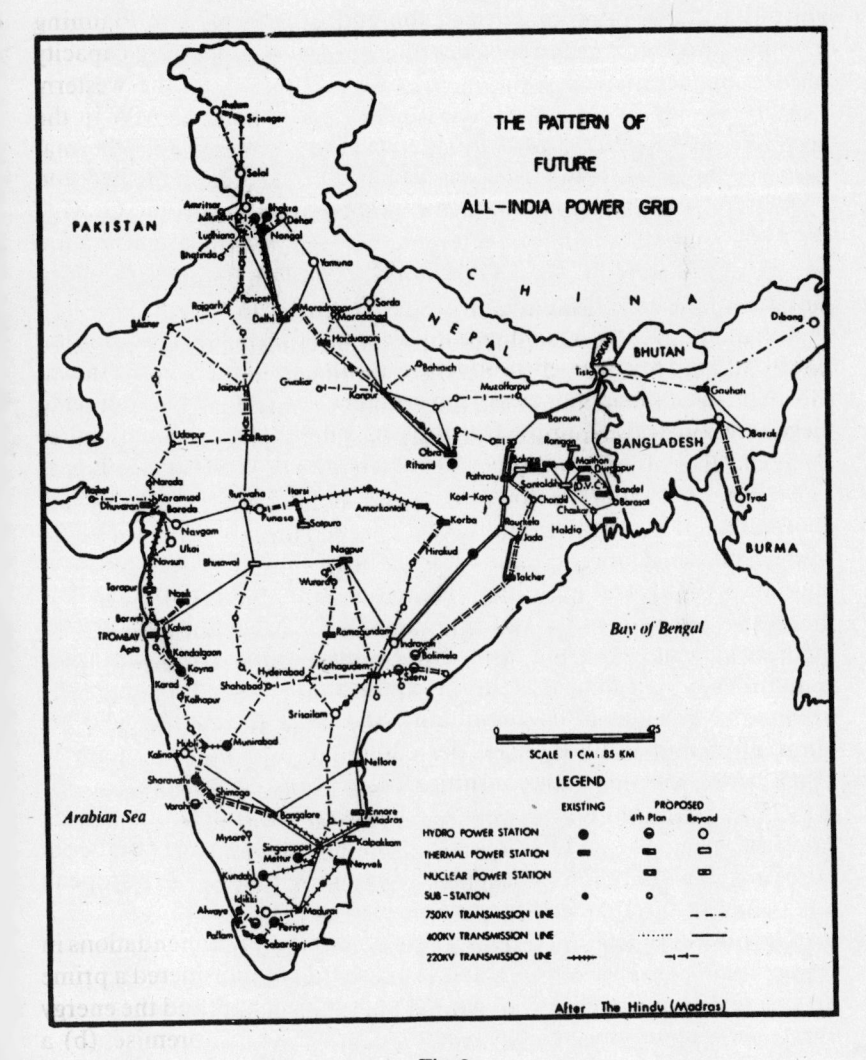

Fig. 8

report should be prepared well in advance in each plan period; (c) the possibility of projecting large-scale mechanized open cast mines in Jharia should be studied; (d) a plan for thermal power generation should be coordinated with the plan for coal production; (e) separate plans should be drawn up for opening export-based coal mines near the ports; (f) all major cities should be provided with gas plants; (g) selection of optimal technology for coal mining should be made on economic grounds using proper weightage for the availability of abundant labour; and (h) a second mine should be cut and opened at Neyvelli (*India: A Reference Manual*, 1976, pp. 243-247). These recommendations were being implemented through a 25-point economic programme initiated by Mrs Gandhi, but after the Janata Government came to power very little was accomplisehd in this respect. After her return to power in 1980, Mrs Gandhi pursued a policy for self-sufficiency in energy.

Petroleum resources are limited in India and are largely confined to the Assam belt, along the west side of the Naga and Manipur hills; to the Surma Valley on both sides of the Indo-Bangladesh borders; as well as along Gujarat and Maharashtra coastal tracts and offshore areas. Petroleum is an indispensible resource for meeting the requirements of power and energy needed for defence equipment and for maintaining the viability of the nation at the time of war or outside threat as well as for development programmes during peace time. The first commercial oil field was established in Assam at Digboi in 1899; however, the British Government was not willing to spend large sums of money for exploration. Besides, oil technology was needed for exploration, and the western oil cartel, once it found large oil fields in western Asia, showed no interest in Indian exploration. The western oil experts flatly said that there was no oil in India and this statement was supported by some theoretical geologists, too. After Independence, the Government of India tried to give a big push to oil exploration but could not succeed because of the lack of oil exploration technology. In 1955, the government purchased an oil rig from Romania and started oil exploration. The Soviet government also supplied some technical assistance; thus, the Oil and Natural Gas Commission (ONGC) was formed in 1956. After the formation of ONGC several foreign oil companies became interested in exploration and signed contracts. In Cambay-Gujarat, oil was struck in the first well in 1958, and since then several successful strikes in Ankleshwar in 1960, in Kalol in 1961, and in Sansad in 1962 helped the exploration efforts. Oil was also found in 1961 at Rudrasagar in Assam, and at Kharsangh in Arunachal Pradesh in 1976. Since 1962, forty-one new wells were discovered. Onshore exploration has been conducted in Assam, Arunachal Pradesh, Gujarat, West Bengal,

Rajasthan, Kerala, the Himalayan region, the Krishna-Godavari-Mahanadi-Cauvery basins, the northern regions of the Vindhyas, and north Goa on the west coast. The survey efforts have intensified and new methods have been employed. The ONGC has geologically surveyed an area of 548,000 square kilometers through various methods, including seismic survey and two satellites for resource survey and has estimated the reserves at 28,500 million tons.

Offshore oil exploration is an important part of the drive to become self-sufficient in petroleum. The continental shelf in India extends over an area of 390,000 sq. km. with a depth of two hundred meters. Bombay High and Bassen are the main areas of exploration besides new areas in the Bay of Bengal where oil has been found in large quantities as well as near the Andaman and Nicobar Islands (Fig. 9). Bombay High is at a distance of 150-200 kms. from the coast, and a well was first discovered on February 1, 1974. Up to March 1976, nineteen wells had been drilled on Bombay High; of these, eleven proved to be oil bearing, one was dry and the remaining were under testing. The ONGC drilled 120 more wells up to 1983-84 in order to have a steady production from this region. Commercial production from Bombay High started on May 21, 1976, initially at a rate of 4,300 barrels per day. It was planned to be gradually stepped up to 30,000-40,000 barrels per day to produce 1.5 million tons to two million tons of crude annually by the end of 1976 and ten million tons per year by 1980 (Verma, 1976, pp. 18-19). The ONGC had drilled 1,173 wells up to March 1975; of these 605 were oil bearing and seventy-nine producing. On the other hand, Oil India Limited drilled 347 wells up to December 31, 1975. The number of drilled wells has been increasing steadily in the public sector and so has the production (Table 6).

Table 6

Oil production in India, 1955-1985

Year	Production (million tons)
1955	0.347
1960	0.451
1965	3.002
1970	6.809
1975	8.283
1978-79 (end of Fifth Plan)	14.000
1980	10.500
1982-83	21.100
1983-84	23.150
1984-85	26.960 (achievable targets)

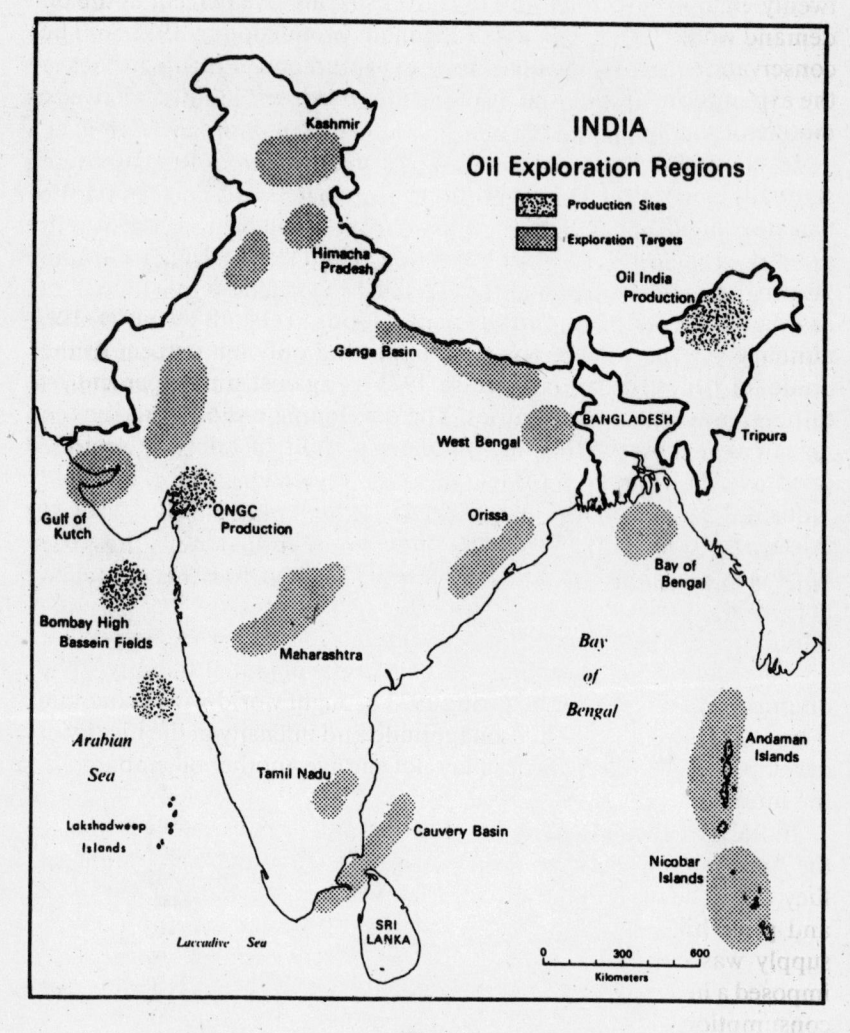

Fig. 9

Planning and Development of Resources

The consumption of oil has jumped from 3.9 million tons in 1951 to 33.05 million tons in 1984; however, the indigenous production has also increased from 0.26 million tons to 23.15 million tons during the same period. It is estimated by the ONGC that oil needs by the end of the Sixth Five Year Plan will be 36-37 million tons for the growing transport, fertilizer, petro-chemicals, power, and other industries. On the other hand, the production from the three regions of onshore oilfields in Assam and Gujarat, and the offshore field of Bombay High may reach twenty-eight million tons, and thus over seventy-five percent of the oil demand would be met through indigenous production by 1985-86. The conservation measures adopted by the government and the priorities in the exploration of oil should lead India towards self-sufficiency by the middle of the Seventh Five Year Plan 1987-88 or earlier.

In November 1973, the OPEC countries raised crude prices substantially and cut their production slightly which affected the industrialized nations greatly, but the developing and underdeveloped nations faced a dilemma of paying high prices for petroleum and keeping the masses satisfied through curbing inflation. It was not an easy task for many economically poor nations to absorb the price hike, although developing nations were importing only ten percent of the crude oil in international trade in 1973 as against ninety percent by thirteen industrialized countries. The developing nations had limited resources to absorb the shock and were short of hard currency to purchase oil from the Middle Eastern countries or sophisticated industrial goods from the developed nations. During the conference of thirteen industrialized countries on February 11, 1974, Dr. Henry Kissinger, then the U.S. Secretary of State, declared that, "the impact of the energy crisis reaches around the world, raising fundamental questions about the future of the developing countries, the prospect for economic growth of all nations and the hopes of global stability." The oil price hike and embargo during 1973 brought world-wide economic depression unparalleled in its magnitude and intensity in the history of development. Many countries may not survive another oil embargo in the future.

India's friendship with the Arab world and its consistent support of the Arab cause in the West Asia wars gave a false hope to Indians that they would be treated as a special friend at the time of the oil embargo and price hike. In reality India was one of the ten countries whose supply was cut by ten percent. To meet this crisis, the government imposed a heavy excise duty on oil and oil products, and a ceiling on the consumption of petroleum by individuals to ten litres per day and this included government vehicles. Owing to these stern measures, oil imports have dropped by over a third, to between Rs. 35 billion and Rs. 40 billion. Crude oil and petroleum products account for less than thirty percent of the country's import bill, as against fifty percent during 1980-81. The imports during 1980-81 totalled 16.248 million tons, which declined to 9.9 million tons (net import after exporting 6.4 million tons) during 1983-84. The self-sufficiency ratio has increased from around thirty percent in 1980-81 to around seventy percent in 1983-84, and self-sufficiency could be attained by 1987-88 at the latest.

Price hikes of five percent by the OPEC nations on January 1, 1977, ten percent in 1978 and 1979, and five percent in 1980 had an adverse impact on India's economy. India is among the countries most affected by the oil price hike, and its oil bill jumped four-fold since the OPEC decisions. However, prices have been stabilized and the oil glut on the world market may bring prices down in the future. Such increase in price by the oil exporting countries has affected the developmental efforts and the stability of the economic conditions of the country. Most of India's oil imports come from Iran, Iraq, U.A.E., and Saudi Arabia. When the OPEC nations increased their price of crude, the Soviet Union offered to supply 5.5 million tons of crude to India over the next four years under the rupee trade agreement; however, this short-term relief was not meant to hinder exploration efforts. The Soviet Union's offer was directly related to gaining friendship with India because India was becoming more self-reliant, and Mrs Gandhi's criticism of the Moscow-oriented Communist Party of India in her speeches might have created alarm among Soviet politicians. However, the offer and supply of crude continued even after the Janata Party came to power in Delhi and continued under Mrs Gandhi's rule ever since the general elections of January 1980. India and the Soviet Union signed a protocol on trade and technology in December 1983, which included lasers, biotechnology, electroslag technology, geology, physics of high temperature and pressures, catalysts, and heat and mass transfer. Under the protocol, it was decided to intensify drilling for oil in the Ranghat-Jaguli-Krishnanagar area of West Bengal and to speed up the repair of wells which were not functioning well in Gujarat and to put them back into production. The Soviet Union also agreed to deliver drilling rigs within the framework of the Seventh Five Year Plan starting in April 1986. India imported 5.82 million tons of crude oil and petroleum products from the Soviet Union during 1982-83. The Soviet Union is the largest supplier of petroleum and petroleum products to India.

Since the oil embargo and oil price hike, Iran and India have developed a close cooperation in the field of development. Iran increased the capacity of the Madras refinery to five million tons and agreed to supply more crude to India, whereas India agreed to supply Iran with steel rails, cement, sugar, and rice. The regime of Ayatollah Khomeini maintains a close relationship with India. Indian technicians are working in large numbers in oil producing countries of the Middle East and engineering goods have been exported to this region from India. However, recently, there is a move in the Middle East to expel some of the Indian and Pakistani technicians from the region, and the Government of India is dealing with these countries on a government to government basis. Cooperation between two neighbouring regions is essential for the stability and survival of both the regions. The national interest would be best served by importing oil from the Middle Eastern countries, since these countries can exchange oil for India's manufactured goods as well as technical and professional assistance. Good relations with the Middle Eastern countries can relieve the strain on the much-needed foreign exchange of India through favourable trade agreements. The OPEC countries have realized that it is advantageous to treat developing nations with special obligations. All intermediaries, especially international oil companies, have to be eliminated to build better trade relations among the oil producing nations and the developing nations. Regional cooperation should also be developed between India and Indonesia so that Indonesian oil can be exchanged for Indian goods; steps are being taken in this direction.

Currently, there are thirteen refineries in India, twelve in the public sector and one in the private sector. The public refineries are at (i) Gauhati-Assam, (ii) Barauni-Bihar, (iii) Koyali-Gujarat (the latter two with Russian assistance), (iv) Cochin-Kerala (Philips Petroleum Company of U.S.; India holds a major part of the shares), (v) Madras-Tamil Nadu (major share owned by the government but with financial and technical collaboration from the National Iranian Oil Company and Amoco, a subsidiary of Pan American International Oil Company), (vi) Bombay-Maharashtra (seventy-four percent shares of government and the rest Esso, which was completely taken over after seven years on January 18, 1974), (vii) Haldia-West Bengal (French and Russian collaboration), (viii) Trombay-Maharashtra (Burmah Shell of London and Esso of New York, taken over on January 24, 1976), (ix) Noonmati-Assam (Romania), and (x) Vishakhapatnam-Andhra Pradesh (Caltex, taken over on October 15, 1976). Koyali will be the largest refinery in India with a refining capacity of 7.3 million tons. Two other refineries have also been completed, one at Mathura-Uttar Pradesh in 1978 with a refining capacity of six million tons to serve the northwest region comprising Jammu and Kashmir, Himachal Pradesh, Punjab, Haryana, Northern Rajasthan, Western Uttar Pradesh, and Northern

Madhya Pradesh. The second refinery at Bongaigaon-Assam was completed in 1977. The private sector refinery is Digboi-Assam (Assam Oil Company). The Oil and Natural Gas Commission has planned an additional refining capacity of twenty million tons bringing the capacity to 48.5 million tons by the end of the Sixth Five Year Plan.

All the refineries will be integrated because ninety-eight percent of the refining is in the public sector, and the rest will be soon taken over. The Government of India has negotiated with the foreign refineries to purchase entire shares and has paid the market price to be fair to foreign companies and governments. India is seeking close cooperation and technical assistance from several foreign companies and governments in the exploration and new drilling of petroleum wells. The foreign companies involved are Atlantic Richfield, Union Oil Company of California, Carlsberg India Groups (The Carlsberg Petroleum Corporation, the Natomas Company, the Crown Central Petroleum Corporation, and the Lone Star Producing Company), the Reading and Bates Oil and Gas Company (the Mapco Inc., and the Terra Resource Inc.)—all American companies; Superior Oil Limited of Canada, and Asamera Group of Canada. The other companies involved belong to Romania, the Soviet Union, France, Sweden, and the Middle Eastern countries. About forty countries showed interest in the exploration; however, when India asked to purchase services for exploration rather than sharing the production, several countries did not bid. India needs to discover more oil in order to become self-sufficient in it; for this additional technical assistance is needed from western and other developed nations. It is difficult to develop trade relations with ideologically opposite blocs and at the same time maintain neutrality; however, India has openly told the negotiating partners to remain out of internal and external politics and work towards the negotiated contracts.

India has to satisfy the growing demand for petroleum products at home by purchasing high priced oil from foreign countries and maintaining the tempo of developmental projects, besides keeping a balance of trade. This can only be achieved through proper planning and skilled negotiations with foreign governments. The Ministry of Petroleum and Chemicals is taking an active part in developmental projects in rural areas as well as in the industrial sectors. To strengthen the agricultural economy, the ministry has established four hundred farm fuel centres to distribute petroleum products to farmers serving rural communities. This will help rural households. Indian farmers, however, will be better served through hydro or solar power rather than petroleum because oil is an exhaustible product and India is in short supply of it.

In the long run, the shortage of power in India can easily be overcome by developing hydroelectric power. Soon after Independence, a number of massive hydroelectric power projects were established, such as Bhakra-Nangal, Damodar Valley, Tungabhadra, Nagarjun Sagar, and several others. Jawaharlal Nehru emphasized that "Dams and other modern developmental projects are the temples of modern India." The future progress of India depends on such projects. At present, hydroelectric energy contributes about forty percent to the total electric power in India. The potential in the country has been estimated by the Water and Power Commission Survey during the period 1953-60 at 41.5 million KW at sixty percent load factor (equivalent to a firm annual energy potential of 216 billion KWh), contributed by 260 specific schemes. There has been an upward revision of estimates by the Commision to 46.5 million KW because of new schemes that are economically attractive (with the rise in energy prices) and because of the improvement of techniques of site exploration and investigation. At present, nearly twenty-two percent (48 billion KWh) of the total economic water power potential has been harnessed; however, when most of the major developmental projects now underway are completed, about forty percent of the country's total hydro potential would be harnessed. The unexploited potential lies mostly in the north and northeastern regions. India's biggest hydro power station, with a 990-megawatt capacity, is located in Himachal Pradesh and was commissioned in 1984. Six units of 165 megawatts each are supplying power to the three power-hungry states of Punjab, Haryana, and Rajasthan. Nearly 177 billion cubic feet of water from the river Beas have been diverted into the Sutlej. The waters are taken through open channels and tunnels, making the entire project the biggest of its kind in the country.

Although hydropower is cheap, it involves an expenditure of huge sums of money on dams and reservoirs and is not a very reliable source of power because one in every three to four years the monsoons can fail. The generation of power depends upon the even flow of rivers throughout the year and India's river flows are directly related to the vagaries of the monsoons. Shortages may occur any time of the year. The government has to act decisively to distribute power without favouring any segment of the society or organization. The opposition and private industry have always blamed governmental machinery for the poor management of power.

Hydropower resources, which constitute the cheapest source of power from the point of view of capital outlay and operating costs, offer vast opportunities for future development. The cost of energy production varies from about two paise per unit to four paise per unit. Potential hydroelectric resources, like all other kinds of resources, are unevenly distributed and some regions are situated more than 480 kilometers from major concentrations of hydropower resources with a total potential of 46.5 million KW; 25 million KW are in the Ganges and Brahmputra basins, where most of the locations being considered are far from load and consumption centres. Existing hydroelectric power facilities are centred principally in Kerala, Karnataka, Tamil Nadu, Orissa, Assam, Arunachal Pradesh, Punjab, and Jammu and Kashmir. Punjab and Tamil Nadu are the leading states in installed capacity.

The annual runoff of the Brahmaputra has been assessed at 382,107 million cubic metres; however, the present utilization of flow is less than one percent of the total available surface flow. Thus, tremendous potential has to be tapped. Another untapped resource region is Jammu and Kashmir. It has probably the largest potential of hydroelectric power. The potential is estimated to be over ten million KW. This potential exists despite the constraints imposed by the Indus Water Treaty which prohibits any storage scheme and entitles the state to have only runoff from the river scheme. The state has so far commissioned projects with generation capacity of less than one percent of its known potential. To furnish cheap and plentiful energy, India has to develop these untapped resources of hydropower.

Atomic power

India has the potential of becoming the richest country in the world in thorium production, with estimated reserves of 450,000 tons, and she is also fairly well endowed with uranium. The known thorium resources in India represent nearly 2.4 billion KWh of energy. The beach sands on the Kerala, Tamil Nadu, and Maharashtra coast have the largest known deposits of monazite in the world. Another huge deposit of monazite has been discovered in the Ranchi Plateau on the border of Bihar and West Bengal. These deposits of monazite contain approximately 50,000 tons of thorium with nine to ten percent concentration, the largest in the world. Monazite concentrates also contain 0.3 to 0.35 percent uranium. Thorium is not a fissionable material, but when placed in an atomic reactor (fast breeder reactor), it is converted into a variety of uranium, uranium-233, which is fissionable (Seshagiri, 1975, p. 118). A new deposit of very rich radioactive monazite zone with a high percentage of uranium content has been found in Lalitpur in Uttar Pradesh. India is the tenth largest country with 34,000 tons of reserves of uranium to produce yellow coke nuclear fuel. Other atomic minerals are beryllium

Planning and Development of Resources

and lithium that are found in sufficient quantity in Bihar and Rajasthan. The scientists from the atomic energy research plant have drawn plans to enrich natural uranium or uranium-233 (obtained from thorium which is available in abundance in India) with plutonium to replace the imported enriched uranium required for the present nuclear power plants. To get plutonium in sufficient stocks, the Indian reactors must be able to convert the uranium 238 (U238) into plutonium 239 (Pu239), and this process depends on the availability of heavy water. Plutonium is a waste product from the power stations. Plutonium can be a substitute for uranium in the future as fuel for reactors, and a core design change to use plutonium has already been under investigation by nuclear scientists. The intention is to make India self-sufficient in the design and functioning of nuclear power plants in India.

Since the establishment of the first reactor, Apsara in 1956, an ambitious programme of nuclear power production has been launched. In 1960, a second reactor was established with Canadian assistance. Jawaharlal Nehru declared that nuclear power was the power for the future of India. The first project at Tarapur (Maharashtra) with a 420 MW capacity was constructed by a U.S. firm in August, 1972. The second is in Kota (Rajasthan) with an installed capacity of 470 MW with Canadian assistance, and the third at Kalpakkam (Tamil Nadu) is being built by Indian scientists with upto ninety percent indigenous material and know-how. A fourth nuclear complex to be established at Narora near Bareilly in Uttar Pradesh is on the drawing board (Fig. 10) and possibly another one in Saurashtra (Gujarat). The Atomic Energy Commission has commissioned nuclear power units totalling a capacity of 2700 MW by 1981. The chairman of the Atomic Energy Commission, Homi Sethna, said in an interview that India plans to build twenty-two atomic power reactors in the 1990s to raise its nuclear power generation capacity to more than 10,000 megawatts. Out of these twenty-two plants, twelve would have a capacity of 500 MW each and the rest 235 MW each. Therefore, nuclear power in India holds a bright future. The research and development work for fast-breeder reactors using plutonium enriched fuel and sodium coolant technology has been undertaken at Kalpakkam which may provide experience in thorium-breeding. Besides, extensive surveys will be conducted to chart out thorium and uranium mining regions. India also expects to become self-sufficient in heavy water needed for its power plants in the next few years through the working and completion of the following plants: Nangal-Punjab (1962), Baroda-Gujarat (1977), Kota-Rajasthan (1977), Tuticorin-Tamil Nadu (1977), and Talcher-Orissa (1977) (Fig. 10).

India exploded an underground nuclear device of less than 15-

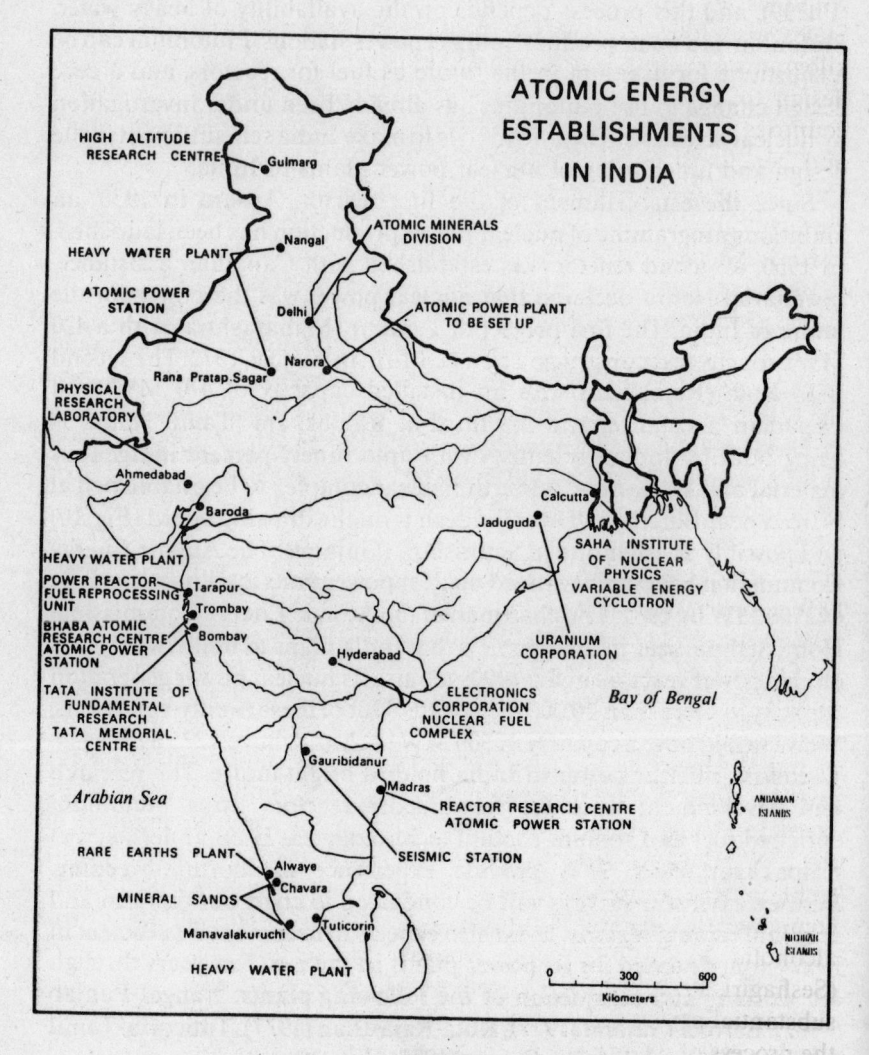

Fig. 10

kiloton magnitude near Pokaran in the Rajasthan desert on May 18, 1974. The explosion neither threw any debris nor contaminated the atmosphere. In the opinion of some western scientists, it might have brought status to India: however, the main aim of the Indian scientists and the government was to use the explosion for peaceful purposes. The western press, especially belonging to the five major nuclear powers, voiced anger at the Indian explosion. Canada cut off aid to India and withdrew all support for the nuclear power programme. The United States also followed suit by blocking the supply of nearly 21,000 kilograms of enriched uranium to India. The Canadian and the U.S. design to hold shipment was a clear warning that the developed countries will make it difficult for developing countries to participate in and benefit from the technological revolution. However, President Carter and the Congress approved the sale of thirty-eight tons of enriched uranium to India in September, 1980; half of it has already been delivered to India. Since then, France is supplying nuclear fuel for the Tarapur plant and the U.S. agreed to supply spare parts.

In case the United States unilaterally cancels the Indo-U.S. agreement of 1963 to supply enriched uranium, the following options could be explored: (a) to seek alternate suppliers of enriched uranium, such as the U.S.S.R., France (members of the NSG), and China; (b) to set up a domestic ultra centrifuge plant to produce enriched uranium with Indian reserves of natural uranium; (c) to use a mixed oxide (MOX) fuel of uranium and plutonium.

The existing uranium resources within the country are sufficient to support the first stage of the nuclear power programme of about 8,000 MW installed capacity of uranium reactors. According to a report of the working group on energy policy, of the 34,000 tons of uranium resources (U3O8) in the country, 15,000 tons are considered economically exploitable at current international prices. Estimates of additional resources are placed at 27,000 tons of U3O8.

India refused to sign the nuclear non-proliferation treaty on the grounds that the treaty discriminates against small nations while favouring big nuclear powers, all of whom are permanent members of the U.N. Security Council, giving them virtual monopoly over nuclear technology. The former Indian Ambassador to the U.N., Mr Trivedi, compared the nuclear non-proliferation treaty to the attitude of the alcoholic Mughal Emperor who wanted to enforce prohibition (Seshagiri, 1975, p. 137). The big nuclear powers are not making any substantial progress in nuclear disarmament nor are they accelerating the process of using nuclear energy for peaceful purposes. India is the only nuclear power which is pledged not to develop nuclear weapons;

however, she does not want to give up the right to develop nuclear energy for peaceful purposes. India would be prepared to sign an agreement aimed at such disarmament that would be applicable to all countries without discrimination. No developing country will tolerate the monopolistic attitude of the superpowers towards nuclear development. The Indian people, irrespective of their political affiliations, consider the non-proliferation treaty as discriminatory and humiliating for non-nuclear powers. They resent what they consider the hypocrisy of nuclear powers which, while significantly contributing towards nuclear proliferation, deliver sermons to others on non-proliferation.

Dr Seshagiri listed seven objections raised by India against signing this treaty. First, non-nuclear nations either have to depend on nuclear power for their security or jeopardize their own security. Second, nuclear technology will be denied to developing nations for peaceful applications. Third, when nuclear explosive energy becomes a full-fledged technology, the non-nuclear weapon states will have to pay to buy the benefits which will drain their foreign exchange reserves. Fourth, the developing nations will be denied the scientific and technological spin-off from the nuclear explosive energy programme. Fifth, the universal inspection procedures would become a hotbed of industrial espionage and other such undesirable activities. Sixth, the entire treaty is discriminatory to India in relation to her size, population and resources. Seventh, it makes a mockery of all limited disarmament because a single blow by a nuclear weapon will be equivalent to the total destruction which took place during the Second World War (Seshagiri, 1975, p. 137). The existing arsenals of nuclear weapons, which according to an authoritative estimate made ten years ago, represents about fifteen tons of TNT per person on the globe, an amount more than sufficient to destroy all life on earth many times over. For example, in the State-of-the-Union message on January 23, 1979, the President of the United States, Jimmy Carter, had made it clear that the American nuclear deterrent would remain strong after SALT II (SALT II was not ratified by the U.S. Congress). He explained that, "Just one of our relatively invulnerable Poseidon submarines—comprising less than two percent of our total nuclear submarine, aircraft and land-based missiles—carries enough warheads to destroy every large and medium-sized city in the Soviet Union" (Jimmy Carter, 1979, p. 228). Carter maintained that the U.S. nuclear power had devastating speed and pinpoint accuracy. In 1979, the United States had forty-one submarines, 376 bombers, and 1,054 land-based missiles, carrying a total of 9,200 war-heads, which increased substantially under the Reagan Administration. The Trident I submarine, which is already operating in the sea, and Trident II, now being tested, are much more sophisticated and powerful than the Poseidons. The target range of Trident I is 6,440 kms., and Trident II will be able to reach 9,660 kms. These sophisticated submarines can accurately strike their targets from a depth of more than 600 meters without being detected, even with sophisticated detection systems. If necessary, the Trident I and Trident II will be able to take shelter at a depth of 600 to 3,350 meters for a long period of time. Now, far more sophisticated space and biological weapons are being developed by the United States and the Soviet Union. The Soviet Union is competing with the United States in the development and deployment of powerful and highly sophisticated nuclear weapons. In certain instances, the Soviet Union is ahead of the United States and in others a little behind. The general public, at least in the democratic countries of Western Europe and the United States, is extremely scared of a nuclear holocaust and consistently opposes the development and deployment of these deadly weapons. And yet the nuclear arms race continues. In what way will India's nuclear projects for peaceful purposes be more disastrous than these arsenals accumulated by the superpowers? Without the total disarmament and elimination of all nuclear weapons from the military warehouses of superpowers, a nuclear disarmament treaty will not reduce the possibility of the total destruction of the human race, and fear of domination by the superpowers of the developing nations will grow with the arms race. The nuclear technology in India will be utilized for the economic development of the country, in mining and prospecting, for building tunnel and irrigation facilities, earth moving, diverting rivers, and building dams. The nuclear reactors may generate enough electricity to supply power to half a million villages and to a large number of industries.

The media, especially television networks, of the western world have brainwashed the viewers in the West into believing that India is only a country of snake-charmers, monkey-dancers, near-naked peasants, side-walk sleepers, and starving people. How can such a poor country afford to spend a tremendous amount of money in producing nuclear bombs? In the first place, the expenditure on the peaceful underground nuclear explosion was less than $400,000 and even the total outlay on the atomic energy programme during the Fifth Five Year Plan (1974-79) was only 0.3 percent ($ 149 million) out of $ 50 billion for the entire plan. The preconceived notion and bias of the western media concerning India's developmental efforts reflects their misreporting on various events in the world. When France and China tested their weapons in the atmosphere, it was a matter of simple reporting in the western media, whereas India's underground explosion was a threat to world peace!

The Indian delegate, Mr C.P.N. Singh, pointed out to the United Nations General Assembly in October 1983 that while nonproliferation efforts continued, the nuclear weapon states carried out, during the previous year alone, more than thirty nuclear tests, of which six were detonated in one day. Contrary to the belief of the superpowers that they are making the world a safer place to live, nuclear proliferation is bringing to the world the possibility of near destruction. India has assured the world that she would not use nuclear explosion for military purposes and that she adheres to the policy of a ban on the development, production, stationing, and use of nuclear weapons. Mrs Gandhi told a meeting of Congress workers in New Delhi on December 23, 1976, that the richer countries or superpowers lectured India on the need to cut down arms spending while they supplied arms to India's neighbours! The supply of arms creates a serious danger to India and peace in South Asia. Mrs Gandhi made a statement in the Rajya Sabha (Upper House of the Parliament) some years ago that nuclear explosions or implosions could be contemplated in the Indian context, if there was need for scientific experimentation.

Solar energy

Harnessing renewable sources of energy at a minimum cost for fighting poverty is vital for the future of the country. India has given top priority to developing solar energy and has planned joint ventures with West Germany and the United States. There are twenty-five solar research centres in India including public sector units, private industrial firms, and educational institutions conducting research to harness energy for rural needs particularly to run irrigation and domestic water supply pumps. Active research is taking place in the development of solar pumps, solar dryers for drying agricultural produce and timber, desalination of water and conversion of brakish water into potable water, solar water heaters, pumping of drinking water, minor irrigation, space heating and cooling, optimization of the photosynthetic process for accelerated growth of plants, educational radio and television sets, and conversion of solar energy into electricity. The three main areas of solar technology on which special emphasis has been laid by the government are: (a) development of solar thermal devices and systems using solar radiation as input energy; (b) development of photo-voltaic devices and systems for direct conversion of solar energy into electricity; and (c) bio-mass and bio-conversion technology. In the initial stage, units of 10-20 KW will be undertaken; however, large size plants in ideal location, such as Rajasthan, based on successes of smaller plants will be designed.

To achieve success in the solar field, India should attain a complete and comprehensive solar map giving area-wise incidence of solar energy, an evaluation of cheaper material for solar devices, a design of simple but efficient collecting and concentrating devices, an invention of methods of production of cheap solar cells and development of suitable storage elements. The country is situated largely in the sunrich belt (tropical region of the earth) and receives on an average 550 calories of solar energy per square centimeter per day. In the arid and semi-arid regions of Rajasthan, the reception is as high as 650 calories. India has a strong case for harnessing solar energy to raise its status as an energy consuming nation. Through her scientific endeavours, she should take the lead in harnessing solar energy to accomplish two important goals, (a) to become self-sufficient in energy, and (b) to export solar technology to underdeveloped countries in the sunny belt.

Other resources

A most important undertaking in terms of energy is the development of bio-gas to solve the fuel problem in rural areas. Nearly half of rural India's fuel requirements (all village homes beyond the reach of the electrification programme) for cooking and lighting can be met by producing high-quality methane gas by fermentation of the dung of the over 200 million cows and buffaloes through gobar gas (bio-gas) plants. Bio-gas produced through the new technological process developed in gobar gas plants is the cheapest gas ranging from 4.74 paise per KWh to 8.25 KWh depending on size from 5000 cu. ft. to 60 cu. ft. plant, respectively. The process can also be utilized for refuse like carcasses, human night soil and agricultural waste. The biggest advantage of these plants is the production of much richer fertilizer than cow dung. After the gas has been drawn, the nitrogen-rich waste contains two percent nitrogen content as compared with only 0.75 percent in ordinary cow dung. In a typical village, the present energy consumption is 500 KWh, but burning cow dung or fire-wood is the most inefficient method of producing this energy. Therefore, the government has granted special loans to establish bio-gas plants in various regions. Haryana has built nearly 17,000 bio-gas plants while the figures for the other states are: Punjab, 5,000, Gujarat and Maharashtra, 23,000. At the end of the Sixth Five Year Plan, there were a total of 130,000 such plants throughout India. Bio-gas plants are to be found in a number of homes in the rural areas of Haryana; very soon this form of energy will be utilized for power pumps.

Other sources of energy development are geo-thermal, wind power, and tidal energy. The prospect of geo-thermal power production in

India is to be found largely in the northwest Himalayan region (the present site at Manikaran in the Pugga Valley and Chumatank in Ladakh), Himachal Pradesh, the West Coast (Konkan coast of Maharashtra), the Narmada-Son Valley, and the Damodar Valley. Geothermal energy is more costly than hydroelectricity but is cheaper than thermal energy. Wind power can be revived and utilized in the pumping of water or for water transport by erecting windmills on boats. Near the coastal areas, tidal energy can be harnessed, especially near the Gulf of Cambay and the Gulf of Kutch as well as on the Hoogly river, with a potential of 106 KWh per year.

Oceans and particularly the Indian Ocean, in the context of depletion of land resources, seems to be an important source for food, fuel and raw materials in the future. In recent years, there is a growing realization that the ocean can become the primary source of food, fresh water, medicines, animal feeds, hard minerals, petroleum, and natural gas and other hydrocarbons. It is also realized that energy can be produced by tides, eddies, currents, and differences in ocean temperature and salinity. Furthermore, the oceans can provide building and construction materials, and even working and living space for the fast growing population of the world. In the twenty-first century, oceans may well play an important role in world affairs, and "maripolitics" may replace the "geopolitics" of the twentieth century as the main element in the thinking of statesmen, military strategists, and political geographers. Power balance may rest with the country or countries that control food, fuel, and raw materials drawn from the sea, rather than just shipping lanes and bases from which to defend them (Glassner, 1978, p. 2). Only six percent of the fish resources of the Indian Ocean is taken off from the ocean and therefore the future prospect for fish harvest seems to be bright. It is interesting to note that the Indian Ocean is located near the "hunger belt," where the majority of the people with protein deficiency and malnutrition live. The Indian Ocean may provide the essential food to this hungry region in the near future. Besides, nearly seventy-five percent of all fisheries are found near the continental mass and are easily accessible to developing nations. About forty littoral states of the Indian Ocean are anxious to preserve the fish stock and exploit them to serve the interests of their protein-deficient populations, whereas only a few distant maritime nations, mostly those whose fishing vessels have sophisticated and capital intensive gear with mobility and adaptability, would like to maintain the freedom of high seas without regard for maintaining sustained fish yield in the Indian Ocean. Because the Indian Ocean is a major unexploited region, it is an obvious target for future exploitation by maritime fishing nations. The sophisticated fishing fleets using "vacuum cleaners" sweep the fish beyond the territorial limits, and as a result the fish resources of the coastal states dwindle sharply. Japan, using sophisticated gear, may come to the Indian Ocean in the near future if restraints are not imposed by the United Nations. The littoral states have also realized the worth of the living resources of the oceans and are thus taking the initiative to safeguard them at any cost.

Another valuable resource of the Indian Ocean is manganese nodules. Although these nodules are not as widespread as they are in the Pacific Ocean, analysis of them has revealed that the Indian Ocean nodules have a higher dry weight percentage of nickel, copper and manganese than those found in the North and South Atlantic Oceans. The largest nation of the Indian Ocean, India is a net importer of copper and nickel, and it has the technical capacity as well as net fixed capital formation that exceeds five billion dollars. India can undertake seabed exploitation of manganese nodules on its own in the near future. Other littoral countries may seek assistance from India or other developing nations for mining these nodules. India is the only Third World country to receive priority contracts for mining the manganese nodules from the oceans. This will be economically, geopolitically, and technologically advantageous to India. These polymetallic nodules contain at least twenty-seven elements in varying proportions, all valuable for industrial use. Manganese nodules are of high grade ore quality, the chief components being manganese (about twenty-five percent), and iron (eighteen percent or higher) (Sukhwal, 1982, p. 49). The best quality nodules are found in water depths of more than 4,000 meters, but nodules are scattered on the ocean floor at depths ranging from two meters to 6,100 meters.

The Indian Ocean is rich in phosphorite nodules, which are made up of sand, gravel, calcarious organic remains, and fossil phosphorite, and are found in areas of great oceanic depth. Sea-floor phosphorite generally contains between twenty percent and thirty percent P_2O_5 and in some areas produce up to thirty-two percent. The Indian Geological Survey claims to have found large deposits near the Andaman Islands. All nations of the world using modern agricultural methods must utilize phosphate fertilizers, but only eight countries of the world hold ninety-eight percent of the reserves. The Arabian Sea is richer in phosphate than the Bay of Bengal. Barium sulphate concretions were dredged from about 1,235 meters off Colombo in the Indian Ocean in the 1880s. These concretions contain over seventy-five percent barium sulphate; other materials found are manganese, calcium, barium, aluminium, iron, silicon, titarium, sodium, potassium, chromium, monazite, ilmenite, magnetite and garnet.

Finally, offshore oil and gas have attracted the attention of all countries throughout the world. Within a decade, it is estimated that more than half of the world's oil will be produced offshore. Fixed platforms are being placed in water depths of 1000 feet and a deep sea drilling system is under design which can take samples of the earth's crust 35,000 feet below the surface of the ocean. Offshore operations are taking place in rich oil fields near Bombay in India and exploration is under way in the Bay of Bengal. The Indian Geological Survey estimates the Bombay high reserves at 700 million tons. The 8.7 billion tons for the offshore areas of India (4.5 billion tons of oil and 4.2 billion tons of oil equivalent of gas) constitute sixty-nine percent of the total potential reserves.

The energy consumption from commercial sources is increasing steadily and is expected to increase in the future. On the other hand, energy from conventional sources such as firewood, cow dung, and vegetative waste will decline in the future with the better utilization of these resources (Table 7). Thus, nation-wide planning and use of conventional resources should be undertaken by the state governments through village panchayats and should be coordinated by the Ministries of Water Resources and Power at the Centre.

Table 7
Consumption of various forms of energy in India

	Commercial energy					Non-commercial energy				
	Coal	Lignite	Oil	Hydro	Nuclear	Total	Cow dung	Wood	Vegetative waste	Total	Grand total
1968-69	19.4	0.6	23.5	4.20	—	47.7	5.50	37.7	9.10	52.3	100
1973-74	19.1	0.8	31.2	4.60	0.90	56.5	4.60	31.7	7.20	43.5	100
1978-79	20.7	0.9	34.1	5.65	1.65	63.0	4.00	27.0	6.00	37.0	100
1980-81	20.6	0.95	36.0	6.18	1.78	65.6	3.68	25.3	5.58	34.5	100
1983-84	21.3	1.0	39.3	7.50	2.40	71.5	3.00	20.8	4.70	28.5	100
1985-86	21.6	1.1	41.0	8.10	2.70	74.5	2.70	18.5	4.30	25.5	100

The establishment of power stations for rural areas has direct political significance. Indian cities were partially electrified before the First Five Year Plan, and during the Second Five Year Plan the electrification was completed. The electrification of villages, on the other hand, was ignored during the planning process in the earlier years of Independence. The future development of power resource and a more

Planning and Development of Resources

equal regional distribution of electricity can bring political unity to the country. In 1951, only 3,687 towns and villages were electrified; the number increased to 333,687 villages by March 1, 1984, that is, fifty-eight percent of the total villages in India with an estimated population of 470 million. In addition, all urban centres with a total population of 160 million (23.3 percent of the total population of India) have been electrified. Thus, 81.5 percent of the total population of India enjoyed the benefits of electric power by March 1984. By the end of the Sixth Five Year Plan, total electrification in India is anticipated. Haryana, Punjab, Delhi, Chandigarh, Kerala and Tamil Nadu have managed to electrify all their villages. It goes without saying that electric power is vital to the agricultural and industrial sectors of the Indian economy. The energized pump sets are expected to increase from 6,400 in 1947 to 5.5 million by the end of the Sixth Five Year Plan, while total installed capacity was expected to increase to 139 billion KWh at the end of March, 1984. This improvement will make life easier and more prosperous for the people and in the process help to bring about unity and stability in the nation. The rates fixed for electricity in the agricultural sector are much lower than those charged in the industrial sector.

It is important to note that region-wise the development of power has been on the basis of available resources. While in the Ganges-Brahmaputra basins, hydroelectric power facilities have been developed, in the Chota Nagpur Plateau the emphasis is on thermal power from coal, and in Rajasthan it is atomic energy. The all-India grid system which is yet to be completed will eventually fix the electricity rate, making the supply of electricity steady and efficient. A sense of unity will develop among the people, and finally the unity of the nation will be achieved.

An acute problem facing India's economy is the power shortage. Power shortages retard industrial growth, force machines to lie idle, cause unemployment, lead to recession in industry, as well as adversely affect agricultural production. The Federation of Indian Chamber of Commerce and Industry (FICCI) believes that a ten percent power shortage can cause an annual production loss of Rs. 70 billion on a national scale. A ten percent shortage is quite normal in India. A World Bank study estimated that the power shortage had reduced the annual economic growth rate in India between one percent and three percent per year during the period 1982-84. At various times in the years 1983-84, the power shortages faced were: Rajasthan—forty-five percent, Karnataka—forty percent, Bihar—forty percent, Orissa—thirty-five percent, Jammu and Kashmir—thirty-three percent, and Uttar Pradesh—twenty percent. In the entire eastern region, including West

Bengal, Orissa, Bihar and Assam, capacity utilization of power in 1983-84 was less than thirty-five percent.

During a three-month period in the year 1983, power cuts cost The Steel Authority of India Limited (SAIL) an estimated sum of Rs. 1.8 billion, at a time when steel was being imported. At Becco Steel Casting Private Limited in Bhilai, the power went off eleven times during one day, and there was no power for a total period of over seven hours on one day in 1983. The Mettur Chemicals have relocated their plant from Mettur, Tamil Nadu to Andhra Pradesh owing to power shortages; there is no power shortage in Andhra Pradesh. Such instances of power shortage are common, and affect industry, commerce, transportation, households, and the political behaviour of the general public. When industries face an undependable power supply, production drops, workers remain idle, wages exceed production, and the whole economy suffers.

Several factors contribute to this power shortage in India. First, discipline among workers is lacking. Employees do not work and overtime bills sometimes are paid for up to twenty-three hours of a workday. The bills in some electric boards total up to forty percent of the revenue. Drivers, who earn Rs. 1100 per month as their normal pay, make three times as much in overtime. The Chairman of the Andhra Pradesh State Electric Board mentioned at a conference that the people who need to be trained are not so much the staff as the Members of Legislative Assemblies and Members of Parliament who insist that all kinds of unqualified people be employed at power stations; politicians exert pressure on the authorities to hire their relatives or acquaintances, rather than employ trained personnel. In most of the electricity boards, there is no professionalism; corruption is rampant, over-manning is a disease, and political interference is a daily fact of life. The result is that, for every megawatt of installed capacity, the electricity boards hire on an average seven people. The international norm is less than two.

Second, the quality of coal used is very poor—at times with fifty percent ash content. This type of coal not only pollutes the environment but also damages the equipment. Third, innumerable river water disputes have held up numerous hydro power projects. Interstate disputes over power sharing are a common feature and as a result, some states face shortages while others have sufficient power. The failure of the monsoons and unreliable rainfall also contribute towards increasing power shortages. Power is in greatest demand before the arrival of summer monsoons, but the water level in rivers and dams then is at the lowest, causing acute shortages. Fifth, the equipment in power

Planning and Development of Resources

plants is of inferior quality, and in some plants equipment is outdated. Besides, workers do not care to clean the equipment regularly. When the maintenance work is delayed or ignored, the breakdown of equipment becomes more frequent and repairs costly. Finally, political decisions play an important part in the power shortage problem. The state politicians are interested in keeping power for their own State in order to catch votes for their re-election; they block the transfer of power. What makes matters worse is that the central government favours some states over others because of vested interests.

To solve the problem of power shortages, the Planning Commission has considered power generation the single biggest item of investment in the Seventh Five Year Plan, accounting for twenty percent of the total outlay. The government now plans a stupendous eighty percent increase in power generation during the Seventh Five Year Plan period. The objective is to raise the power availability from 154 billion units in 1983-84 to 280 billion units by 1989-90. The added capacity will be over 27,000 megawatts, and the investment over the five-year period will be Rs. 670 billion.

To avert power shortages, consumers have resorted to portable generators; Yamaha of Japan plans to start manufacturing these generators in India. Small-and medium-sized industries are installing captive generation equipment for a dependable power supply. It is estimated that the captive power capacity in the country now totals 3,000 megawatts, which is nearly seven percent of the national total. This is increasing at a fast rate. The private sector should play a greater role in power production and the government should encourage private investment in the field of power development. In most cases, the public sector and old plants in the private sector have performed poorly.

However, there is a bright spot in India's power production. The National Thermal Power Corporation (NTPC), the central public sector undertaking runs the Singrauli Super Thermal Power Station in Uttar Pradesh, Korba in Madhya Pradesh, and Ramagundam in Andhra Pradesh with utmost efficiency. The NTPC employs less than two men per megawatt, and aims to bring that to less than 1.5. It has commissioned, on time, ten units with a total capacity of 2,000 megawatts. Work is underway on projects that will yield an additional 7,060 megawatts, and by the turn of the century, its installed capacity is expected to increase by 27,270 megawatts—equal to the total thermal capacity in the entire country in 1983-84. The plants run ninety-nine percent pollution free. There is, however, no interference by the politicians in the functioning of the plants. The professional engineers, technical workers, and labourers work harmoniously with total efficiency. The public sector must follow the example of this corporation.

Industrial resources, development and distribution

Industrial capacity and industrialization are the basis for political power. Most developing nations realize that the key and most conspicuous determinant of political power is a highly developed manufacturing industry, as was true in the case of the Soviet Union about fifty years ago. A nation enjoys several advantages from manufacturing. First, industrialization creates a higher production ratio through mechanization and as a result raises the standard of living and improves the economic condition of the citizens of a nation. Second, it helps to prevent a dangerous dependence on foreign sources for strategic supplies. A nation's security cannot depend on the goodwill of others. For example, India has learned from experience that the United States and the Soviet Union cannot be trusted for support as exemplified during the Indo-Pakistan conflict in 1965 and 1971 and during the Chinese attack in 1962, respectively. Third, a nation should free itself from economic and political reliance—especially on financial aid, weapons, machinery, food, and industrial goods—on other nations through industrialization and become self-sufficient. A state must possess basic resources and the necessary skills to convert these resources into various manufactured goods. In case of deficiency in resources and skills, international trade arrangements with ideologically and politically suitable nations should be developed without losing freedom. Fourth, manufacturing industries can produce weapons at the time of war. Fifth, industries bring prestige to a nation in the modern world. Finally, the industrialization of developing countries may help to bridge the gap between the "have" and the "have not" nations in economic terms.

British policy discouraged the expansion of Indian manufacturing through general restrictive measures and a variety of specific economic and political controls (Miller, 1962, p. 247). Industries were oriented towards domestic consumption and export of raw material for British manufacturing plants, and external trade was tied up by colonial rule to the markets of the British Empire. Investment in social overheads was designed to aid the British merchants; thus the state guaranteed investments in railway and irrigation schemes, extraordinary measures to extend the cultivation of raw cotton, remodelling of land regulations to suit European settlement and investment, expenditure of public funds to encourage European entrepreneurship—all examples of judicious interventionism (Chopra, 1975, p. 447). The British were mainly interested in encouraging labour-intensive industries, such as textile manufacturing or industries that relied on local raw materials, such as jute processing, sugar refining, food processing and leather goods. The sophisticated industrial goods were to be supplied by British industries, with India serving as a market for British finished goods. The major industries were located at the three easily accessible ports of Calcutta, Bombay and Madras. At the time of Independence, only two percent of Indian workers found employment in industry, manufacturing and mining, producing less than six percent of the national income. By 1984, industrial production had expanded seven-fold. Owing to the "laissez faire" doctrine applied to India, the British Government did almost nothing to facilitate industrial growth. The result of this policy was that the modernization of India lagged far behind world trends. At the time of Independence, India was described as a non-industrial, peasant country, but now she can no longer be portrayed as a non-industrial nation. By all means peasant farming is still a very important part of the landscape. Soon after Independence, the Indian leaders realized that, apart from striving for agricultural self-sufficiency, industries should be developed to stabilize the economy of the country.

A number of Indian industries have undergone revolutionary changes since 1947, which is nothing short of an economic miracle. Two major resolutions have helped in changing the industrial landscape in India. The Industrial Development and Regulation Act of 1951 and the Industrial Policy Resolution of 1956 demarcated the spheres of operation of the government and private enterprise in the field of industry. The Planning Commission was set up to supply the entire range of producer and consumer goods (except highly specialized luxury goods) for a vast population; however, goods are now manufactured in India. Highly sophisticated industrial products, at one time available only to consumers of industrial nations, are plentiful in Indian markets now. Through integrated and planned industrialization, India has developed a high level of technological sophistication in such industries as textiles, sugar, iron and steel, machine tools, railway wagons and locomotives, automobiles, television sets, electronics, computer manufacturing, chemicals and explosives, cement, transportation equipment, aircraft manufacturing, shipbuilding, and domestic goods. The development and progress of the machine tool industry has been spectacular. In 1955, India produced goods worth less than one million dollars, whereas this figure increased to $500 million at the end of 1984 with more than 260 machine tool units producing various kinds of goods. India is the third largest producer of steel in the East and ranks tenth among the industrialized nations of the world. Its cotton textiles, tea, bicycles and several agro-industrial products are among the best in the world. In the case of jute, the country is a leading producer and a first ranking processor. India makes fighter planes, transport planes, tractors, tanks, diesel fishing vessels, freighters of small tonnage, naval warships, gigantic machine building plants, equipment for large hydro and thermal power plants, electronic and telecommunication equipment, and nuclear power plants and their parts. The tanks and fighter planes used during the Indo-Pakistani war in 1971, when India defeated the Pakistani military forces in only fourteen days, were manufactured in India. Three major automobile manufacturing companies have planned to produce 120,000 cars annually. In essence, India has made tremendous progress in various fields of industry, and the value added showed more than a nineteen-fold expansion from 1951 to 1984. India is no longer content merely to produce raw materials for the industrial West but would like to compete in the world market for sophisticated industrial goods. The industrial development in the last thirty-seven years has made India a power to reckon with in southern, southeastern, and southwestern Asia and in the world at large.

In spite of this tremendous industrial achievement by India since Independence, certain preconditions were not fulfilled. These unfulfilled conditions, especially in the early years of industrial planning, were that vested interests of the private sector proved to be very powerful, capital goods industries were superimposed on a basically market-oriented economy run by profit-motivated business, and there was an inadequate market within the country for the expanded output of heavy industry. At the time of Independence, India was confronted with the formidable task of wiping out poverty, ignorance, disease and inequity, and building up rapidly an infrastructure of basic industries, which could generate wealth and expand economic opportunities for millions of people of the country (Fazal, 1976, p. 13). The policies laid down in successive Five Year Plans, especially in the Fifth and Sixth Five Year Plans, stated that the existence of poverty is incompatible with the vision of an advanced, prosperous, democratic, egalitarian society implied in the concept of a socialistic pattern of development. In fact, it holds a potential threat to the unity, integrity and independence of the country. Elimination of poverty must, therefore, have the highest priority (Draft Five Year Plan). Two major concepts dominated the industrial priority policies: (a) economic self-reliance, and (b) economic equity. A key feature of industrial planning has been to spread industrial establishments throughout the nation, while continuing to strive for the most economical location. Most of the new locations have been selected according to raw materials available. In an underdeveloped economy, where generation and distribution of surpluses are limited, the vast financial, manpower, and material resources which are beyond the capabilities of non-governmental agencies need to be mobilized through public savings and fiscal measures, and investment has to be coordinated by government machinery for optimum utilization. On this basis, the public sector was given extra incentives in the early years, and the growth of this sector was phenomenal; however, private sector investments were equally encouraged. The Government of India established several financial institutions to finance the public sector. These included the Industrial Reconstruction Corporation of India in 1955, the Life Insurance Corporation of India in 1956, the Unit Trust of India in 1964, the Industrial Development Bank of India in 1964, the General Insurance Corporation of India in 1971, and State Industrial Development Corporations in various states. These institutions sanctioned over Rs. 150 billion for the public sector through the end of 1982 and over Rs. 110 million for the private sector. Owing to an enormous increase in financial assistance to private firms, public financial institutions have acquired a sizable proportion of shares in several big companies (in some companies it exceeds fifty percent). Thus the Government can quite effectively steer private enterprises towards serving public interests, and if the company fails to serve the public interest, fails to make a profit, or acts irresponsibly, it could be nationalized in keeping with the goals of a planned economy. Such takeovers of sick industries by the Government have been common on the Indian industrial scene. The result was that the private sector in India increased its share from barely Rs. 300 million in 1951 to Rs. 100 billion in 1984. The interrelationship between the public sector and the private enterprises became complementary and co-functional towards a common goal of maximizing output.

The capital goods produced by the heavy industries can be absorbed only if there is a long-term perspective of extending the public sector to the entire industrial sphere. This, in turn, requires a progressive specialization of production. Shifting the emphasis to more consumer goods industries needs to be accomplished. In the earlier years of planning, the main problem was that policies were not being implemented according to plan. In the best interest of long-run growth of the economy, it was essential not to shift the emphasis away from a policy of industrialization but rather to create such political preconditions as were necessary for the successful implementation of the policies. The successful implementation of the industrial policies would help to bring about a socialistic pattern of society.

The socialistic pattern of development proposed implies that the basic criterion for determining economic growth must not be private profit, but social gain. Economic activity should be geared towards general welfare, instead of individual gain. The pattern of development and the structure of socio-economic relations whould be so planned that they result not only in appreciable increases in national income and employment but also in greater equality of wealth. (*Three Pillars of Democracy*, 1964, p. 16). The socialistic pattern of development is probably more useful for heavy industries than for agricultural goods industries where a large percentage of the people are involved. Small-scale and agro-industries should be encouraged so that a large percentage of the seasonal labour force can be employed during the off-season.

Progress made since Independence has not changed the regional distribution of heavy industries. In fact, there is a marked imbalance in the level of industrialization in the various regions and this might continue to remain so because all regions cannot be developed as heavy industrial regions, as they might not be suitable for heavy industrial establishments. The major areas of industrial concentration are: (a) the western region, where forty-seven percent of the total industrial labour force is engaged in large-scale industrial establishments; (b) the eastern region, forty-two percent; and (c) the southern region where only 10.5 percent is engaged in large-scale industrial establishments (Karan, 1964, p. 338) (Table 8). The northwest and northeastern regions hardly have any industrial establishments.

Industries are developed in any area primarily because potential resources are available there rather than for political considerations. Potential resources include the ready availability of power, water resources, raw materials, skilled labour, an efficient banking system for huge investment and deposits, easy and cheap transportation facilities, etc. Some political influence, however, is being exerted in decisions concerning the location of new plants. It is not unheard of for the senior ruling party and influential opposition leaders to exert influence in establishing industries in their home constituencies. Most of the large industrial complexes are situated near such urban centres as Calcutta, Bangalore, Ahmedabad, Madras, Cochin, Delhi, Hyderabad, Kanpur, Bombay, Bhopal, and Vishakhapatnam (Fig. 11). These areas have geographical advantages for establishing industries which include superior transportation, good marketing systems, raw materials, skilled labour, and other relevant facilities. However, the strategy for industrial planning has been to decentralize industries and to promote growth in many centres throughout the country, including small cities and villages.

The steel industry is a prime power industry, and no nation in recent decades has risen to world status without steel manufacturing plants.

Table 8
Present regional production and future potentialities of industrial resources in India

Region (State)	Potentialities for future development	Actual production specialities
Northeastern (Assam, Manipur, Tripura, Nagaland, and Arunachal Pradesh)	Petro-chemical, wood-chemical, tea.	Oil refining. Jute*
Eastern (West Bengal, Bihar, Orissa) 42 percent**	Diversified—coal, metallurgical, iron and steel, heavy machine building, fertilizer, petro-chemical, jute, glass, and food processing. Textile* food processing (tea)*	Jute, coal, metallurgical, petro-chemical, fertilizer, iron, and steel. Glass*
Southern (Andhra Pradesh, Tamil Nadu, Karnataka, Kerala, Goa, Pondicherry, Mahe, Yanam, Andaman and Nicobar Islands, Lakshadweep, Minicoy and Amindivi Islands) 10.4 percent	Wood chemicals, light engineering, ferrous metallurgical, coal chemical, ship building, aircraft, food processing, machine building. Petro-chemicals*	Textile, machine building, light engineering, chemcial, aircraft, ship building. Food processing*
Central (Uttar Pradesh and Madhya Pradesh)	Food processing, sugar, ferrous and non-ferrous metallurgical, engineering. Chemical*, agro-based industry*	Ferrous metallurgical, heavy electricals, paper. Textile*, leather*, glass*
Western (Maharashtra, Gujarat, Diu, Daman, Dadra and Nagar Haveli) 47 percent	Textile, sugar, petro-chemical, diversified engineering, machine building, manufacture of petro-chemical instruments, automobile, wood and coal. Chemical*	Textile, petro-chemical, engineering, automobile, atomic energy. Chemical*
Northwestern (Punjab, Rajasthan, Himachal Pradesh, Haryana, Delhi, Jammu and Kashmir, and Chandigarh)	Agro-based industry, hydro power industry, wood chemical, wool, silk, non-ferrous metallurgical. Chemical*, cement*, ceramic*, and light engineering*	Cotton, wool, silk, chemical. Small scale industries*, engineering*

*Indicates minor importance.
**Percentages are calculated from the large scale industrial establishments in India. Percentages refer to the total number of workers employed in major industrial establishments all over India.

India: Economic Base And Political Patterns

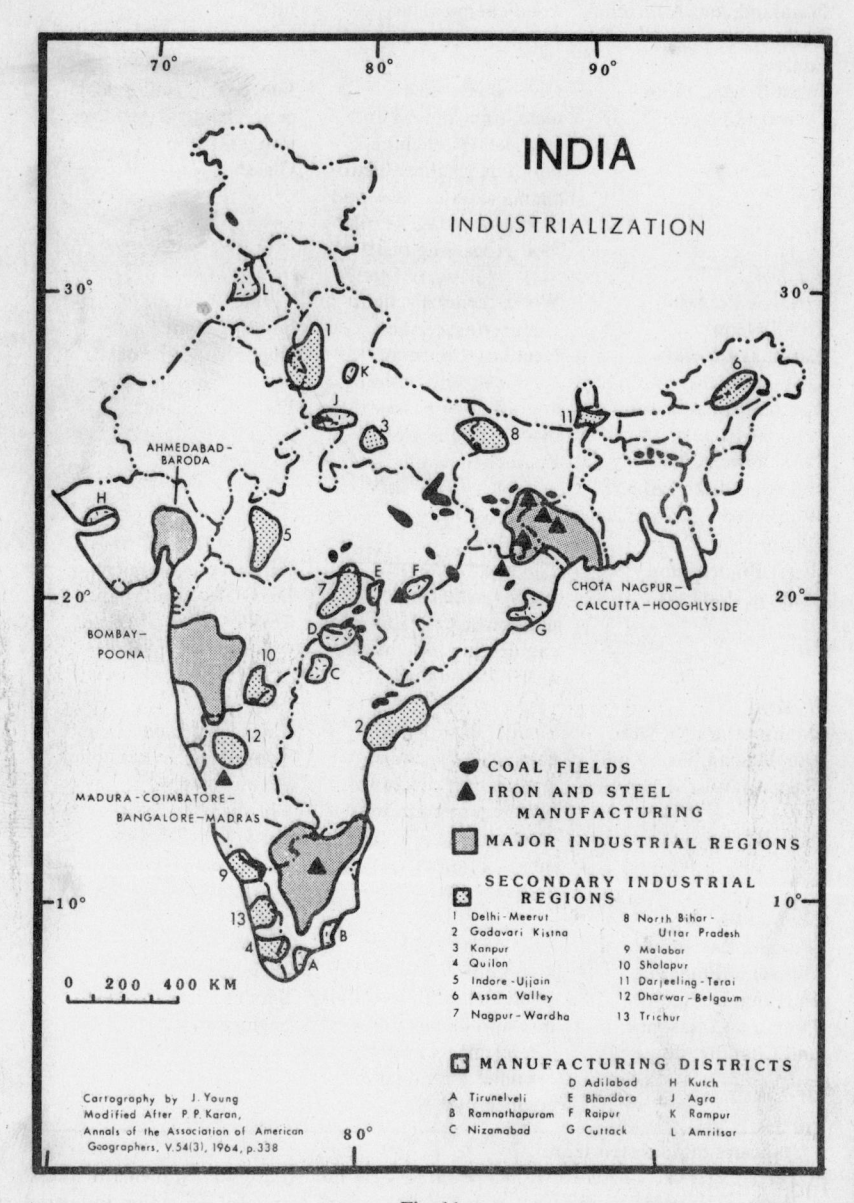

Fig. 11

Industries manufacturing iron and steel products in India are steadily increasing in number. During the first thirty-three years of Independence, production in the engineering industries went up ten-fold and the output in 1984 was in excess of Rs. 6.00 billion. The overall growth rate of industrial production increased by 5.2 percent during 1983-84, and was as high as seven percent for the first three months of fiscal year 1984-85.

The market for Indian machine tools includes not only the developing countries of South and Southeast Asia, the Middle East, Africa, and South America but also technologically advanced countries like the United States, Great Britain, and West Germany. The export of engineering goods now occupies the number one position among items exported to over a hundred foreign countries. India exported computer software worth Rs. 120 million in 1983-84 to a large number of developing and industrialized countries, including the United States and the Soviet Union. The Planning Commission has decided to assign a major role to the electronics industry in the Seventh Five Year Plan to improve agriculture, rail and road transportation, communications, power, space, oceanography, and education. A projected growth rate of more than ten times that achieved in the Sixth Five Year Plan is being considered. A major emphasis will be on the development of telecommunications in the electronics sector for which the government has set aside Rs. 130 billion in the Seventh Plan.

India is now manufacturing MIG-21M and MIG-21B planes without any external assistance. It is anticipated that the MIG-25 and MIG-27 will be produced as well. However, India would like to diversify her defence purchases, rather than depend primarily on the Soviet Union, and she would like to be self-sufficient in her defence needs by manufacturing defence equipment at home. India has made an agreement with Britain for the supply and manufacture of Jaguar aircrafts and with France for the Mirage-2000. Thus, the country is not only becoming self-sufficient, but is also producer of sophisticated industrial goods. India is also acquiring the MIG-29 from the Soviet Union, which is the most advanced fighter aircraft in the world, with Mach 2.3 speed; it is an all weather, counter-air fighter with "look down shoot down radar capability" and weapon system and is beyond the visual range of air-to-air missiles. It is equal to or better than America's latest fighters, the F-16 and F/A18.

The major iron and steel plants established in the public sector since Independence have substantially increased the quality and export of steel goods. Four major steel plants have been established with foreign collaboration since Independence; since the completion of the projects, the foreign involvement has declined drastically (Table 9).

Table 9

Large iron and steel plants established after independence

Name of plant	Location	Collab- oration	Ingot steel	Saleable steel	Increased capacity
Durgapur	West Bengal	U.K.	1.6	1.3	3.40
Bhilai	Madhya Pradesh	U.S.S.R.	2.5	2.0	4.00**
Rourkela	Orissa	West Germany	1.8	1.3	4.00
Bokaro*	Bihar	Indigeneous	1.7	1.4	4.75
IISCO	Kulti-Burnpur, W. Bengal	Private sector	1.0	0.8	3.00
TISCO	Jamshedpur, W. Bengal	Indigenous	2.0	1.5	4.00

Rated capacity (in million tons)

*Bokaro plant was built from indigenous design and material with minor assistance in beginning from the USSR.
**5.3 million tons by the end of the 1980s.

Besides the four major steel plants in the public sector (Bhilai, Durgapur, Rourkela and Bokaro), there are two small public sector steel plants. The one at Bhadravati, which was established in 1923 under the private sector, has now been taken over by the government, while the Indian Iron and Steel Company (IISCO), established in 1919 at Kulti-Burnpur, was taken over by the government in 1976. The total production of steel is coordinated by the Steel Authority of India Limited (SAIL) and the Ministry of Steel and Mines at the central government level. One major private sector steel plant is the Tata Iron and Steel Company (TISCO), which was established in Jamshedpur in 1907. In addition to these public and private sector steel plants, there is an alloy steel plant at Durgapur, West Bengal, in the public sector; it has an annual capacity of 100,000 tons of ingots, but is being expanded to 160,000 tons. Another plant, Visvesvaraya Iron and Steel Limited (VISL) at Bhadravati, Karnataka, has a capacity of 77,000 tons of alloy and 47,000 tons of ingots, and is jointly owned by the Government of India and the State of Karnataka. There are also 169 electric arc furnaces, called mini steel plants, with a total capacity of 4.4 million tons per annum. Of these, 145 are in production and produced 2.5 million tons of steel ingots in 1982-83; the other units are in various stages of implementation. In the pre-Independence days, India was producing

Planning and Development of Resources

one million tons of pig iron and one million tons of steel ingots; the capacity reached 14.6 million tons in December, 1983. The six integrated steel plants account for 11.4 million tons; the remaining comes from the ore furnaces and mini-steel plants. The Steel Authority of India (SAIL) is going ahead with expansion plans that will increase the total capacity to twenty-four million tons of pig iron by 1989-90; the plans involve modernization and expansion of existing units and installation of new steel plants to keep pace with the upsurge in demand. A target of 21.3 million tons of ingot steel production has been envisaged for 1989-90.

Future planning is oriented towards attaining a production level of seventy-five million tons of steel by the end of the century when the national requirement is expected to reach fifty million tons. Each of these four large steel plants was established in its present location in one of the four different states on the basis of availability of resources. There was an agitation in Andhra Pradesh to establish a steel plant in Visakhapatnam, but in the beginning the request was turned down by the central government for economic reasons. After reconsideration by SAIL, the construction of the plant was approved, and right now the construction of the Visakhapatnam steel mill is under way. Since the construction of a new steel plant is considered a status symbol, agitations in different states of the country became common during the late 1960s and early 1970s. The Steel Ministry has prepared a White Paper on the long-term development of the steel industry. A new steel plant at Salem (Tamil Nadu) was commissioned in 1981 to produce 32,000 tons of cold-rolled stainless steel with a capacity to rise to 220,000 tons. The paper stresses the importance of early completion of the three southern steel plants, namely Paradeep in Orissa (under study), Vijaynagar in Karnataka (under study), and Visakhapatnam in Andhra Pradesh (work is progressing towards completion). Another study for establishing steel plants in the Bailadilla region of Madhya Pradesh and in the Surajgarh area of Maharashtra has been completed by Meteorological and Engineering Consultants (MECON) for SAIL. Two other proposed plants are under study, one at Mormugao (Goa) on the west coast and the other at Hospet in Karnataka. These additional plants will not only make India self-sufficient in steel and steel products, but increase the prospects of export and thus add to the foreign exchange reserves of the country.

Russian economic and technical assistance in building two of the four steel plants has created fear in the minds of the general public that the Soviet Union might sometime dominate the internal politics of India. An attempt was made to get American financial and technical assistance for the establishment of the Bokaro plant; however, the terms laid down by the United States were not acceptable to the Indian government. Bokaro was planned as a wholly Indian enterprise after the withdrawal of U.S. aid for it. Soviet assistance was subsequently drawn upon for its speedy construction. About eighty-five percent of the equipment for Bhilai was imported from the Soviet Union, but the position is exactly the reverse in the case of Bokaro where most of the planning, designing, and construction was carried out by indigenous methods. It can be called the first truly swadeshi (indigenous) steel plant in India. The concentration of income, entrepreneurs and technical skills in the more highly developed regions has created a greater imbalance in the spatial economic structure of the country as a whole.

New investors frequently avoid the Chota Nagpur Plateau region, especially the Calcutta area, because of political unrest. Labour difficulties are rampant in the Calcutta region, and approximately 900 "gherao incidents" (workers locking management personnel in their offices) have occurred since the coalition government came to power in 1969. The leftists, in a kind of election strategy, charged that the dominant position in West Bengal business and industry had passed into non-Bengali hands, and thus convinced the voters of their right to either gain control of industry or at least have a fair share of the profits. After the imposition of the Emergency in 1975, the industrial relations climate improved considerably, and there was a great sense of discipline leading to an increase in production. The number of man days lost owing to strikes and lockouts decreased form 40.3 million in 1974 to 21.9 million in 1975 and 12.8 million during 1976. The Janata government came to power in March 1977; consequently, the man-days lost increased substantially from 12.8 million in 1976 to 25.3 million in 1977, 28.3 million in 1978, and 43.5 million in 1979. When Mrs Gandhi came to power in 1980, the man-days lost declined to 21.9 million in 1980. It again increased to 44.3 million man-days (including 19.3 million owing to the Bomaby textile workers' strike) in 1983. After Mrs Gandhi came back to power, she indicated that a problem which was high on her agenda was to create a climate of cordial relations between labour and management. Owing to stability and a sense of discipline in the industrial sector, the first quarter of 1976-77 showed a record increase in production of about sixteen percent, an all-time high compared to a 0.2 percent decrease in 1974. The public sector, which is considered an instrument for development in a socialistic pattern of society, showed a spectacular growth of fifteen percent in 1975-76. Between 1967 and 1974 in the western and southern states of Gujarat, Maharashtra, Karnataka, Tamil Nadu, Andhra Pradesh, and Orissa, investment conditions were more stable and, therefore, foreign investment increased. In Tamil

Nadu, Kerala, and Orissa there were non-Congress administrations, but there were fewer economic troubles than in West Bengal and Bihar. The conditions in industry deteriorated in 1979-80, causing a reduction in the growth rate by about two percent. The average annual growth rate in industry in the seventies was only five percent a year and this was also possible because of two peaks—ten percent in 1976 and eight percent in 1978. In fact industry entered the eighties riddled with problems such as a maze of controls, power cuts and labour indiscipline. One of the major hindrances in achieving the projected targets for industrial production was insufficient power. An erratic power supply is one of the main reasons for the fall in the output of an industrial plant. The Rourkela steel plant in Orissa received less than twenty percent of the power it needed for seven months in 1983-84 and ran at forty-three percent capacity instead of eighty-one percent in 1982-83. This was due to poor monsoon rains that adversely affected hydroelectric power production. The demand for electricity has increased twenty-five-fold since Independence. The Chairman of SAIL explained that money will be spent over the next five or six years to build power plants within SAIL's five mills; this is expected to ensure self-sufficiency up to eighty percent, rather than depending on public utilities to supply power to these plants. In addition to a fall in hydroelectric power in 1983-84, the workers in coal mines went on strike, resulting in a loss of man-days totalling 1,044 million—a staggering number. It is expected that in the eighties industry will be able to achieve a growth of about ten percent per year on an average (unattainable goal), agricultural development at four percent, while GNP would increase at 6.8 percent and per capita income would exceed over Rs. 3000 by 1990.

The Indian government has made a conscious effort to plan a programme of industrial development that is regionally balanced. Regional imbalance could create areas of economic inequalities which could become centres of dissatisfaction and dissent. This situation could prompt the Opposition to demand a measure of self-government or special economic treatment as was evident in the case of Tamil Nadu and West Bengal. Regional, linguistic, ethnic and cultural differences abound in India; thus India must consider economic equality among various regions as the precondition for achieving political, social, and cultural equality. It is important that disparities in the levels of development between different regions should be progressively reduced, but efficiency should not be sacrificed for the sake of equitable distribution. No country can really afford being equitable about distribution of industries because each region differs in the availability of raw materials, labour, transportation facilities, and other ingredients for establishing industrial units. Maharashtra may be regarded as industrially the most advanced State, followed by West Bengal, Gujarat, Tamil Nadu, Uttar Pradesh, Bihar, Madhya Pradesh, Karnataka, and Andhra Pradesh. These nine States together account for seventy-eight percent of the factories, seventy-six percent of the fixed capital, eighty-two percent of the employment, eighty-three percent of output, and eighty-five percent of value added (Sharma, 1976, p. 11).

In the western region, which stretches from Ahmedabad to Bangalore through Baroda, Bombay and Pune, large non-industrial areas existing between cities are being built up rapidly as new industrial plants are being established. The shift of industries is towards the south across the Vindhyas. The main industries of the western region are cotton textile and cotton yarn manufacturing, chemicals, petrochemicals, food processing, pharmaceuticals, and engineering goods. Cotton textile is the prime industry in this region, with the existence of over 700 textile mills, some of which are idle and beyond repair while others are running satisfactorily. The textile strike in 1983-84 made several textile mills inoperative; a number of them were considered "sick" and were taken over by the government. At the opposite end of the peninsula, the eastern region of the Chota Nagpur Plateau (Orissa-Bihar-West Bengal tri-state area) was the premier industrial region in India with iron and steel, metal manufacturing, transportation equipment, jute goods, and chemicals as major industries. This region is turning into an industrial backwater, especially the Calcutta-Asansol area. At the time of Independence, West Bengal was the most industrialized state in the country; however, there has been a definite geographical shift in industrial concentration from the east to the west. A large number of industries around Calcutta are "sick" industries and many Calcutta-based industrial houses, including the houses of Birla and Goenka, have shifted to Bombay and other places. The ruling party in the State of West Bengal, the Communist Party of India (Marxist) has blamed the central government, ruled by the Congress (I), for ignoring industries in West Bengal and for being responsible for the deindustrialization of the State. In the southern region, textiles and light engineering goods are centred around Madras though industries are expanding inland also.

A second major shift in emphasis is from such core industries as steel, textiles, and coal which have been declining in importance, not only in India, but throughout the world to computer-related industries, electronics, automobiles, cement, chemicals, and machine tools. A third shift is from the public sector investment to the investment in the private sector, including foreign investments (especially from overseas Indians).

The private sector in India has certainly proved to be more enterprising and profitable than the public sector (Jay Dubashi, 1984, p. 60). A fourth shift is from industries which have domestic and national concern to those which have world-wide multinational dimensions. Private and public sector industries are expanding into foreign markets. Similarly, foreign entrepreneurs are investing in Indian industries. The recent liberalization policy by the Government of India has encouraged outside investment in all types of industries.

There are too many industries with poor performance levels such as textiles, sugar, steel, and coal that may ultimately prove to be harmful to the economy. In addition, the clustering of industries in certain areas and the lack of industries in other creates serious social and political problems, besides inequitable distribution of economic resources. Thus, spatial diversification, as well as diversification according to industries, must be undertaken with utmost caution, weighing all the pros and cons for future development. Political considerations, where powerful politicians favour their own region at the expense of overall national developmental interest, should not dictate the industrial shifts or the establishment of new industries. New industries are being developed near large urban centres all over the country; for instance, shipbuilding at Visakhapatnam; machine tools, aircraft, and telecommunication industries at Bangalore; heavy electricals at Bhopal; machine building at Ranchi; and fertilizer, leather goods, and oil refining at Kanpur. Other industrial concentrations are being developed in Cochin, Mysore, Hyderabad, Kota, and Amritsar (Fig. 11). These scattered industrial developments are attracting workers from adjacent areas, thereby transforming the economic base and improving the political stability of the various regions of the country. The regional migration to work and the resulting better economic conditions should eventually bind people together and enhance the loyalty of the workers to the region.

Finally, another very important step that has been taken by the Planning Commission is to decentralize the pattern of development of the ubiquitous industries to fit the ideal of a socialistic society. The Commission recommended that a large number of small towns, widely distributed over different parts of the country, should be developed into industrial townships with planned provision for small scale and light industries (Dua, 1967, p. 8). India still remains predominantly a country of village and small-scale industries, and these industries are essentially artisan enterprises. They use agricultural and other indigenous products and are more acceptable to rural people and at least partially fill in the gap created by the unequal distribution of heavier industrial concentrations. These craft industries employ more than two million persons, of whom nearly 0.9 million work in the handloom industries, which is more than the total number of workers employed in the organized industries and mining put together. The number of small-scale units registered on a voluntary basis at the end of 1984 was about 600,000, accounting for about forty percent of the production in the registered manufacturing sector. The gross output was Rs. 85 billion at the end of 1984, with 185 items exclusively produced in the small-scale industrial sector.

The ubiquitous industries provide work to seasonally unemployed persons and thus help to create political stability and improve the living conditions of the rural population. Moreover, work is provided in the villages where women can also share in the craft industries. The wide dispersal of the ubiquitous industries will aid in lowering the dependency ratio and increase overall productivity. As a result, the per capita income may increase and the GNP may rise as well.

Before Independence, the Indian economy was virtually stagnant. The rate of growth since Independence has been more than three times that of the pre-Independence era of the twentieth century. The general index of industrial production increased from 54.8 in 1950 to 187 in 1983. whereas the index for the basic and key industries and overall production of industrial goods increased seven-fold. The industrial infrastructure for a successful industrial society has been created by increasing the number of national highways, railway route lengths, shipping tonnage, electric power generation, iron and steel output, cement production, chemical and pharmaceutical goods, oil refining, automobile manufacturing, ship building, aluminium industry, textile and synthetic fiber production, electronic computer-based products, and defence industrial production. The main basis for this development was to attain self-sufficiency in every sphere.

Important achievements for Indian planners have been the creation of trained manpower, the growth in science and technology, and the development of the technical and managerial abilities to run the modern industries. The spectacular growth of industries has reduced imports of industrial goods and technical manpower, thus saving foreign exchange. Although the standard of living is low, the savings by households has increased from 7.3 percent in 1950-51 to 21.1 percent in 1981-82. This rate of domestic savings is better than that of any of the non-Communist developing countries in the world. Wholesale prices increased moderately in recent years compared to other developing countries, and some industrialized nations as well.

By the above analysis, it seems that everything is rosy on the Indian economic scene. However, the picture is not so bright on the industrial scene in India, particularly in the case of the mining and fuel sectors. The first problem is the less than average performance of the public sector in primary industries such as coal, steel, electric power, railway transport, telecommunications, banking, and insurance. If mining, industrial, and power-based industries are to succeed, they should take advice from academicians outside the government establishment and enlarge industries in the private sector so as to create a competitive spirit.

Second, the rapid growth of population by over 135 million during 1971-81 has put more strain on industrial production; consumer demand has increased substantially and the consumers have also become more educated and sophisticated. Besides, India has to maintain an adequate level of exports to earn foreign exchange. The growth of the population has created another problem in that a large number of people live below the poverty line, with fifteen percent of the people being severely destitute. The unemployment levels in agriculture, manufacturing industries, and service industries have soared because of the rapid growth of population. It is estimated that twenty-five percent of the engineering graduates will not be able to find employment during 1984-89. Medical doctors, technicians, and other trained personnel are facing the same fate and may continue to suffer unemployment in the future. Approximately fourteen million more people per year will require an additional food supply, 2.6 million houses, four million jobs, 126,500 schools, 372,500 teachers, and 180 million meters of cloth, which are beyond the production capacity of India's overburdened economy. In a labour intensive economy, it is apparent that preferred technology, giving higher values of net output and employment per unit of scarce input of capital, should have been adopted, rather than marginal output per worker, favouring large-scale industries.

The efficiency of mines, factories, and farms should be improved and the workers should be paid according to their performance, that is, a production-oriented economy should be introduced. Highly paid bureaucrats and public officials should be made accountable to the public, and they should produce their share of economic output. Yet, despite many handicaps, India's economic performance is unmatched by any developing democratic nation.

NOTES

Jay Dubashi, "The Economy, Industrial Climate; Subtle Shift," *India Today*, Vol. 9, No. 5 (March 15, 1984), 60. (60-61).

Jimmy Carter, "State of the Union, 1979, "*Vital Speeches of the Day*, 45, No. 8 (February

1, 1979), 228.

P.N. Chopra, ed., *The Gazetteer of India, Vol. III; Economic Structure and Activities* (New Delhi: Gazetteer Unit, Ministry of Education and Social Welfare, Government of India, 1975), p. 410.

Draft Five Year Plan, 1974-79 (New Delhi: Planning Commission, The Government of India, 1973), p. 6.

D.R. Dua, *Small Scale Industries and Handicrafts* (New Delhi: Sarvodya Publishers, 1967), p. 8.

Mohd Fazal, "Public Sector in India: A Changing Picture," *Indian and Foreign Review*, Vol. 13, No. 6 (January 1, 1976), 13.

Martin Ira Glassner, "A Special Issue on the Law of the Sea," *Focus*, Vol. 28, No. 4 (March-April, 1978), p. 2.

Pradyumna P. Karan, "Changes in Indian Industrial Location," *Annals of the Association of American Geographers*, Vol. 54, No. 3 (September, 1964), 338. (336-354).

P.P. Karan has selected industrial districts where 1500 or more wage earners were employed in manufacturing. These districts were termed as industrial districts for the purpose of delimiting Indian industrial regions.

E.W. Miller, *A Geography of Manufacturing* (Englewood Cliffs, New Jersey: Prentice-Hall, Inc., 1962), p. 247.

N. Seshagiri, "The Bomb: Fallout of India's Nuclear Energy Programme," *Indian and Foreign Review*, Vol. 5, No. 2 (November 1, 1967), 16.

A.P. Sharma, "India's March Towards Industrial Progress," *Indian and Foreign Review*, Vol. 14, No. 5 (December 15, 1976), 11.

B.L. Sukhwal, "India's Role in Recovering the Polymetallic Nodules from the Ocean Floor and the Law of the Sea Treaty," *The Indian Geographical Journal*, Vol. 57, No. 2 (December, 1982), 49. (47-57).

C. Taylor, C. White, and M. Gullerson, *India: Economic Issues in the Power Sector* (Washington, D.C.: South Asia Regional Office, The World Bank, 1979), p. (i).

Three Pillars of Democracy (New Delhi: Ministry of Community Development and Cooperation, The Government of India, 1964), p. 16.

Kewal Verma, "Towards Self-Sufficiency in Oil Production," *Indian and Foreign Review*, Vol. 8, No. 24 (October 1, 1976), 18-19.

CHAPTER 5

Transport, Communication and Trade

Transportation and communication
Transportation and communication are two of the main ingredients necessary to accelerate the pace of economic progress and to establish a stable nation. In many instances, both these factors play a key role in promoting economic growth, and in all cases they set the limits to progress (Owen, 1968, p. 1). The levels of mobility always correspond to levels of economic development; for example, collecting raw material and distributing manufactured products to the market or to consumers require adequate, cheap, and reliable transportation facilities. The Indian economy has undergone far-reaching structural transformation in recent decades through development and expansion but this could not have been accomplished without changes in the size and structure of the transportation system. The phenomenal progress in transportation has been attained through planned development, in spite of huge population base, diversified economic conditions, and sheer vastness of the Indian subcontinent.

External transportation is aimed at providing access to foreign sources of raw material, food, and technological goods; internal transportation, on the other hand, is concerned with movement within a nation state. During the Indo-Chinese war in 1962, China was able to win because the Indians were faced with poor transportation and bad communications in the difficult Himalayan terrain. After the defeat of the Indian forces on the northern borders, India realized the need to purchase equipment from the United States and as a result, today the Indian forces are better equipped in mountain areas than they were in 1961. India has undertaken the speedy construction of a railway line up to the Himalayan border, because it realizes that transportation has great strategic value. During the Bangladesh crisis in 1971, the quick and efficient transportation of people and equipment proved a valuable factor for Indian forces winning the war. The defence of a country is impossible without adequate transportation and communication facilities. Strategic roads, strategic railways, strategic naval shipyards, and strategic airports strengthen the military power of a nation state. India has given topmost priority to these factors while enlarging its transportation system.

A well-developed transportation network is regarded as a prerequisite for national unity. It enhances the cohesion and integration of the state by facilitating the circulation of goods and ideas. An improved network of transportation has helped India to overcome various knotty problems in recent years. For example, (a) in politically unsettled regions of the country, roads and rivers alike were infested by bands of robbers who hampered trade and travel. The Chambal valley in Madhya Pradesh, areas in Rajasthan, and Uttar Pradesh have been prime examples of areas which have been neglected in terms of transportation. Assam and the Northeast are other regions of instability owing to lack of transportation facilities; (b) the isolation of rural areas owing to poor transportation has been the root cause of backwardness and lack of harmony among various diversified regions in the country; (c) the economic isolation of even adjacent districts prevents the transfer of foodgrains from surplus areas to famine-infested ones. Harvests in some parts of the country were at times so plentiful, but ironically it was more expensive to carry grains to the market than to sell them locally at a cheaper price. During the initial years of Independence, the country had to cope with the acute problem of transporting people and materials. India is still deficient in transportation and communication facilities; though, in recent years, the situation has improved to some extent.

The British developed a network of highways and railways for military movement, administrative needs, and defence requirements for the rapidly growing British Raj in India. The first railway train in India rolled on the track on April 16, 1853, between Bombay and Thana covering a distance of thirty-three kilometers. At the time of Independence, the total route mileage of railway track was 33,985 kms. However, India inherited a railway system which was shattered by economic depression, worn out by abnormally heavy use during the war, and dismembered by Partition. Since Independence, tremendous progress has been made in railway transportation. The railway system in India is the biggest state undertaking and the world's second largest network under a single management, second only to that of the Soviet Union, and the biggest in Asia, with a route length of 61,400 kms. in 1982-83. The railways are India's largest nationalized undertaking, with assets totalling over Rs. 67 billion, and providing employment to over 180,000 (A.B.A. Ghani Khan Choudhury, 1984, p. 5.). The Indian railways provide the principal mode of transportation in the country, reaching out to extreme corners of the country. The growth of the railways has been closely linked with the country's economic, agricultural, and industrial development; the railway network connects mines, coal fields, oil zones, industrial plants, power plants, ports, and transports passengers and material to far-flung destinations in the service of the nation. It carries ten million passengers daily as well as 6.5 million tons of freight over 61,000 kms. Trains run over 1.3 million kms. per day on an average, that is, about three-and-a-half times the distance from the earth to the moon. The railways will carry 225 billion passengers per year by the end of the present century.

The railway system has been expanded, equipped, and modernized to deal with a phenomenal increase in traffic, and has shifted progressively to high volume and high density operations. The unprecedented growth of the railways from 1950-51 to 1981-82 was an indication of the progress made by India. For example, the number of originating passengers went up from 1,284 million to 3,704 million, originating goods from 93 million tons to 220 million tons of revenue earning traffic, net tonnage kilometers from 44,117 million to 174,202 million, the capital-at-large from Rs. 8,270 million to Rs. 66,980 million, and route kilometers from 53,596 to 61,400 during the period 1950-51 to 1981-82. The railways carry more than half the total passenger traffic in the country and two-thirds of the freight traffic. In 1981-82 the railways possessed over 11,000 locomotives, including 6,292 steam, 2,638 diesel, and 1,157 electric locomotives, 40,000 passenger coaches, and more than 540,000 wagons of two dozen different types. By the end of 1982-83, almost 5,800 route kilometers were electrified.

When India became independent, there were as many as forty-two different state/company railway units; they were later integrated to form the Indian system. The Indian railway system comprises not a single rail line, but a large number of zones with different gauges, that is, broad gauge, meter gauge and narrow gauge. The system is now organized into separate zones, each governed by a general manager and coordinated by the Railway Board under the Ministry of Railways. These zones are as follows: Central Railway headquartered at Bombay, Eastern Railway at Calcutta, Northern Railway at New Delhi, Northeastern Railway at Gorakhpur, Northeastern Frontier Railway at Maligoan (Gauhati), Southern at Madras, Southcentral Railway at Secunderabad, Southeastern Railway at Calcutta, and Western Railway at Bombay. Some of the narrow gauge tracks have been converted into meter gauge ones, and some meter gauge tracks into broad gauge ones. The railway equipment and manufacturing infrastructure is sufficient for the needs of the country and in fact equipment is being exported, along with consultancy services to countries, such as Hungary, Poland, Canada, France, East Africa, Nigeria, Ghana, Algeria, Zambia, Iraq, Iran, Saudi Arabia, Syria, Turkey, Burma, Thailand, Sri Lanka, the Philippines, and New Zealand.

The Indian railways use the central traffic control system through microwave techniques, ultrasonic devices for testing the tracks and axles, and 120 channel micro-wave radio relay links between important stations. This has resulted in quicker communication and faster and better collection of data. Computers have been installed in the production units at the Chittaranjan Locomotive Works, West Bengal; the Diesel Locomotive Works, Varanasi; and the Integral Coach Factory, Perambur in Madras. The introduction of computerized seat reservations from March 1, 1985, is a further step towards modernization of the Indian railways. Modern safety devices such as track-circuiting, axle counters, and automatic warning systems are being installed to ensure safe operation. There are over 5,800 kilometers of electrified railway lines which is increasing rapidly. The World Bank has granted a loan of $280.7 million to electrify 3,000 kilometers of major trunk routes connecting New Delhi, Bombay, Madras, and Calcutta. The estimated total expenditure on the project will be $1.2 billion. High speed trains, such as the Rajdhani Express, on the Delhi-Calcutta and Delhi-Bombay routes, with speeds of 120 to 130 kilometers per hour and a potential of 160 kmh, have been introduced. After the Emergency in 1975, ticketless travel, which was a big problem, declined by ninety-five percent in contrast to the pre-Emergency era, while petty thefts and stealing of railway property were checked, stations were cleaned, racketeering in reservations ended, and efficiency and punctuality improved. The Indian railways rank first among the largest five railways in the world so far as safety record is concerned, in spite of the fact that it carries the heaviest passenger load. It has earned the status of a railway pioneer among Third World nations, particularly because it provides cheap, speedy, and comfortable train services for millions of people who undertake long distance journeys every day.

Railway travel and the distribution of railway lines often get mixed up with politics. For example, as a means of attracting the attention of the government to a particular regional-political problem, it has become the practice of groups of individuals to disrupt railway movement. Agitators all over the country vent their anger making the railways their first target. Damage to railway property has been increasing year by year. If the Minister of Railways is not popular with the troublesome groups, they sabotage the railway system to get him out of office. L.N. Mishra was killed in a bomb explosion at Samastipur railway station on January 2, 1975, an incident which shocked the Indian people. As a means of agitating against a language policy during the 1960s, students in some of the southern states burned railway coaches and set fire to railway stations.

The lack of an extensive railway network in Assam, Arunachal Pradesh, Orissa, Jammu and Kashmir, Rajasthan, and the southern states leads to difficulties in distributing food in these areas during times of shortages, and it also hampers efforts to control rebellious groups (Fig. 12). Also uneconomical lines cannot be discontinued because of local political pressures. The opposition parties and groups take advantage of discontent among railway workers by helping them organize rallies and strikes. On May 8, 1974, railwaymen went on strike, disrupting railway service and passenger traffic. The Government of India urged the workers to come back to work but the labour leaders refused; therefore, the government ordered the military to run the trains and terminated the services of those who took part in sabotaging railway property. Finally, the workers came back to work on May 28, 1974, because of financial constraints. The government, however, agreed to increase their pay and bonus according to the inflationary rates. In essence, the unity of the country can be strengthened by the further development and integration of railway lines throughout the country. Some of the unfinished projects have been delayed due to shortage of funds and frequent ministerial changes at the Central level. In spite of these minor delays, the railway sector has performed extremely well in India.

The Indian road network is one of the largest in the world. The total length of the network was over 1.5 million kilometers in 1981 including unsurfaced roads as against 400,000 kms. in 1951-52. More than ninety percent of the total length of the two-lane national highway has been completed. Since 1955-56, the number of commercial vehicles has increased by 400 percent while the road mileage by 350 percent. During the same period, the number of passengers increased five-fold, and by 1966 roads accounted for nearly as much intercity travel as railways. Road development has to be expanded in rural areas because eighty-one percent of India's population lives in 591,800 rural villages. Up to 1970, only one out of every three of these villages was a distance of more than eight kilometers from an improved road, while only one out of nine villages was served by an all-weather road. However, the objective of the Sixth Five Year Plan was to link all villages in the country with a population of 1500 and above with all-weather roads. By March 22, 1982, 43.6 percent (258,000) of villages, small or large, were connected with roads.

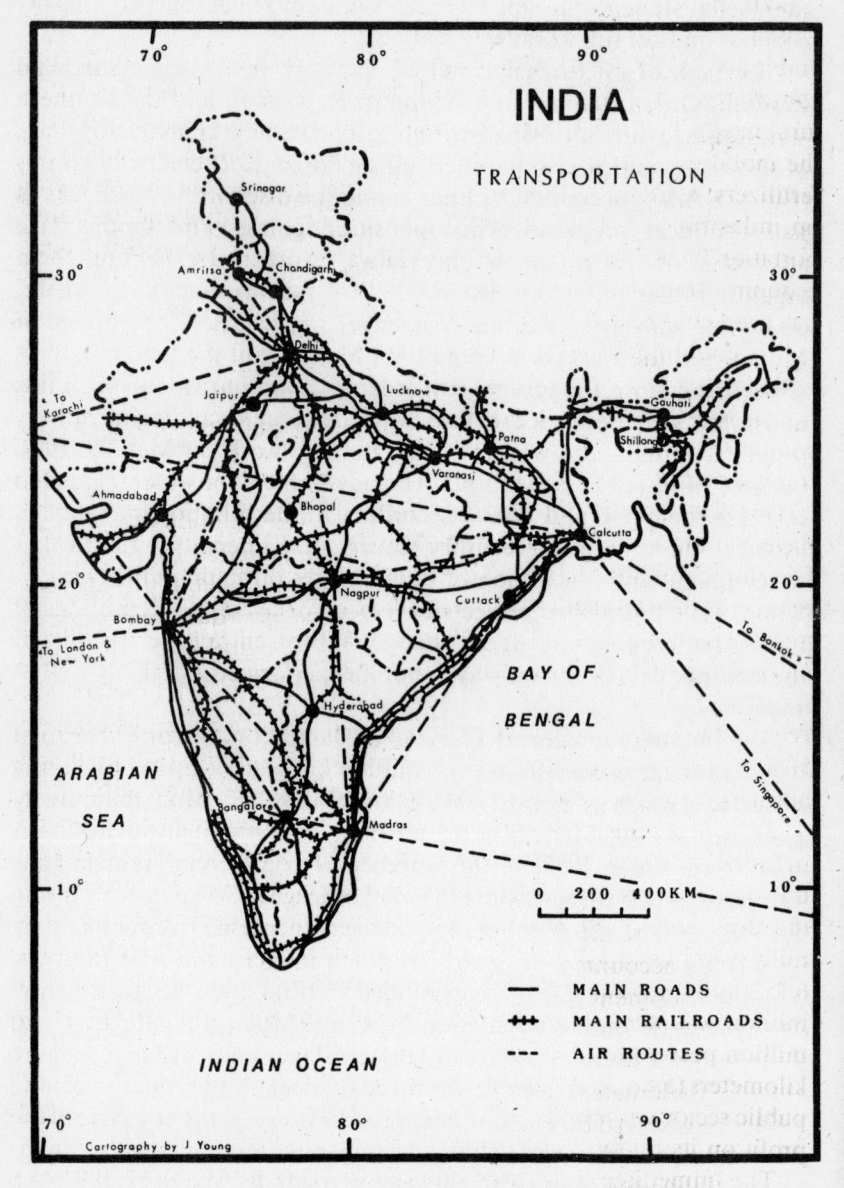

Fig. 12

Transport, Communication and Trade

The government also plans to connect all villages with a smaller population. Haryana became the first state to connect all villages with all-weather roads at the end of 1976.

The inadequacy of road connections in Uttar Pradesh, Assam, Orissa, Northeastern states, Western Rajasthan, Jammu and Kashmir, and parts of some of the southern states is an important factor contributing to the shortage of pump sets, fertilizers and other agricultural needs. This inadequacy in roadways also has a direct bearing on the mobility of people, agricultural and rural development, supply of fertilizers, seeds and foodgrains, exploitation of mineral resources, and on industrial deliveries and retail trade. The lack of adequate transportation facilities leads to cultural stagnation and social, political, and economic fragmentation in the country. The road transportation system has been coordinated with the railways, and zones have been designated to coordinate the national system of roads. Several states have nationalized bus transportation, and others are following suit. A mass transit system with coordinated schedules and fares is necessary for a country like India where a large number of people depend upon mass transportation.

On the northern borders of the country, political and strategic factors have prompted speedy construction of roads. The Border Road Development Board (BRDB) was set up in 1960 to accelerate the economic development of the north and northeastern border areas by making them accessible through road construction. The BRDB aimed at constructing 7,500 kms. of new roads, improving 6,250 kms. of existing roads, and surfacing 11,330 kms. of roads with a width of 6.1 meters. The Board has constructed the world's highest road from Manali in Himachal Pradesh to Leh in Kashmir. Road building activity in the border areas was given an impetus by the 1962 war with China.

Besides rail and road travel, air travel is an increasing phenomenon in India. Air travel, however, is not a major feature of the internal Indian transportation system nor is it likely to become a regular feature even in the next generation, because it is eight times more expensive than railway or bus travel. In 1982, Indian Airlines (domestic travel) carried 6.152 million passengers, 67.5 million tons of freight, and flew 44.9 million kilometers. On international routes, Air India carried 2.140 million passengers, 364.9 million tons of freight, and flew 48.2 million kilometers (*Statistical Outline of India*, 1984, p. 93). Both these airlines are public sector undertakings. Air India was the only airline which made a profit on its international routes for the last several years.

The immediate concern of all political parties and the public is the development of aircraft for the defence of the country. There is popular demand for India to build its own fighter planes in order to defend its borders from hostile neighbours. Transportation is considered a key to political stability and national security. After the 1962 war with China and the 1965 and 1971 conflicts with Pakistan, India built airports with defence capabilities near the border states in the north and the west. The problem is that incidents of piracy and hijacking by criminals wanting political refuge or asylum are happening too often. Political blackmail has recently gained notoriety. When an Air India plane was hijacked, the Government of Pakistan cooperated with the Indian authorities in handing over the plane and helped in freeing the passengers. However on one occasion when the hijackers were freed by Pakistan, friction was created between the two governments. Illegal air piracy should be condemned, and a united effort by the international community should be launched to dismember such groups.

Rail and road transportation handle most of the passenger travel; however, for heavy goods, the cheapest means of transportation is by ships or water traffic. India has a vast coastline of about 6,000 kms., dotted with various types of ports and natural harbours. In all, there are over two hundred ports, a large number of them minor or intermediate ones. There are ten major operational ports in the country, which include Bombay, Calcutta, Haldia, Cochin, Madras, Mormugao, New Mangalore, Paradip, Tuticorin, and Visakhapatnam; an eleventh one at Nhava Sheva (across Bombay harbour) is under construction. The planners envisage the extension and improvement of major existing ports to make them more efficient. Since Independence, few sectors of the Indian economy have registered as spectacular a growth as shipping. India possesses as many as 340 vessels, the number having increased twenty-fold since Independence. Next to Japan, India has the biggest maritime fleet in Asia, ranking fifteenth in the world. The expansion not only is quantitative in nature, but is characterized by diversification and sophistication. Indian ships now carry nearly forty percent of the country's maritime tonnage. The traffic at the major ports has increased from sixteen million tons in 1947-48 to over 96.11 million tons in 1982-83, a six-fold increase. The shipping industry, which is in the public sector, is a highly capital intensive one, requiring heavy investment of capital. The Shipping Corporation of India, the largest shipping company in the world, carries goods all over the world. India also has 14,150 kms. of navigable waterways, but only one-fifth is used by oceangoing steamers. Water transport, the cheapest means of transportation, may prove to be the most efficient for India if progress in this direction is maintained.

Telecommunications network plays an equally important part in the political geography of the country. Post offices, the telegraph and telephone systems, and radio and television stations are the media through which political propaganda is spread and the government tries to wield influence over its citizens. Opposition parties also register their disapproval of government policies through these mass media networks. The post and telegraph service is the second largest state undertaking in India, besides being the largest public utility service in the world. The number of post offices increased from 76,800 in 1960-61 to over 150,000 in 1983-84. In fact, it is hoped that all the census villages in the country (575,936) will have letter boxes by the end of the Sixth Five Year Plan. By March 31, 1979, mail delivery had been provided in 99.79 percent of the census villages. The remaining villages are expected to be covered during the Seventh Five Year Plan. The telecommunication equipment industry formerly reserved for state enterprises has been opened to the private sector, but its share has been restricted to forty-nine percent. The private sector has been permitted to manufacture switching and transmission equipment, which may remove obstacles in the rapid development of modern communications in the country by eliminating equipment shortages and eventually reducing the reliance on imports. In the process, it may also bring efficiency to this sector of the economy. Instead of relying on imports, the industry can enter into private collaborations with foreign multinational corporations, and thereby encourage indigenous production of telecommunication equipment. The private sector has been allowed to manufacture telecommunication equipment, computer-to-computer equipment, teleprinters, telex, machines, telephones, entire micro-wave network systems, transmission and switching systems, and fiber optics communication systems. This is a step in the right direction towards eliminating shortages in the telecommunication industry. The ultimate objective is to provide a daily delivery service to all villages. All first class mail is transported by air in the country. To handle the growing volume of mail, the Postal Index Number (PIN) code was introduced in 1972 with six digits to identify departmental delivery offices. The post offices handle nearly seven billion letters a year. There are two unique services provided by the post offices in India that cater to the needs of the rural people. First, they provide saving bank accounts to the people, the total deposits being larger than in any bank in India. Second, it delivers money orders to individuals at their residences.

The telephone department is the weakest link in the postal and telegraph systems in India. There is a direct dialing system from India to Great Britain, while this system was extended to other countries also by the end of 1980. Telex lines and teleprinters have been introduced to speed up the delivery of telegrams; telegrams are also delivered on phones. The number of telephone exchanges increased from 540 in 1951 to over 31,000 in 1984 and number of telephones from 680,000, to over three million over the same period. Plans are under way to eliminate the waiting lines for telephone connections and progressively reduce manual exchanges and eliminate them completely by 1986. However, efficiency has to be improved in the department. An investment of over Rs. 130 billion for expansion of telecommunications has been proposed during the Seventh Five Year Plan, and a target of over 760,000 telephone lines to be installed by 1990 has been fixed. The entire demand for telex connections of 90,000 lines is also to be met during the Seventh Plan. Under the plan, rural areas will also be linked by telephone, with one phone available within at least every five kilometers throughout the country.

The radio is probably the principal medium through which Indian political leaders communicate with the public. India's radio stations cover about ninety-three percent of the population by medium wave alone. The ultimate objective was to reach out to the entire population by 1984. Radio programmes have been used regularly to educate the public in national and international issues. Since radio stations are run by the government, the Opposition doesn't really have a forum.

India also introduced television broadcasting and programming in 1959 at Delhi. Television coverage has increased through the implementation of the ATS-6 Satellite Instructional Television Experiment (SITE) project. In its initial stage, 24,000 villages in the six states of Bihar, Orissa, Madhya Pradesh, Rajasthan, Andhra Pradesh, and Karnataka were covered. Several sub-stations, each with a 80 km. service radius, were installed. Up to 1983-84, 30,000 villages received television coverage. There were 1,672,600 television sets in India, and the number is rising rapidly. The number of coloured television sets, video recorders, and accessories increased at a fast rate, being manufactured indigenously, as well as being imported from Japan. Television has an audience of thirty to forty million, which was expected to increase to seventy percent of the population by the end of 1984 if the planned targets were met. However, television tends to be a publicly subsidized source of entertainment for the urban rich. In urban areas, imported programmes are relayed, which brings advertisement money. The Government of India and state governments plan to use television for village development and improvement in education, as well as for family planning education.

Solid state television sets, both coloured and black and white, are manufactured in India. Provision of television facilities to India's total population in the next ten years or so would be of great significance for national integration and would go a long way in promoting social and economic schemes and family welfare units. In the initial stages, total coverage of India's population by television could be through community sets rather than by individual television sets.

To achieve the goals of telecommunications, India has launched an ambitious space programme whose main objective is to achieve self-reliance in spacecraft manufacture and launch vehicles, complete interlinkage between the launch vehicles, increase satellite applications, and expand development and utilization programmes. The major missions proposed for 1985-90 include: the launching of the Augmented Satellite Launch Vehicle (ASLV)—330 pound class satellite—and Stretched Rohini Series Satellite (SROSS) from Sriharikota Range in Southern India (SHAR) during 1985; the launching of the Indian Remote Sensing (RS) satellite from the Soviet Union in 1986; and the development of a new state rocket, the Polar Satellite Launch Vehicle (PSLV), designed and built by Indian scientists, to put a 2,200-pound multipurpose satellite into an orbit above the earth in 1987-88, from SHAR.

India has built facilities at Hassan in Karnataka to guide and control its own satellites orbiting the earth. The space programme has made use of both U.S. and Soviet technology and equipment. India has three multipurpose INSAT satellites (Indian National Satellite System) from the Ford Aerospace and Communication Corporation, Palo Alto, California, in the United States; specifications were set by India's Department of Space. The INSAT-IA was launched on April 10, 1982, but abandoned on September 6, 1982, owing to its failure resulting from fuel loss caused by a jammed valve in the oxide line and a malfunction of the craft's solar sail, which was to provide it with power. The INSAT-IB, which was launched on August 30, 1983, faced minor problems initially, but these were overcome; and the satellite is now working satisfactorily. The INSAT-IC is being procured and is expected to be launched in 1986. The cost of procurement and launching is $103 million. All these satellites were built by the Ford Aerospace Communication Corporation and launched by NASA. The INSAT system will bring phenomenal services and will serve as data gathering device for weather forecasting. Each INSAT satellite is fitted with 8,000 two-way telephone links which would revolutionize the telecommunication services and promote economic development. The satellite's meteorological data, relayed by thirty earth stations, could help farmers and oil drilling ships plan their work schedules. These satellites can provide round-the-clock, half-hourly observations of weather systems, including cyclones, sea surfaces, and cloud temperatures over the entire country and adjoining land and seas areas. It could lead to rapid strides in adult education, family planning, shipping, ocean fishing, irrigation, industry, planning, power generation, and agricultural feedback in rural areas through the expansion of television coverage. There will be at least two additional television channels, which will cover the whole of India. At present, there are small individual stations but with these two channels, the whole subcontinent will be covered.

The Soviet Union assisted India in its space programme, under which regular weekly meteorological soundings were conducted from the Thumba launching site since 1970 using Soviet M-100 rockets. An ambitious space programme is aimed at helping India to improve telecommunication as well as weather forecasting facilities, and to take television to millions of homes across the country. India launched its first satellite (Aryabhata) on April 19, 1976, with Soviet assistance. Immediately after the successful Aryabhata mission, the Indian Space Research Organization (ISRO) was able to design, fabricate, and launch, with Soviet assistance, the two experimental earth resource satellites, Bhaskara I and II, on June 7, 1979, and November 20, 1980, respectively. India has already successfully launched six experimental satellites. The exploitation of space offers India exciting possibilities which would eventually raise the standard of living of the people. The Indian space programme is expected to spend $1.551 billion during the Seventh Five Year Plan. However, some politicians belonging to the Opposition have criticized the expenditure, arguing that the money would be better spent in fighting poverty. Undoubtedly, in the long run, exploration and utilization of space is an economical proposition which would bring prosperity to the masses.

The Soviet Union helped in launching three Indian experimental satellites between 1979 and 1981, and India proposes to launch its first Remote Sensing Satellite (RSS) on a Soviet vehicle in 1986. It would be as advanced as the latest U.S. Landsat-class satellites and would photograph India's land mass and crops. On April 3, 1984, an Indian Cosmonaut, Rakesh Sharma, went into space in the Soviet Soyuz T-11 spacecraft. Thus, India became the thirteenth country to join the exclusive group of those world's nations which have sent their people into space. The United States has requested India to send a scientist into space along with American scientists on a future flight. The remote sensing experiment "Terra", conducted by Sharma in the fields of forestry, land use mapping, cartography, oceanography, geology and mineral resources, and coastal zone monitoring will be useful for future economic planning. Detailed photographs have been taken of over forty percent of the country including the coastal areas adjoining the country (First Indian Launched Into Space: News Report, 1984, p. 10). This information will be useful as a resource inventory and will assist in the exploration of land and sea resources.

Communication and transportation facilities have helped to improve the internal cohesion of the country and have also helped to broaden knowledge of and interest in international relations with the outside world. Modern communications can play an important role in educating farmers, improving farm techniques, lowering the rural and urban birth rate, bringing cultural diffusion among various cultures, and uniting the nation into one cohesive nation state. Major changes in the attitude of the people can be brought about by the use of the communication network, changes which will improve the general standard of living and create a better image of the country among the various nations of the world.

During March 1976 and February 1980, a conference of the press agencies of non-aligned countries was held in New Delhi with the idea of forming a non-aligned news agency. Such an agency was expected to encourage a free exchange of news and ideas among non-aligned nations. The formation of the news agency received a favourable response from various national newspapers which hoped that the agency would eliminate bias and distorted coverage by foreign correspondents as well as domination by the western commercial news agencies.

The success of the tourist industry in a country is directly dependent upon the progress made in the transportation and communication field. Tourism is the world's largest and most rapidly expanding industry with three-directional importance for the developing nations. First, it is a foreign exchange earner; second, it acts as a catalyst to internal development; and finally, it is the most important means of social and cultural diffusion among the nations of the world. Jawaharlal Nehru once said, "We must welcome the friendly visitor from abroad not only for economic reasons, for tourism brings foreign exchange, but even more so because this leads to greater understanding and mutual appreciation." The tourist traffic rose from 139,800 in 1960 to 1,288,200 in 1982, nearly a nine-fold increase, and this figure was expected to reach 1,500,000 by 1985. Indian tourism is oriented towards its cultural, spiritual, aesthetic, and holiday aspects to attract western tourists. A number of five-star hotels have been set up, some with international tie-ups to provide comforts and services to tourists. Tourism is one of the top ten foreign exchange earners of the country bringing in $7.5 billion in 1982.

Foreign trade

The nature and extent of foreign trade of a country depends directly on the general economic conditions of the country, its internal and external political problems, and even governmental stability. A booming foreign trade can be a source of power for a nation state. British power during the late nineteenth and early twentieth century was built on foreign trade. Today, the oil rich Middle Eastern countries are building their nations on the foreign wealth acquired through oil sales. Similarly, Japan's prosperity owes much to the development of foreign trade. India could also follow the same pattern; with thirty-nine years of independence, India must however seek affiliations and trade relations with ideologically similar partners to survive as a democratic nation. Besides, she must build her trade alliances in such a way as to create a diversified export market for her growing industrial goods while following the policy of non-alignment. India became a signatory to a general agreement on tariff and trade which was ratified by seventy-seven nations in 1970. These nations account for more than eight percent of the world's trade tonnage.

India's major trade partners have been the United Kingdom, the United States, and Japan. New trade partners are emerging in areas such as the Middle East, Africa, the European Common Market, Eastern Europe, and the Soviet Union. Up to 1973-74, wheat and fertilizers were the two main items of import from the United States. However, there was strong political opposition from the leftists and other Opposition parties to Mrs Gandhi's government importing such large amounts of wheat from the United States. The leftists maintained that India's planning process had not been based on sound economic principles. The virtual dependence on the United States for wheat, they alleged, had lowered the nation's prestige by portraying India as a hungry nation. This dependence could not have been more obvious than when the United States threatened to cut off wheat shipments to India during the Indo-Pakistani war in 1965. The direct reaction was that Prime Minister Lal Bahadur Shastri requested the people of the nation to go on fast and even grow foodgrains in the backyard or in clay pots if need be rather than face humiliation. Threats of this type and uncertainties in the food supply could prove to be dangerous at a time of national crisis. Ever since 1975, there has been a sharp decline in food and fertilizer imports which has helped the nation to build its foreign exchange reserves.

The United Nations identified India as the country hardest hit by the oil crisis. Even though oil and petroleum product imports declined in quantity since the 1973 oil embargo and subsequent price hike by the OPEC countries, the total amount paid for petroleum imports increased sharply. The import of petroleum, fertilizers, and foodgrains accounted for fifty-six percent of the total value of imports in 1974-75. Other major items of import were chemicals, electric machines, cotton, iron and steel, and newsprint. The total imports have increased from Rs. 11.22 billion in 1961-62 to Rs. 150 billion in 1983-84, an increase of over 1300 percent.

The value of exports, on the other hand, increased from Rs. 6.42 billion to Rs. 100 billion, a 1500 percent increase during the same period. A negative balance of trade has increased from Rs. 4.79 billion in 1960-61 to Rs. 50 billion in 1983-84, more than a twelve-fold increase (Fig. 13). Items exported are engineering goods, handicrafts, leather and rubber, hides and skins, jute manufactures, iron ore, tobacco, oil cakes, cashew kernels, rice bran, fruit and vegetables, electronic software, diamonds, jewellery, opium, sugar, coffee, coir, cotton textile, tea, and spices. At the time of Independence, India was exporting agricultural raw materials such as cotton, jute, spices, sugar, tea, mineral ores and leather goods. In the eighties, India's exports have diversified to include engineering goods, railway cars and locomotives, television cables, machine goods, chemicals, crude oil and iron and steel. The comparatively cheap but skilled labour force gives India an edge over other countries. India possesses sufficient raw materials and infrastructure as well as trained manpower to produce industrial goods for export. An encouraging development in recent years has been the government's concerted effort to export consultancy services. The foreign exchange earned through these services was Rs. 180 million in 1980-81. A study conducted by the government showed that India is capable of earning one billion rupees by 1984-85 and two billion rupees by 1989-90. At present India is exporting sophisticated industrial goods and services instead of agricultural raw materials as she did under the British rule or during the earlier years of Independence. India must curtail her imports to achieve a favourable balance of trade. It is heartening to note that in recent years India's balance of trade is improving. The only short-term and perhaps even long-term method of reducing the trade gap is by increasing the remittances from overseas Indians. An increase in manpower exports, coupled with the introduction of measures to attract capital investment by Indians living abroad, could help boost the Indian economy and improve the balance of payment position.

A major feature of the export policy has been the creation of export surpluses in the economy. Apart from making the country's external payments position more viable, reserve growth has become an important policy instrument for accelerating investment without running the risk of serious inflation and eventual depression. The policy objective since 1974-75 was to increase the foreign exchange reserves to a comfortable level. The foreign exchange reserves increased from Rs. 7.93

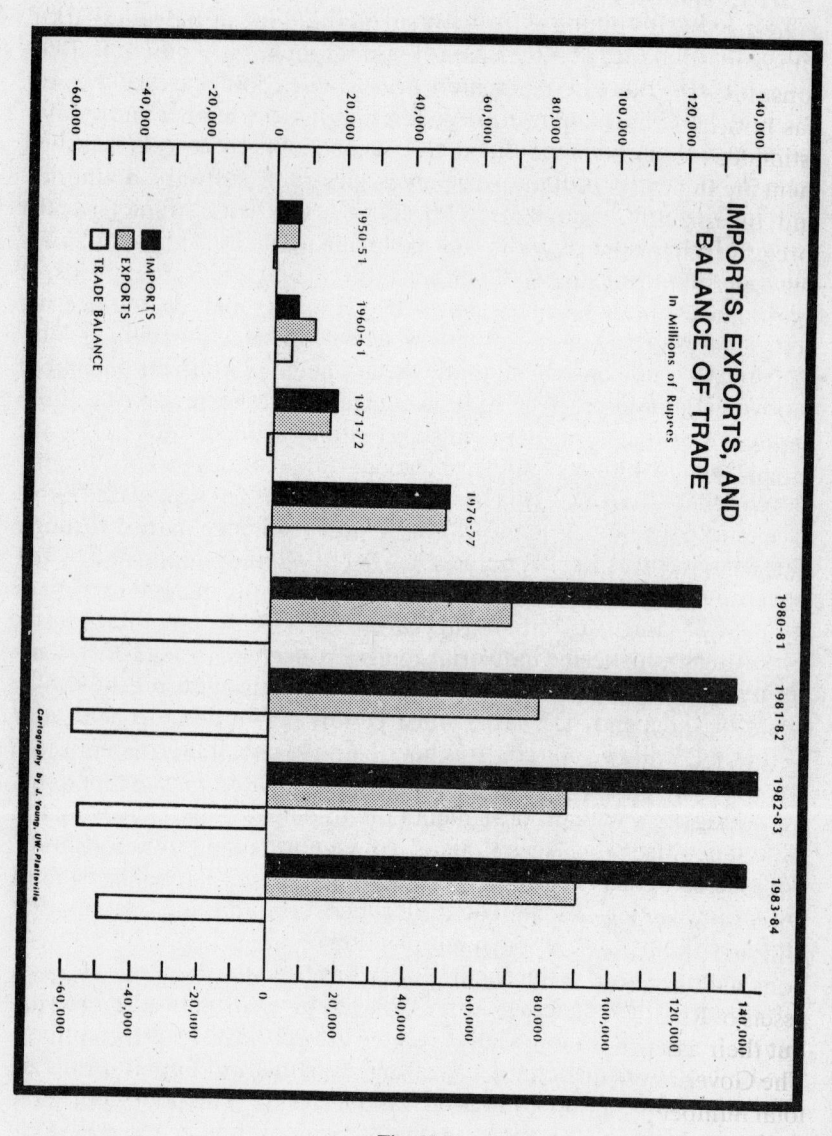

150   *India: Economic Base And Political Patterns*

Fig. 13

billion in 1974-75 to over Rs. 50 billion including gold deposits in the early eighties. Much of this increase was on account of the accumulation of reserves either in bank deposits or in investments in various sectors of the economy by overseas Indians.

A partial remittance by the Indians working overseas increased from a meagre $132 million in 1970-71 to over $5.5 billion in 1982-83 and Rs. 8 billion in the first nine months of 1983-84. This amount, which in effect constitutes the foreign exchange earned by the export of skilled labour, has now outstripped the earnings from the export of other items. An estimated eleven million Indians live abroad in 136 countries. Most of them are highly skilled professionals and their remittances to families and investments in various industrial ventures have added to the foreign exchange reserves. Their assets have been estimated to be between $60 billion and $90 billion. If the current trend continues, the remittances and capital investment by Indians living abroad can be multiplied from the present $5 billion to $15 billion before the end of this decade. As a result of this trend, India's prestige in the world market will improve. Besides, India has never defaulted in the repayment of her loan and interest to any country which is definitely a plus point in India's favour.

The improved relations with Pakistan and the creation of Bangladesh in 1971 has eased the strain of importing cotton and jute from these countries. India should constantly strive to develop good relations with these neighbours who can supply raw jute and long staple cotton at cheaper prices than any other country in the world. For economic and political stability in the area, it is essential that South Asian nations develop good trade and economic ties among themselves and avoid unnecessary differences.

If India wants to be self-reliant and remain non-aligned in her trade relations, she must screen thoroughly foreign investments made in the country and place controls over the activities of multinational corporations. National interests should supercede individual and corporate interests. In 1973-74, there were 540 branches of multinational corporations in India and 188 Indian subsidiaries with total assets of Rs. 30 billion. However, in 1980-81, there were only 311 multinational corporations with assets of Rs. 26.91 billion and 101 Indian subsidiaries with assets of Rs. 24.77 billion. Thus foreign companies declined in number, but their assets have increased from Rs. 30 billion to Rs. 51.68 billion. The Government of India clears foreign collaborations every year. The total number of collaborations during the period 1957 to 1983 was 7,884, the largest number of collaborations occurring in 1983-84, totalling 673; this was due to relaxation on the restrictions on foreign investment initiated by the government. During the Janata government regime from 1977 to 1980, foreign collaboration remained stagnant or declined because of the opposition to multinationals by the Industry Minister George Fernandes. The Coca Cola Company was ordered to stop its operation in India. It is surprising that considering the Soviet Union and India are friends only four collaborations exist between them. The largest number of collaborations in 1983 were with the United States (139), West Germany (129), Great Britain (119), Japan (58), Switzerland (47), France (40), and Italy (30)—all of them democratic nations. Thus, India's alignment in terms of foreign investment and collaborations is in line with the philosophical alignment of her democratic norms.

The larger multinationals have entered into the market with higher investment potential. According to David Rockefeller, an eminent American banker, "India has handled its economy well and India's attitude has become more favourable towards foreign investment. India is a place which is more hospitable for doing business." The remaining corporations belong to various other nations, mostly democratic in nature. The Socialist bloc countries deal directly with the government for trade agreements. Therefore, India has to allow foreign companies to invest, but in accordance with a strong national commitment to improve the economic conditions of the masses, rather than keeping the foreign companies satisfied. After the assassination of Mrs Gandhi on October 31, 1984, by two of her Sikh body guards, her elder son, Rajiv Gandhi, was sworn in as the seventh Prime Minister of India. He won an impressive victory in the Eighth General Elections held in December 1984 with more than three-fourths of the seats in the Parliament. In early days of his administration, Rajiv Gandhi liberalized the economic policy and encouraged foreign investment in India. He encouraged foreign and domestic companies to invest in high technology and computer-based industries to make India a technologically advanced country.

Even during the last days of Mrs Gandhi's rule, the Ford Motor Company of the United States opened an auto assembly plant in Madras. Ford supplied engines for trucks and the assembly remains under the management of Indians. India has also collaborated with Suzuki Motor Company of Japan to produce a small car Maruti. Maruti Udyog Limited was first formulated by the late Sanjay Gandhi, the younger son of the late Mrs Indira Gandhi, who died in a plane crash. The company has been taken over by the government. The factory opened on schedule and produced 20,000 cars in 1984-85 and is scheduled to produce 40,000 in 1985-86 and 100,000 in 1988-89. The orders for 135,000 vehicles have already been received for delivery to customers. The total cost of the project is estimated at Rs. 2,269 million. Rajiv Gandhi emphasized to foreign investors that India has a large market, stable political system and highly trained technical manpower which will be an ideal environment for foreign investment.

Developmental efforts of the Third World countries, especially India, rest on the availability of secure low-interest loans or grants for development. During 1974-75, the total loans granted to India by various countries and international agencies reached Rs. 14,484 million, along with grants of Rs. 1,898 million for a total of Rs. 16,712 million. Loans increased to Rs. 25,250 million in 1982-83 while grants reached Rs. 4,233 million, totalling Rs. 29,448 million. The largest loans during 1982-83 were given by the International Bank of Reconstruction and Development (IBRD)—Rs. 108,700 million, the I.D.A.—Rs. 7,621 million, the United Kingdom—Rs. 2,859 million, and the United States—Rs. 674 million. The Soviet Union and the East European countries did not extend any loans or grants to India. Only mutually beneficial trade continued.

The World Bank has approved three loans to India totalling $641.7 million for projects to increase fertilizer production, electrify part of the Indian railway system and to expand the availability of hydroelectric power in the western region of India. The first loan of $203.6 million is expected to finance the construction of a fertilizer plant at Vijaipur in Madhya Pradesh. The total cost of this plant, including a gas-based ammonia unit, two urea units and an integrated power and steam generation unit, will be $638.6 million. The second loan of $280.7 million is to electrify 3,000 kilometers of major railway trunk routes between New Delhi, Bombay, Madras, and Calcutta. The estimated total expenditure on the project is $1.2 billion. The third loan of $157.4 million, along with $143 million credit from the IDA special fund, will finance the Bodhgot hydroelectric project in Madhya Pradesh as well as the western region of India. The total cost of the project is $1,238 million. Even with this amount of aid, India was one of the countries that received the least aid from other countries. India has managed its external debt prudently and has earned a reputation of credit worthiness in the international market. The government has attracted more foreign investment, especially from overseas Indians, to meet its growing demand for foreign currency. The total external assistance, bilateral and multi-lateral, was roughly $3 billion a year.

The United States offered $87 million as development assistance and $105 million under the PL-480 programme in 1984-85. India is, however, cautious enough not to take loans or assistance if it means jeopardizing her independence in foreign affairs. For the sake of national pride, a country must assert its independence in dealing with foreign countries, and not give up its freedom. Japan pledged $200 million as aid to India for the year 1984-85. This borrowing from the international agencies and foreign governments has aroused criticism from the Opposition who maintain that the borrowings have been excessive. They argued that India was being sold to foreign countries and they asserted that future generations would be burdened with heavy debt payments. India's external debt is $19.8 billion, of which $19.6 billion is publicly guaranteed and $0.2 billion private and nonguaranteed. At present, the annual debt servicing is nearly $1 billion, or nine percent of the earnings from exports and is not invisible. India will need net external resources of the order of $15 billion in the next five years or about $3 billion annually to fulfil the projected targets of the Seventh Five Year Plan. This is necessary to stimulate exports and attain self-reliance.

In conclusion, it is vital for the economic progress. stability and viability of India as a democratic nation to evolve a cheap and efficient transportation system and to enlarge communication facilities. These facilities can play an important role in promoting national integration and can help in reducing fissiparous tendencies among various groups and regions. The main thrust in the coming years will have to be on achieving self-sufficiency through import substitution in a number of critical areas. Improved export performance will be necessary to reduce the current account deficit and improve the debt service ratio.

NOTES

A.B.A. Ghani Khan Choudhury, "The Long March of the Indian Railways," *Indian and Foreign Review*; Vol. 21, No. 9 (February 29, 1984), 5. (5-10)

Economic Survey, 1983-84 (New Delhi: The Manager, Government of India Press, 1984).

"First Indian Launched Into Space: News Report." *Indian and Foreign Review*, Vol. 21, No. 12 (April 15, 1984), 10. (8-10)

D.R. Pendse, *Statistical Outline of India, 1984* (Bombay: Tata Services Limited, Department of Economics and Statistics, 1984).

United Nations: Statistical Yearbook, 1981 (New York: United Nations, 1982).

Wilfred Owen, *Distance and Development: Transport and Communication in India* (Washington, D.C.: The Brooking Institute, 1968), p. 1.

CHAPTER 6

Impact of Population Growth on the Economy

THE two most valuable resources of a state are its land and people. The state is, as Frederick Ratzal put it, "ein Stuck Boden, ein Stuck Menschen" (a bit of land and some people) (Norman Pounds, 1972, p. 125). Human resources can hasten the process of modernization because they alone have the capacity to accumulate capital, exploit natural resources, frame policies and execute them, build social and political organizations, besides forming the backbone of national defence. Therefore, the size, quality, and density of population are the basic ingredients for the study of national power potential of a nation state. Population numbers decide the military capability of a country, the extent of labour force available for employment, and the size of the domestic market through their purchasing power. The wealth, vitality, and stability of a state rests on the energy and talent of its people.

Population explosion is a serious problem which India is facing in the second half of the twentieth century. India accounts for about 15.4 percent of the total world population, while it has a little over two percent of the world's land area. With an estimated total population of over 780 million in 1985, India ranks only second to the People's Republic of China. Although India has approximately one-third the area of the United States, it is the home of a little less than three times the population of the United States. In fact, the total population of India accounts for eighty-five percent of the population of the seventy states of Africa and Latin America put together. Such a vast population creates numerous economic and political problems for the country.

India's population is increasing at a very rapid rate of 2.25 percent per annum. During the decade 1951-61, the absolute increase was 87.1 million, while it was 109 million during 1961-71 and 135.86 million during 1971-81. Over one-third of the net increase of 445 million between 1901 and 1981 was during the decade 1971-81 alone, and about two-thirds during the post independence era. The 1961-71 decade recorded the highest rate of population growth in India's demographic history, while the absolute increase was 196.1 million during the two decades 1951-71. The rates of growth were 21.64 percent and 24.80 percent during the decades 1951-61 and 1961-71, respectively, that is, thirteen million persons are added to the population every year which is equivalent to the entire population of Australia. The growth rate, however, declined slightly during the decade 1971-81 although the total population increase was much higher than it was in earlier decades owing to a high percentage of young people entering the reproductive age. Based on the 1981 growth rate, the natural increase is calculated as twenty-eight persons per minute, 1,680 per hour, 40,320 per day, 282,240 per week, 1,128,960 per month, and 13,547,520 per year in India. India's rate of population growth, however, is not exceptional in relation to the rate of growth in Japan or for that matter in such Western European countries as Great Britain, West Germany, the Soviet Union, or the United States; all of them at times have exceeded India's percentage increase (Norton Ginsburg, 1958, p. 465). The present percentage rate of increase is also far lower than that of the Latin American and African nations. The rapid increase in population growth was especially notable during 1951-81 because of a drastic decline in death rates and a slow decrease in the birth rate (Table 10); the net increase was moderate in the earlier periods owing to the higher death rate. Indian officials estimate that the population will stand at 758 million by 1986, and one billion by A.D. 2000. Four important features about India's population are important to take note of: the huge absolute increase, the continuing high level of natural fertility, the rapidly decreasing death rate, and the persistent poverty of the masses.

The effect of this high increase in population in the past two decades is evident in the increased dependency ratio and the high rate of unemployment which have together nullified much of the progress achieved through the planning process. More and more workers are being added to the labour force. According to the 1981 census, 49.4 percent of the total population was in the 0-14 age group, 44.2 percent in the 15-59 age group, and 6.4 percent in the age group 60 and above (Fig. 14). In absolute terms, there are 327.1 million children up to the age of nineteen years and when they enter the reproductive age, the potential rate of growth of population will be much higher even with proper family planning programmes and incentives. The number joining the labour force will also increase at a faster pace than in the previous decades. In 1981, there were 222.5 million employed workers, 177.5 million males and forty-five million females. This constitutes 57.6 percent of the male population and fourteen percent of the female population, an aggregate of 33.4 percent of the total population. There were also 22.1

Impact of Population Growth on the Economy

Table 10

India: population increase, rural urban growth, and birth and death rates, 1901-1981*

Census year	Population (millions)	Population in millions Rural	Population in millions Urban	Percentage of change during the preceding decade	Birth rate per thousand during the preceding decade	Death rate per thousand during the preceding decade
1901	238.4	212.7	25.7	—	—	—
1911	252.0	226.1	25.9	5.73	49	43
1921	251.3	223.2	28.1	0.30	49	47
1931	278.9	245.5	33.4	11.00	46	36
1941	318.6	275.6	43.0	14.23	45	31
1951	361.0	297.6	62.4	13.31	40	27
1961	439.2	360.3	78.9	21.64	42	23
1971	547.9	438.9	109.0	24.80	40	18
1981	683.8	525.5	159.78	24.78	37.2	15

*Data collected from various census tables and Dr. S. Chandrasekhar, *Infant Mortality, Population Growth, and Family Planning in India* (London: George Allen and Unwin, Ltd., 1971) and D.R. Pandse, *Statistical Outline of India* (New Delhi: Tata Services Limited, Department of Economics and Statistics, 1984).

million marginal workers, 3.5 million males and 18.6 million females. In 1982 employment increased to 23.393 million in the organized sector, that is, excluding self-employed people. It is estimated that 1,000,000 Indians enter the job market every year, and this figure is increasing every year. There were 21,953,000 registered unemployed people in 1983, besides unregistered unemployed people in various age groups. Every worker has to support at least two non-working members (66.6 percent of the total population is non-working); as a result, the per capita income gets reduced. Any gradual increase in per capita income gets neutralized by the growth of population. Owing to a higher dependency ratio, nearly eighty percent of the people who live below the poverty line do not get enough calorific intake for healthy living. The increased dependency ratio lowers the per capita income and places a great strain on the working population. The tragedy is that the strenuous efforts made by the Government of India in the field of irrigation, land reclamation, and food output have been largely cancelled out by the growth of population. A better standard of living and even two square meals for everyone depend upon limiting the numbers. For the twelve

INDIA
AGE DISTRIBUTION OF POPULATION, 1981'

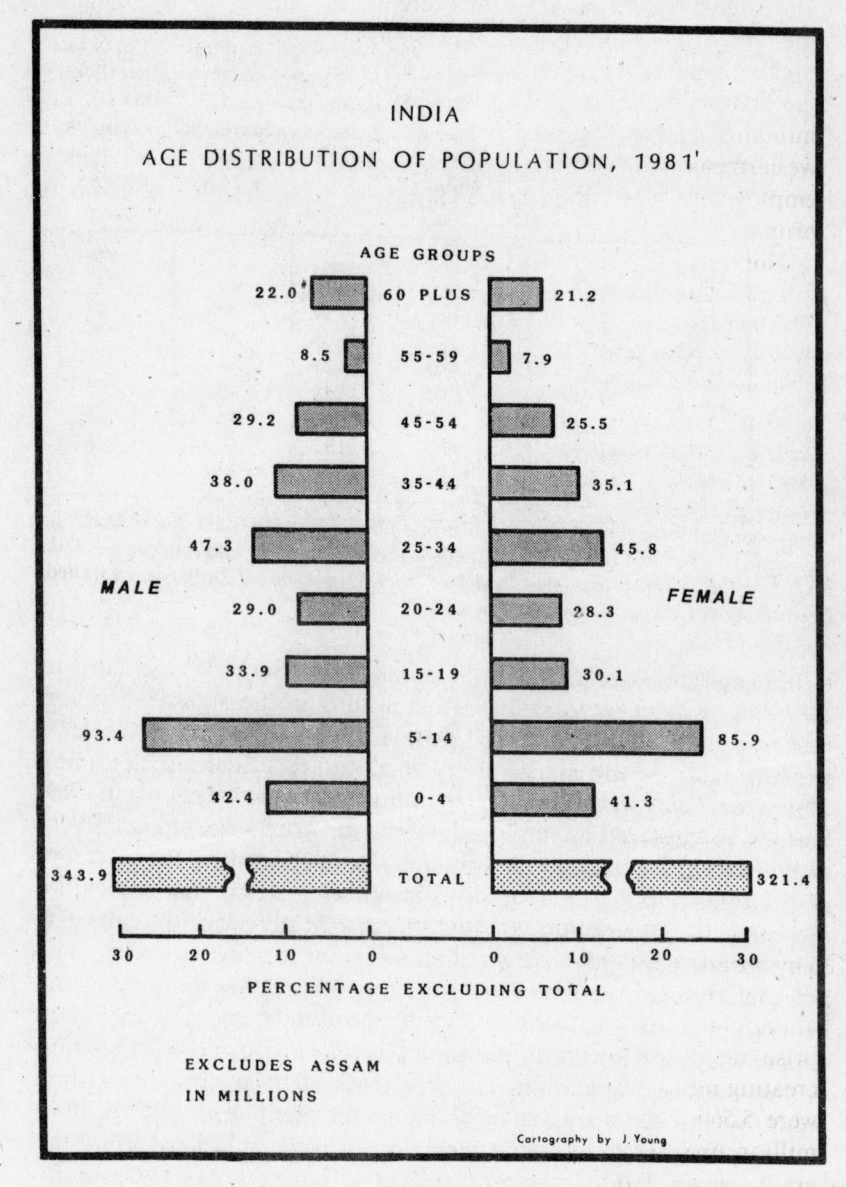

MALE	AGE GROUPS	FEMALE
22.0[#]	60 PLUS	21.2
8.5	55-59	7.9
29.2	45-54	25.5
38.0	35-44	35.1
47.3	25-34	45.8
29.0	20-24	28.3
33.9	15-19	30.1
93.4	5-14	85.9
42.4	0-4	41.3
343.9	TOTAL	321.4

30 20 10 0   0 10 20 30
PERCENTAGE EXCLUDING TOTAL

EXCLUDES ASSAM
IN MILLIONS

Cartography by J. Young

Fig. 14

million persons added to the population every year, the additional resources which are needed are 116,000 schools, 343,000 teachers, 2,315,000 houses, 174,238,000 meters of cloth, 11,579,000 quintals of food, and 3,700,000 jobs (Sukhwal, 1984). In the western industrialized nations, the ratio of working population to the non-working population is much higher than it is in the case of India; therefore, fifty to seventy percent of the economic growth in the western nations is contributed by their human resources. Besides, production per worker is much higher in western countries than it is in India because the majority of workers are employed in the secondary and tertiary sectors rather than in the primary sector.

Not only the size of the labour market but the quality of the labour force is also an important criterion in evaluating the power of a state. The level of health and nutrition, age structure and sex ratio, literacy rates and education, and skill and ability are basic ingredients for a productive labour force. Sixty-one-and-a-half percent (161 million) workers were self-employed, out of which 128.1 million or 49.1 percent were cultivators and 12.4 percent (32.3 million) were non-cultivators in 1980. A higher percentage of cultivators, fifty-nine million, owned up to only two percent of the land in 1976-77 and thus were not surplus producers. The number of matriculate job seekers (unemployed) between 1971-81 increased from 1,297 million to 5,008 million, undergraduates (B.A., B.Sc. degree and diploma holders) from 605,000 to 2,325 million, graduates and post-graduates (M.A., M.Sc., and Ph.Ds) from 394,000 to 1.685 million, at an average increase of over 400 percent in each category. The number of students graduating at different levels in 1981 were: 37.8 million matriculates and higher secondary diploma holders, 220,000 non-technical diploma holders, 1.14 million technical diploma holders, and 9.5 million college and university degree holders at graduate and post-graduate levels. The increase in educational level could not produce a productive labour force; rather, the growth of educational personnel created huge white-collar unemployment because education and employment were not fully coordinated through the planning process. The social traditions of India have looked down upon manual labour and thus developed a craze for white-collar jobs among the educated Indians. Besides, government and private enterprise neglected the less developed areas of employment, thereby creating more imbalance in the employment of lower level jobs. There were 5.560 million unemployed high school diploma holders, 2.439 million undergraduates (Bachelor degree holders), and 1.769 million graduates and post-graduates in 1978, that is, 49.5 percent of educated persons were unemployed. There are large numbers of unskilled workers and landless labourers who usually do not register in unemployment agencies, thus the number of unemployed workers is actually much higher. Besides, the educated unemployed are discouraged after a long search for employment and withdraw from the job market. Such a large number of unemployed workers creates unrest in the streets, youths become disenchanted with the government, idleness takes hold among productive citizens who become a burden on the national economy and the society. Nearly one million trained engineers are unemployed now. A large number of technical personnel are working in the Middle Eastern countries; as a result, they brought in $180 million 1980-81 through consultancy services; this amount may increase to Rs. 2000 million by 1989-90. The engineering graduates are theoretically well trained through old textbooks, but they lack practical training. A large number of unemployed doctors open private clinics in urban areas where health facilities are already available, instead of practicing in villages; most of them are used to city life and find it hard to adjust to the hard life in the villages. Moreover, the medical education is old-fashioned and is unrelated to the basic health needs of the country. India produces 32,000 technical personnel, 14,000 engineers, 10,000 doctors, and 7,000 scientists annually. This number is increasing steadily because the lack of employment opportunities drives high school graduates to colleges. Unfortunately, high school, college, and post-graduate curriculum has no coordination with the manpower needs of the country. Unemployment is the highest among graduates in humanities and science. There were nearly seventeen million unemployed people in 1981, despite the fact that the Government of India created twenty-five million additional jobs between 1971 and 1981. The unemployment problems will be further aggravated if all females belonging to the working age group were to enter the job market; at present, most women are housewives. A high rate of unemployment can pose a threat to social stability. Very often political, economic, and social groups instigate unemployed workers and students to stage riots, demonstrations, and strikes, and even to destroy public utilities in order to turn the tide of public opinion in their favour.

The uneven distribution of population has an important bearing on the economic and political differences in the country. Density merely represents an arithmetical ratio. The capacity of land to support people varies according to the resources of the land and depends on the technical capacity of people to develop and use those resources. Overpopulation can adversely affect national power by restricting the availability of capital for investment. Half of the population of India lives on less than one-quarter of the available land, and one-third is concentrated on less than six percent of the land. The average density according to the 1981 census was 216 per square kilometer. This represents a density approximately eighteen times greater than that of Africa, Latin America, North America, and the Soviet Union. Densities are greatest in areas with abundant water, such as the alluvial plains of the Ganges and the coastal lowlands, in particular the rice lands of Kerala and West Bengal. By contrast, parts of the dry interior are relatively sparsely populated. The Ganges Valley, still predominantly agricultural, has a density of population comparable to that of many western industrialized nations. Interestingly enough, governments of all of the densely settled states of north India have changed more frequently than they have in other regions. These changes are owing to dense population and problems associated with it, for instance, economic backwardness.

The rather marked urban growth rate and the village to city migration pattern of the Indian population have a variety of political effects. Though India continues to be a predominantly agricultural and rural country with 76.3 percent of the population living in 575,936 villages (census villages), the proportion of urban population has been increasing faster than the rural population from 11.2 percent (25.8 million) in 1901 to 23.7 percent (159.7 million) in 1971. Moreover, during 1971-81, the rate of urban growth at 46.4 percent was much higher than that of the rural growth rate (11.97 percent). While the rural population increased by 240 percent from 1901 to 1981, the urban population increased by 600 percent during the same period. Tamil Nadu, Maharashtra, West Bengal, and Gujarat are the most urbanized states in the country. These states draw more than their share of industries and attract greater investment of private capital, thereby achieving a notable improvement in their standard of living. In the elections in Tamil Nadu, it is the urban, industrial, and commercial entrepreneurs who are successful rather than the more numerous rural agriculturists. However, the Janata Party's electoral triumph in north India during the 1977 parliamentary elections was based on rural votes; the rural voters suffered more harassment by family planning officials than the urban sophisticated masses, particularly in the northern states. Similarly, Congress (I) victory in 1980 general elections was the result of the support of the rural and weaker section of the society.

Internal migration is not of great importance in India. The comparative immobility of the Indian people has long been obvious from the official census reports. In every Indian census, nearly ninety percent of the population have been enumerated in the districts in which they were born (Gunnar Myrdal, 1969, p. 387). Five percent of the people did move to the adjoining districts for better job opportunities in more industrialized areas. With the increase in transportation and communication facilities, availability of job opportunities in distant places, and the decrease in family attachment due to industrialization, this trend is changing and more and more people are migrating to states other than their own. The traditional social restriction to their birthplace has decreased; however, local and regional feelings among the people still exist. Except during times of national emergency, the tendency towards separation is evident in many of the regions and states of India. A greater sense of national unity and integration throughout India is one of the main objectives of any government either at the centre or at the state level. Most of the migration that is taking place is near such large urban areas as Bombay, Delhi, Calcutta, Bangalore, Madras, Hyderabad, and Kanpur. The percentage of urban population according to the 1981 census was 60.4 percent for the category of big cities with a population of 100,000 or more; 11.6 percent for towns between 50,000 to 99,000; 14.4 percent for 20,000 to 49,999; 9.5 percent for 10,000 to 19,999; 3.6 percent for 5,000 to 9,999; and 0.5 percent for all towns below 5,000. The faster growth was registered in the new steel towns, oil towns, port cities, and other industrial-urban complexes mainly through immigration of workers. This resulted in overcrowding of big cities and the rise of new slum areas. The traditional support which the Congress Party enjoyed for the last thirty years from the slum dwellers in large cities was wiped out because Mrs Gandhi's slum clearance programme in New Delhi and other places brought bitterness among the poor people who were living in slums but were near their work place. The creation of new residential quarters for these poor people away from the inner city cost them additional expense in bus travel. This movement from their traditional living places infuriated them, and thus they voted against the Congress Party in 1977 parliamentary and other municipal elections. Within thirty months, they again voted for the Congress (I) Party because the Janata Party did not fulfil the promises made during the election campaign. According to the U.N. Yearbook, most of the big cities of the world have registered a population decline in recent years. Among them are Tokyo, New York, London, Moscow, and Seoul. People moved from the central city to suburban areas, a pattern which is still to be noticed in India. The concentration of population created unrest in large cities and aided the downfall of the Congress Party in the urban areas. The higher percentage of migration to urban areas has also created a severe unemployment problem and increased the incidence of riots and crime in the big cities. Another type of migration is that which takes place when a severe regional drought condition arises; however,

Impact of Population Growth on the Economy

this is only a seasonal migration rather than a permanent one. Such migration results in acute food shortages in the cities to which the hungry migrants turn for emergency relief, and they disrupt the peace and stability of municipal administration. Additional internal migration, especially mobility from one area to another, will tend to unify the nation and strengthen the idea of nationhood. As one means to this end, the Government of India has made it compulsory for all Indian Civil Service personnel (Indian Administrative Service, Indian Police Service, and Indian Administrative and Accounts Service) to be assigned to posts in states other than their home state.

Emigration is becoming more important on the Indian political scene. Large numbers of engineers, doctors, technicians, professional and skilled workers are migrating from India to the United States, Canada, Great Britain, and the West European industrialized nations, thus causing a brain drain in the country. Furthermore, the Middle Eastern countries with their very large revenue from the sale of oil are attracting skilled and semi-skilled workers from India. These workers remit their earnings to India, adding to the foreign exchange reserves of the country. In 1980, there were 10,951,000 Indians living abroad, 871,400 in Africa, 1,503,900 in America, 6,976,600 in Asia, 634,500 in Europe, 615,900 in the Middle East and 349,300 in Oceania and Indonesia. International immigration increased when Bangladesh became an independent nation in 1971. Nearly ten million refugees came to India during the war, and some of them stayed even after the war was over. This put an extra burden on India. The native Assamese in the State of Assam are agitating for the expulsion of these immigrants from Assam, and a large number of people have been killed in numerous demonstrations. Some people migrated from Uganda, Southeast Asian nations, and Sri Lanka—all areas with a concentration of people of Indian origin. The Tamilian problem is an acute one, which is creating a rift between India and Sri Lanka.

Another important demographic factor is the sex and age ratio. According to the 1981 census, for every 1,000 males there are 935 females in India. Females are less educated, and most of them remain housewives; thus their talents are not being utilized properly. The desire to have male children also leads to the formation of large families. The vast population of India is a serious concern not only to the Indian educated elite but also to the government, groups, and individuals in other friendly nations of the world. Indian leaders became alarmed during the early years of Independence about the population explosion in the same manner as the Japanese became conscious of it after the Second World War. India joined Japan as the second sizable nation in the world to inaugurate a series of efforts to control the number of births. The important feature in India's population was a drastic decline in the death rate from forty-four per thousand in 1901 to fifteen per thousand in 1981, whereas the birth rate declined more slowly from 45.8 per thousand in 1901 to 41.2 per thousand in 1971 to 37.2 per thousand in 1981. Thus, a check on the birth rate was imperative. Ever since Independence, the government sponsored family planning programmes to reduce the rate of growth of population. The government offered incentives to people to adopt birth control methods to bring down the birth rate from 37.2 per thousand in 1981 to twenty-five per thousand at the end of the Sixth Five Year Plan (1985). Some of these incentives included (i) raising the marriage age to twenty-one years for males and eighteen years for females. The Parliament passed a law to this effect in the 1977-78 session, but enforcement of this law has always been a problem; (ii) freezing the number of legislative seats of the lower House of Parliament at 543 up to A.D. 2001 and also the size of state Legislatures up to A.D. 2001 on the basis of the 1971 census, so that the regions which follow strict family planning programmes will not be penalized by a lower representation in legislative bodies; (iii) passing laws in some States to restrict the family size to three children as was done during the Emergency. The States which passed such laws were Maharashtra, Haryana, Punjab, and Uttar Pradesh; (iv) offering monetary compensation to people undergoing sterilization; (v) giving those village Panchayats which perform the largest percentage of sterilizations a reward of Rs. 10,000 annually (during the Emergency); and (vi) legalizing abortion. As a result, the number of abortions went up from 44,000 in 1973-74 to 130,000 in 1978-79. However, during the Emergency some harsh measures were used including forced sterilization by some officials as part of the family planning drive, with the result that mass fear developed among the people about sterilization. From January to September, 1976, more than one million sterilization operations were performed, of which seventy-five percent were vasectomies. Public media campaigns and educational programmes on family planning included posters, films, radio talks, television shows, movies, and posters with such messages as "Two children are respectable, three a menace" and "A small family is a happy family."

With help from the United Nations and various international agencies, the United States and a number of other friendly countries, India has begun the largest officially sponsored family planning programme in the world. About twenty percent of the country's anticipated expenditure on family planning for 1976-77 was met by external sources and this is still increasing. Under this programme,

32.73 million sterilizations have been performed in the country between the period 1952 and 1980. This is more than sixty percent of the total world performance of sterilization. The insertion of intro-uterine loops was 8.56 million, and roughly 4.5 million persons used conventional contraceptives. Nearly a billion condoms were used every year as a preventive method (Table 11). The popularity of condoms is increasing throughout India. Between April 1980 and December 1980, 95.7 million condoms (Nirodh) were sold commercially. Furthermore, 99.6 million condoms, 37,147 jelly-cream tubes, and 16,401 foam tablets were distributed during the same period under the free distribution scheme. Birth control pills are being distributed through 4,525 rural and 2,523 urban primary health centres hospitals. After conducting intensive research, medical researchers have developed a vaccine, a male pill, not only cheaper than condoms (for free distribution), but also a safer method of sterilization. A reversal of the sterlization process has also been discovered which could be an incentive for more sterilization in the future. At the end of March 1982, there were 23.7 million couples protected by family planning programmes representing a total of 25.9 percent of the total number of reproductive couples (118.8 million) in the country. Of these, 20.7 million couples were covered by sterilization, 1.1 million by I.U.D., and 2.0 million by conventional contraception. Since 1956, at least 54.73 million births have been averted. Between April 1983 and January 1984, 3.14 million sterilization operations were performed and 1.23 million I.U.D.s inserted. At the end of the first year in office, the Janata Party could not meet the target of thirty births per 1,000. Voluntary sterilization registered a decline of 91.2 percent between April 1977 and January 1978, the number of I.U.D.s fell by 51.2 percent, and the use of conventional contraceptives declined by 22.7 percent. There are more than fifty million couples in the country with three or more children. Ideally these couples should undergo voluntary sterilization or adopt family planning methods to prevent further births. Studies have shown that the majority of Indians do not oppose family planning in principle. There is no religious prejudice against birth control. Today ninety-five percent of the people in urban areas are aware of the possibilities of family planning, eighty percent accept it in theory, and forty percent practice it; whereas in the villages the comparable figures are only seventy-five percent, forty-five percent, and twenty percent, respectively.

It is expected that during the Seventh Five Year Plan, new measures will be adopted to control population growth. Among the various measures, the major one would include the move towards universal literacy. A rapid expansion in family planning services and improve-

Table 11

(Part — A)

Methodwise number of acceptors of family planning in India, 1976

Year	Sterilization	IUD insertions	C.C. users	Total acceptors
1956	7,153	—	—	7,153
1961	104,585	—	—	104,585
1967	1,839,811	668,979	475,236	2,984,026
1971	1,329,914	475,848	1,962,725	3,768,487
1975	1,349,028	428,438	2,494,960	4,272,426
1976 (Targets)	4,300,000	1,140,000	4,690,000	10,130,000
1976 (Performance)	Over 7 million	(Apr. '76 to Dec. '76)	1 billion in '76	
Total sterilizations since 1952	18,902,698	5,600,000		

ment of basic health services would involve the following: support for research on new contraceptive techniques acceptable to all religious groups, reduction of mortality rate, expansion of immunization programmes to all children, better nutrition and nutrition education programmes, health education for parents in the treatment of common childhood diseases, provision of potable water in slums and rural areas, and education on the benefits of breast-feeding. Other measures include creation of employment opportunities in rural areas, expansion of basic social and health amenities in rural areas, and development of appropriate measures to regulate urban growth. Legislation will be initiated at the central level to raise the minimum age of marriage to twenty years. Programmes to reduce social and economic disparities will be strengthened. Finally, plans were made to revitalize the family planning programme and to reduce the level of fertility and mortality. India has set a target of reducing its annual population growth rate to 1.2 percent by the turn of the century. The population growth rate declined to 1.9 percent by 1983. It is anticipated by Indian census officials and demographers that the population will stabilize by A.D. 2005.

The family planning programme has direct political implications for both public and private expenditures. Opposition to the programme has arisen because people still support the old established tradition of having a number of sons for social security reasons and prefer early marriages to late marriages. While most of the young people in the reproductive age groups are not averse to family planning, it is the older generation who tend to discourage the younger generation from using contraceptives.

Impact of Population Growth on the Economy

(Part — B)
Family planning sterilization targets and performance, 1976

State	Targets	September performance	April-Sept. performance	Percentage of acheivements	April-Sept. 1975 performance	Percentage increase + or decrease — during April-Sept. 1976 over corresponding period last year
Andhra Pradesh	400,000	20,000	104,300	26.61	62.531	+ 66.8
Bihar	300,000	81,276	145,242	48.40	13,374	+ 986.0
Gujarat	200,000	75,274	151,512	78.80	49,796	+ 204.3
Kerala	222,500	102,679	102,746	46.20	34,790	+ 195.3
Madhya Pradesh	267,500	218,561	567,000	212.00	32.815	+ 1,627.8
Maharashtra	562,000	107.099	250,000	44.50	95,989	+ 160.4
Punjab	546,500	25,064	42,545	91.40	19.163	+ 121.9
Tamil Nadu	500,000	77,801	203,220	40.60	119,292	+ 70.4
Uttar Pradesh	400,000	176,273	419.920	105.00	23,358	+ 1,697.8
West Bengal	302.500	190.352	600,000	152.90	34,372	+ 1,645.6
Delhi	29,000	19,274	87,000	302.40	5,911	+ 1,383.5
Goa, Daman & Diu	8,000	N.A.	1,426	17.80	936	+ 52.4
All India	4,299,000	1,254,959 (Some reports mentioned 1.8 million)	3,376,082	78.60	698,117	+ 383.9

Although the economic viability of the country can be threatened in the absence of a strong family planning programme, force should not be utilized in implementing such a programme. The excesses of the family planning drive during the Emergency were responsible for the routing of the Congress Party at the polls. The family planning programme is meant to be a weapon against poverty and malnutrition. Per capita income, urbanization, proportion of non-agricultural workers, and proportion of literate females are significant variables for the success of the family planning programme in India (P.P. Karan and

Christopher Boerner, 1972). In essence, there is a clear association between high level of development and higher performance in family planning. The issues of rural poverty and population growth should be addressed with sufficient force and speed; otherwise the largest democracy in the world may face an acute malnutrition problem and unstable government (Paul W. English, 1977, p. 145). In the absence of family planning, population explosion, as well as serious shortages in all sectors of the economy, may arise. The slogan of Mrs Gandhi during the 1971 general elections, "Garibi Hatao," could not succeed, partially because of population pressure and related problems. The Janata Party changed the family planning policy into a family welfare policy to integrate the welfare of the society through education of the masses, equitable distribution of resources, voluntary family planning and creating a norm of small families, and to improve the health facilities for the lower sections of the society. But it did not work in practice. It remained as a slogan. The policy statement of the Janata Government was to have family planning and population control as vigorously as possible on a voluntary basis and not on a coercive basis. The slogan was never put to practice. The Congress (I) Party has again pushed the family planning programme by increasing the budget for the Sixth Five Year Plan to Rs. 1.1 billion from Rs. 1.45 million during the Fifth Five Year Plan and the planned increase during the Seventh Plan will be much higher. In 1980-81, fifty thousand one-day mass-contact camps were established across the country to help solve personal problems faced by villagers, especially concerning family planning. Such camps have been conducted regularly to advise couples on matters of sterilization and other birth control devices.

In spite of the progress made by the planning process since Independence, the standard of living of the rural masses has risen very slowly. There are several reasons for this slow change. First, population increased at a faster rate than economic progress, especially in rural areas. India was unable to enact and execute strict laws to control population as did Japan in 1948 and China in 1983. This was due to strong opposition by tradition bound groups, the illiterate masses as well as the Opposition parties who took advantage of the democratic form of government, protesting against every government move to curb population in the name of freedom. In fact Mrs Gandhi's defeat in the 1977 general elections is a good example of what the Opposition did. Second, production did not increase in proportion to the size of the work force because, in a number of cases, workers were not employed on the basis of performance; rather on the basis of favouritism and nepotism. Therefore, in some cases undeserving candidates were given jobs, resulting in poor performance. Third, population is considered a productive resource as long as people belonging to the working age group are employed and there is a very low unemployment rate. Not only the quantity but the quality of work force is very important for maintaining a high level of production per worker and bringing the cost of production down. However, in India this is not the case. Only one-third of the population constitutes the work force. Production per worker is low compared with that in Japan and other western industrial democracies. This ratio must change and a large number of unemployed workers should be brought into productive work force by creating additional jobs. To encourage productivity, India should develop a system comparable to that of Japan and the western industrial nations where a worker is paid for productive work, that is, a production-oriented, work force should be developed. Fourth, strikes and lockouts should be banned in the case of essential services and should be kept to the minimum in other industrial sectors. Man-days lost on account of strikes and lockouts increased from 4.9 million in 1960-61 to 77.4 million in 1981-82 (44.2 million man-days were lost owing to the Bombay Textile Workers' strike) and 44.3 million during 1983-84 including 19.3 million as a result of the Bombay textile strike. Such high incidences of strikes and lockouts lead to an increase in production costs and create uncertainties among the economic community. Workers' grievances should be heard but national interest should come first. During the Emergency (1975-77) everyone worked and a mood of discipline developed among workers. It does not mean that India has to resort to that kind of policy; however, discipline must be brought into everyday life of the Indian workers who should take pride in their work.

NOTES

S. Chandrasekhar, *Infant Mortality, Population Growth, and Family Planning in India* (London: George Allen and Unwin Limited, 1971).

Norton Ginsburg, *The Pattern of Asia* (Englewood Cliffs, New Jersey: Prentice-Hall, Inc., 1958). p. 465.

P.P. Karan and Christopher Boerner, "Spatial Patterns of Human Fertility Behaviour in India," *National Geographer*, Vol. 8 (1973), pp. 1-13.

Gunnar Myrdal, *Asian Drama: An Inquiry into the Poverty of Nations*, Vol. I (New York: Twentieth Century Fund Press, 1968), p. 387.

Norman J.G. Pounds, *Political Geography*, 2nd ed. (New York: McGraw Hill Book Company, 1972), p. 125.

B.K. Roy, *Census of India, Population Density Map* (New Delhi: Census of India, 1982).

B.L. Sukhwal. Due to the intense family planning programme during the Emergency between 1975 and 1977, the true figure was twelve million rather than the thirteen million cited earlier. The actual average increase during the 1971-81 decade for each year was 13.58 million. The needed resources for every year would be 121,274 schools, 388,162 teachers, 2,619,809 homes, 197.257 million meters of cloth, 13,103,586 quintals of food, and 4,187,166 jobs.

United Nations; *Demographics Yearbook*, 1981 (New York: United Nations, 1982).

Paul English Ward, *World Regional Geography: A Question of Place* (New York: Harper and Row Publishers, 1977), p. 145.

CHAPTER 7

Conclusions

THE key to the economic prosperity of India over the next few years lies in rapid industrial expansion. The labour force as well as a large number of industrialization units can help to absorb unemployed skilled professionals, thus making them productive members of society rather than dependants upon an already overburdened working population. India, however, should not follow the development model adopted by industrialized nations. The industrialized nations had the advantage of having an abundant supply of natural resources in relation to demand when they started out on economic development. The fossil fuel subsidy was very large, and the free energy from the subsidy triggered a series of fossil fuel-related technological innovations which had a multiplier effect on economic growth. Moreover, if these natural resources were not available at home, the advanced countries such as Britain embarked on a policy of colonialism (Dennis Pirages, 1978, p. 248).

India, however, did not have these advantages when it decided to follow the path of economic development. Even if the resources available are adequate for industrial growth, it takes a long period of time to develop them. India does not have that time. It took nearly three hundred years for the advanced nations to industrialize; India cannot afford such a long time. Nor does it have colonies to subsidize its industries, provide cheap labour and raw materials, nor large markets where finished products can be sold. India cannot acquire territories through military conquest (the same is true now for other countries, including the nuclear superpowers) nor are there sparsely settled regions left in India, that is, no frontiers to explore. On the other hand, India is a very densely populated country where standards of living are low. The people in India are aware of the higher per capita incomes and comfortable life-style enjoyed by the citizens of the affluent nations. Ideally, they would strive to achieve the same standards of living. The point, however, is that the principles by which the industrial societies were governed during their economically progressive periods are no longer applicable in developing societies. For example, in their formative years of industrialization, the industrial societies used child labour, a sixty-hour work week, and subsistence level wages. Developing societies, such as India, have adopted child labour abolition laws, minimum wages, a fixed forty-hour work week, retirement benefits, health benefits, and other economic benefits to workers. Besides, workers are paid according to the time spent at the work place rather than production per hour.

To avoid the ills of industrial societies, such as shattered family lives, mental disturbances, crime, urban squalor, mass unemployment, alcoholism, drug use, and wealth disparities, India should maintain a dual purpose economy, that is, labour intensive agricultural production and a limited sphere of industrial development so as to maintain traditional Indian values and cultural norms. The majority of people in industrial societies cannot claim to be happy because of the tremendous pressure on an average individual. India must develop at least the basic infrastructure to provide medical care, an adequate diet, basic shelter, clothes, education, literacy, and mass communication, and also maintain political democracy. It is apparent, though, that freedom should not be negotiated for anything else. The planning process should strive for a labour intensive economy concentrating on agriculture, rural development and appropriate technologies in facilitating a non-energy intensive, decentralized, non-capital intensive, easy-to-understand approach to economic growth (Nicholas Jaquier, 1976). This approach is appropriate for India because it may help to eliminate social and economic inequalities among various groups, maintain diverse cultural patterns, provide basic human needs rather than the market demand, bringing about overall satisfaction even though there will be less capital and resource consumption than in energy-intensive industrialized nations. A remarkable aspect of the Indian economy has been the structural change from a stagnant agricultural one to a dynamic industrial one incorporating sophisticated technologies. A systematic planning process of the economy has encouraged new entrepreneurs and has prevented the concentration of capital in the hands of a few established business houses. India must strive for self-reliance in all fields of production and adopt a policy of non-alignment in international politics. It should strive for global international trade with the Third World and industrialized nations, continue to promote scientific exchanges with industrialized nations, mass produce small machines for agricultural and service industries, aim at full employment of the agricultural and technical labour force, and use renewable

Conclusions

sources of energy, such as methane gas from cow dung, solar energy, tidal energy, geothermal energy, and wind power for sustained progress. These sources of energy, with small plants distributed throughout India, especially in the villages, may improve the conditions of the rural poor. Politics should be kept out of these economic ventures and proper studies should be conducted to evaluate various resources in different parts of India. This will assist the future planning process. Finally, it is imperative that India take appropriate measures to curb population growth immediately. National interest should be placed before political and party interests in bringing about a reduction in the birth rate. This should be done through education rather than by coercion.

The process of economic development in India since Independence had to face a number of setbacks. A variety of climatic factors have had a significant bearing on the political situation of India—its internal unity or disunity, its economic viability, and its regional disparity. Many of the nation's political problems have been caused by such natural calamities as floods, droughts, and regional shortages of food. Climatic conditions have influenced indirectly the problems relating to the selection of dam sites, conservation of forests, and soil erosion. The real political strength of a nation lies in its stock of natural resources which forms the physical foundation for its industries and other economic activities. Thus, the unequal distribution of agricultural and mineral resources in India has affected the economic viability and political stability of the nation as a whole as well as its various regions. This unequal distribution of resources has created regional disparity and rivalry among the states and has contributed to fragmentation and regionalism in the nation.

The uneven distribution of agricultural resources in relation to population has resulted in some states like West Bengal and Kerala being deficient in food, whereas other states such as Andhra and Punjab having surplus food. Crop failure, due to drought, flood, or other hazards, forces the central government to buy foodgrains from foreign markets; this puts a strain on the already scarce foreign exchange reserves in the country. What is worse is that adverse media reports in foreign countries project India as a country of starving millions.

The unequal distribution of minor resources has posed problems of equitable distribution of industrial establishments in various states. Industrial capacity and industrialization are the cornerstone of political power of a nation state. Most of the large industrial complexes in India are situated near big cities, such as Calcutta, Bombay, Madras, Delhi, Bangalore, Hyderabad, Kanpur, and Visakhapatnam; consequently, these cities have experienced a heavy influx of unskilled workers resulting in labour unrest as well as slum conditions. The problems of unequal distribution of industries were partially met by the central government's efforts to establish industrial plants in various states in response to locally available resources. The central government has tried to provide reasonably equal opportunity for the industrial development of every state. However, because of the unusual concentration of heavy industry in the Chota Nagpur Plateau, that area has developed labour unrest which contributes to political instability in the region. For example, the State governments of West Bengal and Bihar in this region became unstable after the 1967 general elections, and the ministries were toppled several times. Eventually, West Bengal turned to a CPI (M) and Bihar adopted the Janata Party rule after June 1977. During the January 1980 general elections and June 1980 state elections, Bihar voted for the Congress (I), but the CPI (M) maintained their domination in West Bengal. The party's position improved because the state government devoted some efforts to improve the conditions of the lower section of the society, especially the industrial workers.

Industrial expansion has been stifled, not only by the scarcity of essential inputs, such as power, coal and transport services, but also by poor management. Measures for increasing industrial production should include: higher industrial investment, encouragement of private investment and reduction of taxes on industries. Besides, to finance public investment, the government should borrow from banks, because the increase in the yield from government securities could make them a viable alternative for the ordinary investor. A monetary policy that allows a steady growth of the money supply at around twelve percent per annum can contain inflation, create a stable environment for higher investment and sustain growth. It would be beneficial for the government to get rid of the hundreds of meaningless industrial and commercial enterprises through sale or closure. As a result of their losses, these enterprises act as an enormous and continuous drain on resources. However, the vested interests by politicians of the ruling party and the Opposition see to it that these establishments are under the public sector, because they fear that a profitable and independent private sector could create its own power system and endanger the incumbent politicians.

Since India is deficient in certain minerals and fuels, significant sums of money must be expended in importing these items from foreign countries to meet the demand at home. After the oil embargo by the Middle Eastern countries, India faced a crisis of unprecedented magnitude, and its oil bill jumped four-fold. To acquire scarce resources, India has to maintain good relations with various foreign

Conclusions

countries and power blocs, especially with ideologically similar countries, such as the United States, the nations of Western Europe, and the Middle Eastern states. Indian scientists have been forced to find new sources of energy because of the low quality of coal, lack of sufficient quantity of petroleum, and unequal distribution of water-power resources. They are also engaged in finding alternate sources of energy, such as gobar gas, solar energy, tidal energy, geothermal energy, and other non-conventional sources. Nuclear energy was considered necessary to meet the growing demands; therefore, on May 18, 1974, India exploded an underground nuclear device in order to develop nuclear power for peaceful purposes. India also refused to sign the nuclear nonproliferation treaty because it was discriminatory to small countries and favoured the big nuclear powers. She has always supported the total ban on nuclear weapons and fully supports the nuclear disarmament by all nations.

Widespread poverty, regional economic disparities, and political instability can be attributed at least in part to India's immense population and its uneven distribution. India has, however, finally become aware of over-population as a national problem and has started a massive family planning programme under which 32.73 million sterilizations have been performed in the country between 1952 and 1980. Over 23.7 million couples have been protected by family planning and welfare programmes representing a total of nearly 25.9 percent of the total number of reproductive couples in the country. It is heartening to note that between 1956 and 1983, 54.73 million births were averted, a phenomenal achievement for a developing nation. In spite of a massive family planning and sterilization programme undertaken by the government, population has been growing at an alarming rate of about 13.58 million per year. At present the total population of India is over 700 million. The uneven distribution of population has generated several problems for the central administration as well as for the various state governments. Some of the most densely populated states, such as Kerala and West Bengal, have changed their allegiance to Communist governments, hoping somehow to eliminate existing food scarcities, low wages, unemployment, inadequate housing, and generally poor living conditions. The densely settled Northern Plain has become politically unstable since March 1967, owing to regional food shortages, widespread unemployment of educated young people, and the existence of a large number of landless labourers; consequently, the Congress Party was voted out of power.

Underdeveloped countries are demanding an equitable price for their raw materials and the import of technology to develop their own resources to serve the masses. But the industrialized and capitalistic nations are interested in the survival of their own system of neocolonialism to further their aims. The control of raw materials and the markets for their manufactured commodities by the capitalistic nations, through multinational corporations, is carried on with the help of a small number of native elites in underdeveloped and developing nations who are not concerned about poverty. In India, however, the masses are more aware of their condition than are the people in some other developing countries because India, being the largest democracy in the world, chooses her leaders through ballot boxes. In fact, India has achieved technological advancement. India is exporting engineering and industrial goods to several industrialized nations, as well.

India's position as an industrial nation is reinforced by the large pool of scientific and technical manpower and a skilled labour force which ranks as the third largest in the world. This phenomenal progress, achieved during a short period of planning process, has developed the economic independence of the Indian nation, and as a result, India could follow a policy of non-alignment. Consequently, the image of India has improved among the comity of nations.

In conclusion, the bonds of political unity which have been brought into existence in independent India must be strengthened by more social and economic integration. The political future throughout South and Southeast Asia depends largely on one of the two great neighbouring states, Communist China or Democratic India, being more successful in solving its economic problems. Failure in India could mean the end of democracy there and in some of the smaller nations as well. Thus, India must succeed in its planning programmes. Economically, India must progress at a faster rate than China and must control its population if it is to attain success in its democratic ideals. The present family planning programme should be extended, and the masses should be better educated about its techniques and objectives. The last seven general elections have indicated that democracy in India has survived due to maintenance of unity of the nation and the accelerated rate of economic development. In the final analysis, India may improve its position among the comity of nations, especially among the industrial democracies of the West and eventually earn respect among them. Industrial nations have depleted a large proportion of their resources whereas India has started exploration and exploitation of her resources. Also, India's plants are modernized contrary to the outdated plants of the industrial nations except Japan. The country is capable of attaining substantial increases in production from existing capabilities through small investment in modernization

Conclusions 177

and upgrading of existing plants. Thus, the economic future of India looks bright provided the tempo of progress continues.

NOTES

Nicholas Jequier, ed., *Appropriate Technologies: Problems and Promises* (Paris: Organization for Economic Cooperation and Development, 1976).

Dennis Pirages, *The New Context for International Relations: Global Ecopotics* (North Scituate, Massachusetts: Duxbury Press, 1978).

Postscript

SINCE the completion of the manuscript, numerous economic and political changes have taken place in India. Mrs Indira Gandhi was assassinated on October 31, 1984, by two of her Sikh body guards while she was going from her residence, 1 Safdarjang Road, to her office, 1 Akbar Road. Both places are connected by a walkway. Her assassination caused shock waves not only in the Indian nation but in the whole world. Rajiv Gandhi, her elder son, was sworn in as the seventh Prime Minister of the nation. He acted swiftly in appointing a small cabinet of four ministers. Eventually, he was elected unanimously by members of the party in Parliament and the Pradesh Congress organizations of all states. Soon after his election and during his first week in office, Rajiv Gandhi set up a three-man ministerial committee to suggest a way out of the Punjab impasse, invited the leaders of the Assam student movement for talks, set up an expert panel to suggest a new education policy, ordered the creation of National Wasteland Development Board, and created a Central Ganga Authority to clean up the Ganga. He also made it clear to ministers and senior civil servants that he expected results, and that he would give them very little time to achieve these results.

Rajiv Gandhi also restructured some of the ministerial portfolios and excluded some senior cabinet ministers of Mrs Gandhi's cabinet. Pranab Mukherjee, the senior-most minister holding the finance portfolio in Mrs Gandhi's cabinet, A.B.A. Ghani Khan Choudhury, Railway Minister, and P.C. Sethi were excluded from the cabinet. Rajiv Gandhi appointed three new Congress Party general secretaries, re-allocated the portfolios of the existing ones and appointed ten new joint secretaries to give a new look to his administration. He replaced Prime Minister's secretariat personnel including Oscar Fernandes, a Karnataka-born aggressive politician; Ahmed Mohamed Patel, a Gujarati Muslim, the AICC (I) joint secretary; V.S. Venkatraman, a Brahmin from Tamil Nadu, as the special assistant to the Prime

Minister: Montek Singh Ahluwalia, Oxford-educated Sikh to join the Prime Minister's secretariat to take up economic decision-making process; and Arun Singh, a cousin of Rajiv to take up as parliamentary secretary. R.K. Dhawan, the special assistant to late Prime Minister Mrs Gandhi, was asked to resign. Dhawan worked as special assistant to Mrs Gandhi for fourteen years and was her most trusted advisor. Rajiv Gandhi brought younger, energetic, and forward-looking men in his administration.

To improve the economy, Rajiv Gandhi appointed a new finance minister, V.P. Singh, three new members of the Planning Commission (two of the existing members were asked to leave), a new Governor of the Reserve Bank of India, and India's nominee on the executive boards of the World Bank and International Monetary Fund was replaced. The public sector was served notice that it would have to perform and show profit as well as increase production to meet the growing demand at home and additional products for export.

Along with internal organization, Rajiv Gandhi was simultaneously preparing for the eighth general elections. On November 13, 1984, he announced that general elections would be held on December 23, 27, and 28, 1984. The eighth Lok Sabha comprised 542 members, excluding two nominated members by the President of India. General election was not held for twenty-seven seats in Assam and Punjab, the troubled states engulfed in agitation. The Congress (I) Party won 403 seats out of 513 for which elections were held. Except Andhra Pradesh and West Bengal, opposition parties performed miserably, even the party bosses were defeated. The opposition stalwarts like A.B. Vajpayee, Chandra Sekhar, H.N. Bahuguna, Ram Jethmalani, Satish Agarwal, and Maneka Gandhi were defeated by newcomers in politics of the Congress (I) party. In Andhra Pradesh, the regional party of Telugu Desam won twenty-eight seats out of forty and in West Bengal, the Communist Party (Marxist) won eighteen out of forty-two seats, whereas the Congress (I) won only six and sixteen seats, respectively. The Congress (I) won the highest majority of votes and seats of any previous election including the landslide victory of Mrs Gandhi in 1971 and 1980. The party won 78.55 percent of the total seats, more than three-fourths of the majority.

After attaining the absolute majority in the Parliament, Rajiv Gandhi made political history by an amendment to the constitution that will automatically disqualify a legislator if he/she switched loyalties from one political party to another. The anti-defection bill passed unanimously by both houses of Parliament marked the fulfilment of a government pledge that it would provide a healthier political environment in the country. This bill will end an era of "politics without principles," and "politics of Aya Ram Gaya Ram."

In State assembly elections held on March 2 and 5, 1985, the Congress (I) party won majority in eight of the eleven states that went to polls, but lost in Karnataka, Andhra Pradesh, and Sikkim due to local influential political figures leading the parties in these states. However, the Congress (I) still maintained majority in the Lok Sabha and majority of the state assemblies. In the by-elections held in April 1985, the Congress (I) party lost heavily which indicates that Rajiv Gandhi should continuously strive for betterment of the people and clean up the political party machinery as well as administrative set-up to maintain political hold of the country. The voters of India should not be taken for granted; a party must show results through performance rather than slogan mongering. However, it is too early to blame Rajiv Gandhi for all the shortcomings of national politics and economic failures. He is still considered to be a clean politician with progressive ideas and the good of the people in mind.

On the economic front, the Seventh Five Year Plan (1985-90) will remain the same as formulated earlier despite the tight resource position, under which public sector outlay would be $1.5 billion. The Prime Minister explained that the plan outlay should not be lowered because of tight resource position but he emphasized that the country needs more stringent financial discipline, cutting out wasteful expenditure, insistence on efficient collection of taxes, and working towards a tighter system of priorities. He asked planners to give top priority to agriculture and take into account high technologies in formulating the Seventh Five Year Plan for industrial growth. He argued that there is an urgent need to complete the projects on time so as to avoid wasting of resources. Industry must keep pace with new technological advances in the field. The Economic Survey (1984-85) showed that agricultural performance will have to show continued improvement if the economy is to grow at the targeted rate of five percent per year in the Seventh Five Year Plan. In industrial sector, India had the prerequisite of a large domestic market for industrial products, a diversified industrial base, ready availability of business skills, and skilled manpower. Thus, the Indian industry should be able to grow at a rate of eight to nine percent a year compared with only six percent during the Sixth Plan. To maintain such a rate of growth, there should be a tighter fiscal discipline including tighter programming and monitoring of the public expenditure, greater caution in providing subsidies, reducing state overdrafts, and an acceleration of India's export capabilities.

The Prime Minister identified energy, power, communication, transport and high technology areas as potential fields for foreign investments. To foreign investors, India offers a massive market consisting of 780 million people, assured political stability, democratic form of government, forward looking consistent industrial policies, and a broad industrial base which could be an ideal environment for investment. India's record of repayment of loan is outstanding as well. A four-day exhibition, "U.S. Electronics 85" of American electronic companies held in the last week of February 1985 at the Taj Palace Hotel in New Delhi, attracted about sixty-five American companies manufacturing sophisticated electronics equipment. The equipment represented by the American companies included computers, computer peripherals, microprocessor-based instrumentation systems, electronics test and measuring instruments, telecommunication equipment, simulators, electronic bio-medical equipment, and electronics components and instruments. During this exhibition, eleven American companies had signed agreements with Indian software and hardware concerns for collaboration. The amount of business generated through approval of licenses to American companies for exporting products to India totalled $358.1 million in 1984 as compared to $332.9 million in 1983, and this is expanding. Coca-Cola and IBM are negotiating to come back in India; these companies were expelled from India in 1978 by the Janata Government. The Prime Minister said that India missed one bus in the industrial revolution and has not been able to catch up for three hundred years. Maybe we did not get on the second bus, that of electronics and computers, but he thought we can now run behind and be in position when we can jump on. There are at present seventy-five wholly foreign-owned enterprises in the country, of which more than a third were established in 1984. Economic experts believe that this is only a beginning and industrial growth rate should stabilize around ten percent a year by 1990. There is absolutely no reason why India should not aim at a harvest of 400 million tons of foodgrains by the year 2000 and steel output nearer to 100 million tons. The prosperity of India depends upon enlarging the industrial base, maintaining agricultural productivity high, and expanding industrial production aiming at export. India should maintain her population growth at or below the two percent level per annum.

The new annual budget presented by the Finance Minister, V.P. Singh, for 1985-86 included a series of measures aimed at promoting industrial growth, encouraging stock market, cutting personal and corporate taxes, slower growth in defence spending, and encouraging foreign investment including by Indians living abroad. Foreign investors, and not just Indians living abroad, are encouraged by the relaxed investment environment and a policy of *laissez faire* capitalism which is to stay in India and encourages foreign companies to enter and invest in India as well as expand existing investments. Duties on some advanced computers not manufactured in India would be lifted. The government has also announced its intention to simplify drastically the takeover of financially ailing companies by healthier ones. Nearly all political parties were unanimous in approving the changes that the new government has proposed in the economic planning of India. A proposed budget outlay of $82.7 billion for 1985-86 ending on March 31, 1986, with a deficit of $2.79 billion down from the estimated $3.32 billion from the current year was proposed. A healthy aspect has emerged for the last few years regarding India's foreign exchange reserves. In 1973-74 the resources were Rs. 5,808 million, in 1977-78 it was Rs. 52,919 million, in 1984-85 it was Rs. 63,102.8 million, and it is still improving. These reserves are coming mainly from the Indians living abroad.

The new government of Rajiv Gandhi has started a political economy of India with vigour and he hopes to take India into the twenty-first century as a highly industrialized nation, but to what extent he will be able to accomplish his objectives depends upon many complicated and interrelated economic, political, administrative, and social factors. To be successful, he should get cooperation from opposition parties, administrative bosses, and his own colleagues in Parliament. He has, however, started his prime ministership with a zeal to improve the economic conditions and political climate of the country and its people by introducing a new approach to the budget process and five year plans. His aim is to enlarge the private sector of the economy and to improve the performance of the public sector by adopting specific measures for increasing production as well as streamlining the administrative set-up. Most of the economists and private sector investors have been encouraged by his initiatives. The *Wall Street Journal* put it clearly that India is only beginning to realize its vast economic potential. Its policy makers could do more to help, but at least they now seem to have crossed the intellectual hurdle of concluding that markets make smarter decisions than bureaucrats. Therefore, Rajiv Gandhi has adopted a progressive path for the economic future of India.

More than a year has passed since Rajiv Gandhi won an impressive victory at the polls and became the Prime Minister of India. The country is in a buoyant mood on various fronts and people are gaining confidence. Since Independence, most of the prime ministers had difficulty in satisfying the public at home; however, Nehru and Mrs Indira Gandhi were respected in the international arena. Rajiv Gandhi, on the other hand, has gained confidence, and respect at home as well as on the international scene. At home, he solved acute problems facing

Postscript

the nation for years, such as the Punjab crisis, reaching Assam accord, building confidence among people through economic surge, pushing forward in removing political corruption, bringing political stability, and earning respect from the Opposition.

Soon after taking office, he concentrated on solving the Punjab crisis and appointed Arjun Singh, the Chief Minister of Madhya Pradesh, as the Governor of Punjab. Through diplomacy, the Punjab Accord was signed on July 24, 1985, between the Prime Minister and Sant Harchand Singh Longowal. According to the Accord, the principle of continuity and linguistic affinity with a village as a unit has been recognized. Punjab was awarded the Chandigarh Capital Project area that comprises nearly seventy percent of the Union Territory. The town of Mani Majra and the adjacent areas minus the Sukhana Lake will be awarded to Haryana. A commission constituted with the help of linguistic experts will determine the remaining Hindi speaking areas of Punjab, which were to be transferred along with Chandigarh on January 26, 1986. Haryana Government offices have already been cleared. The claims and counter claims for readjustment of the existing Punjab and Haryana boundaries will be settled by another commission.

The agreement recognizes the present usage of water of the Ravi-Beas rivers between Punjab, Haryana, and Rajasthan as of July 1, 1985. The conflicting claims over the remaining waters would be worked out by a tribunal headed by a Supreme Court judge. The ruling would be delivered within six months and would be final and binding on all three states. The division of waters of the Ravi-Beas rivers has remained a problem between three states since the bifurcation of Haryana and Punjab in 1971. This agreement may solve the long existing problems between these three neighbouring states.

Along with the Accord, the Prime Minister declared that elections in Punjab be held on September 22, 1985, before the due date to extend the Presidential rule on October 6; however, on August 20, Sant Longowal was assassinated by two Sikh youths. Thus, the election commissioner of India postponed the Punjab elections from September 22 to 25 to accommodate the period of mourning. The elections were conducted with extreme security measures and were peaceful. The Akali Dal won seventy-three seats—a majority out of 155 seats contested. On the other hand, the Congress (I) won only thirty-two seats, the Bhartiya Janata Party three, the Janata Party one, the Communist Party of India one, and Independent five. There was an unusually high voter turnout of 66.54 percent, which proved that the people of the state, collectively, had no faith in boycotters of elections and the instigators of violence. Surjit Singh Barnala of the Akali Dal (the Sikh religious and regional party) became the Chief Minister and the state is returning to normalcy. Chief Minister Barnala stressed that his government will cooperate with the Centre and crush terrorists. The administration's first policy pronouncement in the State Assembly was that Punjab would remain an integral part of India. The Akali Dal and the government also declared their resolve to give "no quarters to any separatist or sessionist activities" in the state. The government also declared that the State Government would like to have cordial ties with New Delhi based on mutual understanding and accommodation rather than confrontation.

The second important achievement was the settlement of Assam problem on August 15. The All Assam Students Union (AASU) and the All Assam Gana Sangram Parishad (AAGSP) were fighting the foreigners issue. A large number of Bengalis migrated during the Bangladesh movement in late 1960s and early 1970s, culminating in the highest number of migrations in early 1970s. The late Mrs Gandhi was anxious to settle Punjab crisis and the foreigners issue in Assam but was unsuccessful on both fronts. Rajiv Gandhi stressed to settle the Assam issue and finally was successful in signing the Accord. The Accord specifies that January 1, 1986, shall be the base date and year for the purpose of detection and deletion of foreigners. All persons who came to Assam before January 1, 1966 including those whose names appeared on the electoral rolls used in 1967 general elections, shall be regularized. Names of those foreigners who came to Assam between January 1, 1966, and March 25, 1971, will be deleted from the electoral rolls for only ten years, and those entering after March 25, 1975, will continue to be identified and expelled. The international borders shall be made secure against future infiltration by erecting physical barriers like walls, barbed wire fencing and other obstacles at appropriate places. The All Assam Students Union and the All Assam Gana Sangram Parishad will call off agitation, and assume full cooperation and dedicate themselves towards the development of the region. Several clauses referred to in the Accord towards strengthening the economy of the state and creating peace and harmony in the region.

After the Assam Accord, the election commissioner announced that election of fourteen representatives to the Lok Sabha and 126 members to the state assembly will be held on December 16, 1985. There were 116 candidates for fourteen Lok Sabha and 1,128 candidates for 125 assembly seats. The elections were postponed for one seat due to the death of a candidate. Polling was peaceful where Asom Gana Parishad captured sixty-four seats, gaining an absolute majority, the Congress (I) twenty-five, United Minority Front seventeen, Rival Congress Party four, Plain's Tribal Council three, Marxists two, and independents ten.

This is the first time the Congress Party lost control of the Assam State Assembly in thirty-six years. A 32-year-old student leader, Prafulla Kumar Mahanta, took over as the Chief Minister of the state. His two top priorities are to implement the Assam Accord with the Centre and to eradicate corruption from the public life. He also assured minorities that they will be safe under the new government rule. He assured that the government had decided to rehabilitate the families who lost relatives during the six-year agitation campaign. Although Congress (I) Party lost the election, the Prime Minister was confident that the new government would be cooperative towards the Centre and the state will prosper.

The style of functioning of Rajiv Gandhi is quite different from that of his mother, the late Mrs Gandhi. He has not directly interfered and tried to topple the opposition ruled states like Andhra Pradesh, Karnataka, and West Bengal. Similarly, he let his Congress (I) Party lose elections to the Akali Dal in Punjab, and the Asom Gana Parishad in Assam, in the larger interests of these states and the country and as such his down-to-earth, as well as practical, approach has proved invaluable in the solution of problems that were allowed to fester by Mrs Gandhi. He wants to be sure that each state has its own identity and rights and the Centre should not unnecessarily interfere in their internal affairs. Following the Assam Accord, a solution to the insurgency in Mizoram followed with patch-up talks with the Mizo leader Laldenga, resulting in an end to the chronic northeastern insurgency problem.

The biggest achievement of the Prime Minister has been that in an amazing short period of time he was able to bring peace and political stability to the nation that was last year wrecked with furious fighting on the streets and threatened with divisions. He is responsible for ushering an era of domestic tranquility such as the country has not experienced for years. His programmes included the restructuring of an outdated educational system, the cleanup of the Holy river Ganga, and the most dramatic, though controversial, reform in the economic sector, where he has loosened bureaucratic controls, liberalized imports, rationalized taxes, and given an increased role to the private sector to increase the competitiveness of the Indian industry. According to Rajiv Gandhi, his greatest achievement during the past year was to transform the mood of the nation from one of pessimism to optimism. Even the domestic opposition admits that Gandhi's performance exceeded expectations.

On December 28, 1985, Rajiv Gandhi addressed the Indian National Congress Party's centenary celebration and attacked the party for corruption, sloth and avarice. He spoke of "self-perpetuating cliques who thrive by invoking the slogans of caste and religion and by enmeshing the living body of the Congress in their net of avarice." He was equally harsh on other groups and agencies. The bureaucracy, the police, the business community, and even the labour unions came under his attack. He openly declared that he was preparing to clean the house on a large scale. It is probable that aging politicians, bureaucrats, ministers, and party bosses may be removed and younger, energetic, forward looking, and decisive people who share the Prime Minister's ideas and ideals brought in. He spoke like a dissident, he took all the words out of the mouths of the Opposition. The Opposition leaders admit that the Prime Minister's attitude to the opposition parties is contrary to his mother's. He has not adopted a provocative or confrontationist attitude; he is not arrogant like his mother. Some opposition leaders confess that never before have there been so many formal discussions and meetings with the Opposition as under Rajiv Gandhi. In essence, the Opposition is having a hard time finding issues on which to challenge him. Rajiv Gandhi told in an interview with a TV reporter, Jack Anderson of the United States, that he plans to carry out policies that are good for the country without fear of losing power. He consults Opposition and incorporates their ideas in planning and implementation of national policies.

On the international scene, Rajiv Gandhi has impressed the world leaders with his style and aggressive approach in establishing himself as a leader. The western media, which almost shared a mutual hostility with Mrs Gandhi, gives unstinted praise to his leadership. When Rajiv Gandhi came to the United States to attend the fortieth anniversary of the United Nations, he met Rónald Reagan, the President of the United States, and discussed bilateral relations and ways to ease tension as well as reduce involvement of superpowers in South Asia. The United States and India reached for a better understanding between the two largest democracies of the world. He also discussed bilateral and multilateral issues with Mikhail Gorbachev and suddenly went to the Soviet Union while returning to India. In New York, Rajiv Gandhi also met Prime Minister Zhao Zhiyang of China and discussed bilateral issues. An important meeting took place in New York with President Mohammad Zia-ul-Haq of Pakistan, and both leaders reached a consensus to meet again. Rajiv Gandhi addressed the non-aligned meeting in the Bahamas, of which he was the chairman, and met Cuban President Fidel Castro. While returning from the trip, he visited several European capitals and the Soviet Union. He also visited Japan in December 1985.

Rajiv Gandhi became very active with five other nations to not only reduce but to eliminate the nuclear weapons from the surface of the earth. In a short period of time, he has established himself as a leader of the Third World and earned high praise for his leadership from world leaders. On the regional basis in South Asia, he initiated the South Asian Association for Regional Cooperation (SAARC), an organization of seven countries—India, Bangladesh, Pakistan, Sri Lanka, Nepal, Bhutan, and Maldives—representing over one-fifth of humanity. The areas of cooperation among these countries are agriculture, meteorology, tourism. and sports.

The seven-nation association issued a declaration pledging non-interference in each other's affairs and peaceful settlement of the region's disputes. The document urged states with nuclear weapons to sign a non-proliferation agreement that would lead to the complete halt of testing, production and deployment of neuclear weapons and called for an international conference to examine inadequacies of the international economic systems. Rajiv Gandhi told the group members that India welcomes the diversity of the region and reaffirms the sovereign equality of the seven nations, and that he had a profound faith in peaceful coexistence. President Zia visited New Delhi on December 17, 1985, and both leaders pledged not to attack each other's nuclear facilities. Rajiv Gandhi accepted an invitation to visit Pakistan during the first half of 1986. They also discussed the complete normalization of relations between both the countries and settle all the outstanding disputes peacefully. India and Bangladesh have also settled the issue of Ganga waters for the next three years. Similarly, Rajiv Gandhi was instrumental in diffusing the tension existing between the Tamils and Sinhalese in Sri Lanka and proposed to help in permanently resolving this dispute.

In conclusion, Rajiv Gandhi has established himself as a dynamic leader at home solving acute problems, creating viable economic conditions, stabilizing the political system and bringing young people into politics, reducing inbred corruption at all levels, keeping hands off from Opposition-ruled states,. and bringing confidence among the general public. If he survives the dissension of his party and remains safe from terrorists, he may bring India into the twenty-first century. There is already an increasing middle class of over 100 million people, a formidable force, and the largest of any country in the Third World. Internationally. he has proven to be a leader of the Third World countries, champion of the cause of nuclear disarmament, mediator in reducing tension between superpowers, and an ardent supporter of peaceful coexistence and to settle all disputes through bilateral and multilateral negotiations rather than confrontation. He should however, devote ample time and resources to raise the standard of living of the poor and rural areas. In the final analysis, India is fortunate to have a young leader of charismatic style, promptness in solving difficult problems, sense of national obligation, and of a growing international stature.

Bibliography

Books

Agricultural Census of India. New Delhi: Department of Census, Government of India, 1977.

Chandrasekhar, S. *Infant Mortality, Population Growth, and Family Planning in India.* London: George Allen and Unwin Limited, 1971.

Chopra, P.N., ed. *The Gazetteer of India, Vol. III; Economic Structure and Activities.* New Delhi: Gazetteer Unit, Ministry of Education and Social Welfare, Government of India, 1975.

Cole, J.P. *Geography of World Affairs*, 6th ed. London: Butterworths, 1983.

The Constitution of India, Article 262. New Delhi: The Manager, Government of India Press, 1951.

The Constitution of India, Seventh Schedule, Entry 17, List II. New Delhi: The Manager, Government of India Press, 1951.

Cressey, George G. *Asia's Land and Peoples: A Geography of One-Third of the Earth and Two-Thirds of Its People*, 3rd ed. New York: McGraw Hill Book Company, 1963.

Draft Five Year Plan, 1974-79. New Delhi: Planning Commission, The Government of India, 1973.

Dua, D.R. *Small Scale Industries and Handicrafts.* New Delhi: Sarvodya Publishers, 1967.

East, W. Gordon and Prescott, J.R.V. *Our Fragmented World: An Introduction to Political Geography.* London: The Macmillan Press Ltd., 1975.

East, W. Gordon, Spate, O.H.K. and Fisher, Charles A. *The Changing Map of Asia: A Political Geography*, 5th ed. London: Methuen and Company Ltd., 1971.

Economic Survey, 1983-84. New Delhi: The Manager, Government of India Press, 1984.

Garretson, Albert H., Hayton, R.D. and Olmstead, C.J., eds. *The Law of International Drainage Basins.* Dobbs Ferry, New York: Oceana Publications, Inc., 1967.

Ginsburg, Norton. *The Pattern of Asia.* Englewood Cliffs, New Jersey: Prentice-Hall, Inc., 1958.

The Government of India Act, 1935, Entry 19, List II. London: H.M. Stationery Office, 1935.

Hoy, Don R., ed. *Essentials of Geography and Development: Concept and Processes*, 2nd ed. Columbus: Charles E. Merrill Publishing Company, 1984.

India 1975 and 1976: A Reference Annual. New Delhi: The Manager, Government of India Press, 1975.

The Interstate Water Disputes Act, 1956. New Delhi: The Manager, Government of India Press, 1956.

The Interstate Water Disputes Amendment Act, 1968, S. 2. New Delhi: The Manager, Government of India Press, 1968.

JeQuier, Nicholas, ed. *Appropriate Technologies: Problems and Promises*. Paris: Organization for Economic Cooperation and Development, 1976.

Mamoria, C.B. *Agricultural Problems of India*, 7th ed. Allahabad: Kitab Mahal, 1973.

Miller, E.W. *A Geography of Manufacturing*. Englewood Cliffs, New Jersey: Prentice-Hall, Inc., 1962.

Mukerjee, R.K. *Economic Problems of Modern India*, Vol. 1. London: Longmans, Green and Co., Ltd., 1939.

Myrdal, Gunnar. *Asian Drama: An Inquiry Into the Poverty of Nations*, Vol. I. New York: Twentieth Century Fund, Inc., 1968.

Owen, Wilfred. *Distances and Development: Transport and Communication in India*. Washington, D.C.: The Brooking Institute, 1968.

Pendse, D.R. *Statistical Outline of India, 1984*. Bombay: Tata Services Limited, Department of Economics and Statistics, 1984.

Pirages, Dennis. *The New Context for International Relations: Global Ecopotics*. North Scituate, Massachusetts: Duxbury Press, 1978.

Pounds, Norman J.G. *Political Geography*, 2nd ed. New York: McGraw Hill Book Company, 1972.

Rao, V.L.S. Prakasa. *Urbanization in India: Spatial Dimension*. New Delhi: Concept Publishing Company, 1983.

Rau, B.N. *The Indus Commission, 1942*. London: H.M. Stationery Office, 1942.

The River Boards Act, 1956, S. 13. New Delhi: The Manager, Government of India Press, 1956.

Roy, K.K. *Census of India, Population Density Map*. New Delhi: Census of India, 1982.

Seshagiri, N. *The Bomb: Fallout of India's Nuclear Explosion*. Bombay: Vikas Publishing House Private Limited, 1975.

Spate, O.H.K. and Learmonth, A.T.A. *India and Pakistan: A General and Regional Geography*, 3rd ed. London: Methuen and Company

Bibliography

Limited, 1967.
Stamp. L. Dudley. *Asia: A Regional and Economic Geography*, 11th ed. London: Methuen and Company Limited, 1962.
Sukhwal, B.L. *India: A Political Geography*. New Delhi: Allied Publishers Privated Limited, 1971.
Sukhwal, B.L. *Modern Political Geography of India*. New Delhi: Sterling Publishers Private Limited, 1985.
Sukhwal, B.L. *South Asia: A Systematic Geographic Bibliography*. Metuchen, New Jersey: Scarecrow Press, Inc., 1974.
Taylor, C., White, C., and Gullerson, M. *India: Economic Issues in the Power Sector*, Washington, D.C.: South Asia Regional Office, The World Bank, 1979.
Three Pillars of Democracy. New Delhi: Ministry of Community Development and Cooperation, The Government of India, 1964.
United Nations: Demographic Yearbook, 1981. New York: United Nations, 1982.
United Nations: Statistical Yearbook, 1981. New York: United Nations, 1982.
The United States Constitution, Article I, S. 8(ii) Article II, S. 2(2).
The United States Supreme Court Judgment, 373 U.S. 546 (1963), U.S. 340 (1964).
Wadia, P.A. and Merchant, K.T. *Our Economic Problems*, 4th ed. Bombay: New Book Company, 1957.
Ward, Barbara. *India and the West*. London: W.W. Norton and Co., Inc., 1964.
Ward, Paul English. *World Regional Geography: A Question of Place*. New York: Harper and Row Publishers, 1977.
Weigert, Hans W. and others. *Principles of Political Geography*. New York: Appleton-Century-Crofts, Inc., 1957.

Journals and periodicals

Bhagirath. Vol. 17, No. 4 (April, 1971).
Dubashi, Jay. "The Economy, Industrial Climate; Subtle Shift." *India Today*. Vol. 9, No. 5 (March 15, 1984).
Carter Jimmy. "State of Union, 1979." *Vital Speeches of the Day*. 45, No. 8 (February 1, 1979).
Choudhury, A.B.A. Ghani Khan. "The Long March of the Indian Railways." *Indian and Foreign Review*. Vol. 21, No. 9 (February 29, 1984).
The Economic Weekly. July, 1964.
Fazal, Mohd. "Public Sector in India: A Changing Picture." *Indian and Foreign Review*. Vol 13, No. 6 (January 1, 1976).

"First Indian Launched Into Space: News Report,"*Indian and Foreign Review.* Vol. 21, No. 12 (April 15, 1984).

Glassner, Martin Ira. "A Special Issue on the Law of the Sea." *Focus.* Vol. 28, No. 4 (March-April, 1978).

"Harnessing the Land Resources." *Eastern Economist.* Vol. 47, No. 17 (April 28, 1967).

Karan, Pradyumna P. "Changes in Indian Industrial Location." *Annals of the Association of American Geographers.* Vol. 54, No. 3 (September, 1964).

Karan, P.P. and Boerner, Christopher, "Spatial Patterns of Human Fertility Behaviour in India." *National Geographer.* Vol. 8 (1973).

Khan, Rasheeduddin. "Indian Polity, 1966-67: Challenges and Development." *Indian and Foreign Review.* Vol. 13, No. 12 (April 1, 1976).

Menon, N.C. "India's Progress Impresses U.S." *The Overseas Hindustan Times,* Vol. 27, No. 20 (May 13, 1976).

Sethna, H.N. "India's Nuclear Energy Programme." *Indian and Foreign Review.* Vol. 5, No. 2 (November 1, 1967).

Sharma, A.P. "India's March Towards Industrial Progress." *Indian and Foreign Review.* Vol. 14, No. 5 (December 15, 1976).

Sukhwal, B.L. "Geopolitical and Geostrategic Importance of the Superpower Rivalry in the Indian Ocean." *Asian Profile: Asia's International Journal.* Vol. 10, No. 1 (February, 1982).

—"India's Role in Recovering the Polymetallic Nodules from the Ocean Floor and the Law of the Sea Treaty." *The Indian Geographical Journal.* Vol. 52, No. 2 (December, 1982).

"Politico Geographic Analysis of Bifurcation: A Case Study of Punjab and Haryana, India." *Geographical Review of India.* Vol. 36, No. 4 (December, 1974).

"Preliminary Survey of the Development of Irrigational Facilities in the Thar Desert Area: A Case Study of the Rajasthan Canal Project, India." *Problems of the Management of Irrigated Land in Areas of Traditional and Modern Cultivation; I.G.U. Working Group on Resource Management in Drylands.* Edited by Horst G. Mensching. Hamburg, FRG: UNESCO/MAB Programme, 1982.

"River Water Management and Disputes in India." *National Geographer.* 14, No. 2 (December, 1979).

Uppal, J.S. "Economy Took a Big Leap After Independence." *India Abroad.* Vol. 25, No. 28 (April 13, 1984).

Verma, Kewal. "Towards Self-Sufficiency in Oil Production." *Indian and Foreign Review.* Vol. 8, No. 24 (October 1, 1976).

"Who Benefits from Zonal Control!" *Swarajya.* Vol. 12, No. 2 (November 25, 1967).

Index

Afghanistan, 40, 79
Africa, 2, 15, 126, 148, 156, 161, 163: Central Africa, 84; East Africa, 138; South Africa, 86, 87, 94; West Africa, 86
Agarwal, Satish, 179
Agitations, 89
Agra, 46
Agriculture, 4, 14, 15, 16, 32, 82; agricultural experts and scientists, 37; agricultural labourers, 13; agricultural problems, 16-17; agricultural production, 38-39; agricultural resources, distribution of, 173-174; climatic conditions and, 17-25; water supply, irrigation and, 28-30
Ahluwalia, Montek Singh, 179
Ahmedabad, 122
Ahmednagar, 20
Air travel, 141-142
Ajoy basins, 54
Akalis, 75
Akali Dal, 183, 184, 185
Algeria, 87, 138
All Assam Gana Sangram Parishad (AAGSP), 184
All Assam Students Union (AASU), 184
All India Congress Committee (AICC), (see Congress)
America (see also U.S.A.), 102, 163; North America, 161; South America, 125
Amindivi islands, 35
Amritsar, 131; Golden Temple in, 20
Anantpur, 22
Andaman and Nicobar islands, 35, 97
Anderson, Jack, 186
Andhra Pradesh, 20-21, 24, 27, 28, 35, 45, 58-65, 76, 78, 87, 88, 89, 116, 127, 128, 130, 144, 179, 180, 185; Andhra Pradesh State Electric Board, 116

Ankeleshwar, 96
Apsara, first reactor, 105
Arab World, 99
Arabian Sea, 113
Arizona, 52
Arjun Singh, 183
Artisans, rural, 32
Arun Singh, 179
Arunachal Pradesh, 35, 96, 104, 139
Aryabhata, first satellite, 146
Asia, 4, 83, 120, 136, 142, 163; Western Asia, 96, 99
Asom Gana Parishad, 184, 185
Assam, 22, 27, 35, 45, 74, 76, 89, 99, 104, 116, 136, 139, 141, 163, 178, 185; Assam Accord, 184, 185; Assam problem, settlement of, 184
Association of Iron Ore Exporting Countries, 86, 89
Atlantic Ocean, 113
Atomic Energy, 104-110
Atomic Energy Commission, 105
Augmented Satellite Launch Vehicle (ASLV), 145
Australia, 36, 49, 52, 86, 87, 94, 156

Bahamas, 186
Bahuguna, H.N., 179
Bajajsagar Dam, 77
Bangalore, 122, 131, 162, 173
Bangladesh, 2, 40, 48, 52, 79, 96, 151, 163, 187; Bangladesh crisis, 135
Banks, nationalization of, 31
Barak river, 76
Barcelona, 51
Bareilly, 105
Barnala, Surjit Singh, 183, 184
Baroda, 130
Bastar, 86
Bay of Bengal, 113, 114

Beas, 54, 75
Becco Steel Costing Private Limited, 116
Beleswar Kemtrassaur, 89
Bellary, 22
Bengalis, 184
Bhakra, 75, 76, 103; Bhakra Nangal Management Board, 78
Bharat Coking Coal Limited, 92
Bharatiya Janata Party, 183
Bhaskara I and II, 146
Bhave, Acharya Vinoba, 27-28, 30
Bhima, 78
Bhoomidan, 27
Bhopal, 122
Bhutan, 52, 79, 187
Bihar, 17, 20, 22, 24, 27, 28, 35, 45, 73-75, 78, 84, 86, 88, 89, 92, 93, 104, 105, 115, 116, 130, 144
Bijapur, 22
Bio-gas, 111
Bokaro, 92, 128
Bombay, 18, 97, 119, 122, 130, 142, 162, 173
Bonai, 86
Bonded Labourers, 25; Bonded Labour System (Abolition) Ordinance (1975), 26
Border Road Development Board (BRDB), 141
Brazil, 23, 87
Britain, 5, 125, (*see also* Great Britain)
British Colonial policy, 5
British Government, 118, 119
Buenos Aires, 51
Burdwan, 92
Burma, 138

CPI (M), 174
Calcutta, 119, 122, 128, 130, 142, 162, 173
California, 52
Cambay, 96
Canada, 16, 36, 49, 51, 52, 76, 88, 102, 107, 138
Carter, President, 88, 107, 108
Castro, President Fidel, 186
Cauvery, 54, 56-58, 76
Cauvery Valley Authority, 58, 76, 78
Central Board of Irrigation and Power, 77
Central Ganga Authority, 178
Central Water and Power Commission, 77

Central Water Irrigation and Navigation Commission, 66
Chambal Control Board, 78
Chambal river basin, 30
Chambal Valley, 136
Chanda, 92
Chandigarh, 35, 115, 183
Chandrasekhar, 179
Charan Singh, 28
Chatarprabha, 78
Cherrapunji, 45
Chhatarpur, 89
Chattisgarh, 86
Chikmagalur, 89
Chile, 87
China, 2, 8, 82, 83, 91, 94, 107, 109, 135, 155, 168, 176, 186; Chinese attack in (1962), 118
Chittaranjan Locomotive Works, West Bengal, 138
Chota Nagpur plateau, 84, 87, 93, 115, 128, 130, 174
Choudhury; A.B.A. Ghani Khan, 178
Coal, 91-93; production, 92; Coal Mines Authority Limited, 92
Cochin, 131, 142
Colonialists, 5
Colorado, 51
Columbia, river, 51
Communication, 135-147
Communist Party, 183
Comparative economic structure, 1
Congress, 26, 28, 36, 110, 161, 162, 167, 168, 174, 179, 180, 183, 184, 185, A.I.C.C, 11
Cooperative farming, 28
Cooperation, international, 79
Cooperatives, 32
Crop: crop productivity and crop regions, 32-40
Cuba, 186
Cuddapan, 22, 76
Cultural factors, 48-50

Damodar Valley, 86, 92, 103, 112
Damodar Valley Authority, 78
Deccan plateau, 84
Delhi, 22, 35, 46, 70-71, 75, 78, 115, 122, 162, 173
Desai, Morarji, 28
Devagondanahalli, 89
Dewan, Professor H.R., 84

Index

Dhawan, R.K., 179
Disel Locomotive Works, Varanasi, 138
Diu, Daman and Dadra Nagar Haveli, 35
Dravida Munnetra Kazagham (DMK), 1, 18
Drought, 17, 18, 23, 41

East, 1
East Bengal, 1, 8
East Pakistan (now Bangladesh), 4
Economic porgress, 11-15
Economic world, 87
Egypt, 51
Emergency (1975), 8, 9, 13, 14, 37, 41, 42, 128, 164, 167, 169
Emigration, 163
Employment, 83
Energy: consumption of various forms, 114; process, 111-112
Essential commodities, fall in price of, 12
Europe, 118; Eastern Europe, 86, 87, 153; Western Europe, 109, 175
Export policy, 149-150

Family Planning Programmes, 164-168, 176
Famines, 17, 18, 20, 22, 45, 48
Farakka Barrage, 48, 51, 78, 79
Farmers, 22, 24, 40
Federal Republic of Germany, 16
Federation of Indian Chamber of Commerce and Industry (FICCI), 115
Fernandes, George, 152
Fernandes, Oscar, 178
Fertilizers, 30-32
Fertilizer Corporation of India, 31
Flood, 16, 17, 18, 20, 22, 23, 41
Food: national policy of, 36-37; shortage, 33; strategy for self-sufficiency in, 40
Food for Work Programme, 41
Foodgrains, 37
Ford Motor Company of United States, 152
Four Points programmes, 11
France, 88, 102, 125, 138, 152
Fuel: Fuel Policy Committee, 94; fuel and power resources, 91-104; fuel resources, 90-104

Gabon, 87
Gandak Control Board, 78

Gandhi, Indira, 7, 10, 11, 14, 18, 24, 29, 42, 75, 88, 96, 100, 110, 128, 148, 152, 162, 178, 179, 182, 184, 185, 186
Gandhi, Maneka, 179
Gandhi, Rajiv, 152, 153, 178, 179, 180, 182, 184, 185, 186, 187.
Gandhi, Sanjay, 152
Ganga, 178; Central Ganga Authority, 178
Ganga and Rajasthan Canal Projects, Rajasthan, 32
Gangasagar, 78
Ganges Valley, 161
"Garibi Hatao" (Remove Poverty) slogan, 18, 168
General Insurance Corporation of India, 121
Geneva, 86
Germany, 110
Ghana, 138
Goa, 35, 86, 87, 97, 127
Godavari river, 48, 54, 61-65, 76; Godavari **Water dispute tribunal, 63**
Gold, 88
Gorbachev, Mikhail, 186
Government of India Act (1935), 53
Gramdan, 27
Great Britain, 84, 89, 125, 152, 156, 163 (*see also* Britain)
Green Revolution, 40
Gujarat, 18, 22, 23, 27, 30, 35, 37, 45, 65-68, 68-71, 77, 78, 87, 93, 96, 99, 111, 128, 130, 161
Gulf of Kutch, 112
Gulhati, N.D., 59
Gurgaon, 22

Hamburg, 51
Harmon Doctrine, 51, 54
Haryana, 17, 18, 22, 27, 28, 32, 35, 54, 70-73, 75, 76, 78, 84, 89, 93, 111, 115, 164, 183
Helsinki conference, 51
Hemavati, 56
Himachal Pradesh, 27, 35, 71-73, 75, 76, 78, 84, 112
Himalayan region, 97, 112; border, 135
Hindu Code Bill, 23
Hirakud, 78
Hungary, 138
Hyderabad, 122, 131, 162, 173
Hydropower resources, 103-104

IBM, 181
INSAT Satellites (Indian National Satellite System), 145; INSAT-1A, 145; INSAT-1C, 145;
Indian Bureau of Mines, 88
Indian Iron and Steel Company (IISCO), 126
Indian Ocean, 2, 112-114
Indian Remote Sensing (RS), 145
Indian Space Research Organisation (ISRO), 146
Indo-Chinese war, 135
Indo-Gangetic plain, 23
Indo-Pakistan conflict (war) in (1965) and (1971), 37, 118, 120
Indo-Pakistan Indus Water Treaty of (1960), 75
Indonesia, 40, 163
Indus, 51; Indus Commission in (1941), 53; Indus Water Treaty, 51, 79, 104
Industrial Development and Regulation Act of (1951), 119
Industrial Development Bank of India, 121
Industrial Policy Resolution of (1956), 119
Industrial Reconstruction Corporation of India, 121
Industrial resources, 123
Industrial societies (Industrial nations), 171-174
Industrial structures, 1
Industrialization, 118, 119, 122, 171
Industries, 118-119, 120, 121, 122, 125, 128, 129, 130, 131, 132, 133, 171-174; heavy industries, 82
Inflation, 9
Ingedinala, 89
Integral Coach Factory Perambur, Madras, 138
Inter-State Water Dispute Act (1956), 53, 66; Inter-State Water Dispute Act (1968), 54
International Bank of Reconstruction and Development (IBRD), 50, 51, 153
International Court of Justice, 51
International Law Association, 51
International Monetary Fund, 179
Iran, 100, 101, 138
Iraq, 100, 138

Iron Ore and Steel, 83-84
Irrigation, 18, 28-30, 32, 44, 47-48; Irrigation, artificial, 47; Irrigation Commission, 29; Irrigation projects, 56
Italy, 152

Jagjivan Ram, 37
Jammu & Kashmir, 22, 27, 35, 70-71, 75, 76, 84, 104, 115, 139, 141
Janata Party, 24, 161, 162, 168, 183; Janata Government, 7, 14, 41, 96, 152, 181
Japan, 4, 16, 23, 86, 144, 148, 152, 154, 156
Jayakwadi, 78
Jethmalani, Ram, 179
Jharia, 92, 96
Johnson, President, 37

Kabini, 56
Kakapara, 78
Kalasapura, 89
Kalol, 96
Kalpakkam (Tamil Nadu), 105
Kampuchea, 79
Kandaleru reservoir, 76
Kanpur, 122, 131, 162, 173
Karamnasa, river, 73
Karnataka, 22, 27, 30, 35, 49, 56-65, 78, 89, 104, 115, 126, 127, 128, 130, 144, 145, 180, 185
Kashmir, (*see* Jammu and Kashmir)
Kattalai Bed Regulator, 56
Kenya, 79
Keonjhar, 86
Kerala, 17, 18, 22, 27, 33, 35, 49, 56-58, 61, 78, 97, 104, 115, 129, 161, 175
"Khalistan", 20, 75
Kharasangh, 96
Khomeini, Ayatollah, 101
Khosla, (Dr.) A.N., 66
Khosla Commission, 44, 67
Kissinger, Dr. Henry, 99
Konkan, 23
Korba, 92, 117
Kosi River, 20, 78
Kota (Rajasthan), 105, 131
Krishna river, 48, 58-60, 76; **Krishna Delta canal, 58; Krishna Godavari basin, 54, 97; Krishna Valley Authority, 60; Krishna Water Dispute Tribunal, 59, 76**

Index

Krishnaraja Sagar Dam, 56
Kuddapa (Cuddapah), 22, 76
Kumaon, 86
Kurnool, 22, 76; Kurnool-Cuddapah canal, 58

Laos, 79
Lakshadweep, 35
Lakshamanathirtha, 56
Laldenga, 185
Lalitpur, 89, 104
Land: land legislations, 25-28; land reforms, 25-28; land resources, 16; landowners, 24
Landless labourers, 24, 25, 27, 32, 166, 175
Laos, 79
Latin America, 155, 156, 161
Leone, 87
Life Insurance Corporation of India, 121
Lok Dal, 14
Longowal, Sant Harchand Singh, 183

Madhya Pradesh, 22, 27, 30, 35, 61-69, 71-73, 76, 77, 78, 86, 87, 89, 92, 127, 130, 136, 144, 183
Madras, 56, 60, 77, 100, 119, 130, 142, 162, 173
Mahanadi, 54; Mahanadi-Cauvery basins, 97; Mahanadi Delta Scheme, 78
Mahanta, Prafulla Kumar, 185
Maharashtra, 20, 27, 30, 35, 58-68, 76, 78, 86, 87, 93, 94, 96, 104, 111, 127, 128, 130, 153, 164
Mahi, 35, 54, 77, 78
Malaprabha, 78
Malaysia, 84, 86
Maldives, 187
Manganese, 87
Manipur, 27, 35, 74, 76, 96
Mardeora-Hirapur, 89
Maruti Udyog Limited, 152
Marxists, 184
Mauritania, 87
Mauritius, 40
Mawsyuran, 45
Mayurakshi, 78
Mayurbhanj, 86
Meghalaya, 45
Merchant, 17
Metals, non-ferrous, 88-89

Meteorological and Engineering Consultants (MECON), 127
Mettur Chemicals, 116
Mettur High Dam, 56
Mettur Reservoir, 56
Mexico, 50
Mica, 87-88
Middle East, 2, 79, 84, 99, 101, 102, 125, 148, 160, 174, 175
Mineral Division of the atomic energy, 88
Mineral Exploration Corporation, 88
Minerals, distribution of, 89; mineral resources, regional production and future potentialities, 83-91
Minicoy, islands, 35
Mishra, L.N., 139
Mizoram, 185
Mohammed Ibrahim, Hafiz, 59
Money lenders, 31, 32
Montevideo, 51
Mormugao, 51
Mormugao, 142
Mukherjee, Pranab, 178
Musakhand projects, 77
Mysore, 56, 57, 86, 131

NASA, 145
NSG, 107
Naga Hills, 96
Nagaland, 35
Nagarjunasagar, 78, 103
Nangal, 105
Narmada river, 29, 48, 54, 65-68, 69, 77; Narmada-Son Valley, 112; Narmada Valley Development, 67
Narora, 105
National Coal Development Corporation, 92
National integration, 30
National Thermal Power Corporation (NTPC), 117
National Wasteland Development Board, 178
Navagam Dam, 66, 77
Nehru, Jawaharlal, 103, 105, 182
Nellore, 76
Nepal, 79, 187
New Mangalore, 142
New York, 51
New Zealand, 138

Neyvelli, 96
Nhava Sheva, 142
Nigeria, 52, 138
Nile, 51
Nira canal, 58
Nuclear energy, 6, 105; nuclear energy plant, 88; nuclear explosions, 109, 110; nuclear technology, 109

OPEC, 100, 101, 148
Oceans, 112-114
Oceania, 163
Oil, 96-101; Oil production in India (1955-1985), 97
Oil and Natural Gas Commission (ONGC), 96, 97, 99
Oil India Limited, 97
Organisation of Oil Producing and Exporting Countries, 92
Orissa, 31, 35, 61-65, 74-75, 76, 78, 84, 86, 87, 89, 104, 115, 116, 128, 129, 139, 141

Pakistan, 4, 5, 8, 41, 51, 79, 83, 94, 101, 151, 186, 187; Pakistani war in (1965), 148
Paradip, 142
Paris Peace Conference (*see* Peace)
Patel, Ahmed Mohamed, 178
Peace Conference of Paris Commission (1919-20), Barcelona, 51
Peasants, 28
Pench Valley, 92
Periyar, 76
Peru, 87
Petroleum, 93, 102; petroleum resources, 96
Philippines, 138
Physical factors, 45-48
Planners, 82
Planning; balanced, 82; process, 82-83
Planning Commission, 11, 16, 59, 63, 119, 131
Plans: Five Year Plans, 120; first, 5-9, 29, 47, 48, 59, 62, 82, 99, 114; second, 114; fifth, 7, 12, 29, 31, 109, 120; sixth, 7, 8, 12, 29, 31, 42, 48, 111, 115, 120, 139, 164; seventh, 99, 100, 117, 143, 144, 146, 154, 165, 180
Pochampad Dam, 64, 78
Pokaran in Rajasthan, 107
Poland, 4, 138

Polar Satellite Launch Vehicle (PSLV), 145
Pondicherry, 35
Post and Telegraph Service, 143
Poverty, 42, 120, 175
Power shortages, 115-117
Prescott, 1
Prices, 14, 32, 33; rise in wholesale, 8
Private sector, 6
Public distribution system, 33
Pullambady Scheme, 56
Pune, 130
Punjab, 17, 18, 20, 22, 27, 28, 32, 35, 41, 45, 53, 70-73, 75, 76, 78, 84, 89, 93, 104, 111, 115, 164, 178, 184; Punjab Accord, 183; Punjab crisis, 183

Radio, 144
Rail, 136, 139, 142
Rainfall, 17-18, 20, 45
Rajasthan, 17, 18, 20, 22, 27, 30, 35, 45, 54, 65-73, 75, 76, 77, 78, 87, 88, 92, 97, 111, 115, 136, 139, 141, 144, 183; Rajasthan canal project, 75; Rajasthan Canal Board, 78
Ramaganga, 78
Ramagundam in Andhra Pradesh, 117
Ramghat Jaguli-Krishnanagar, 100
Ranchi plateau, 104
Raniganj, 86-92
Ratnagiri, 86
Ratzal, Frederick, 155
Ravi, 54, 75; Ravi-Beas rivers, 183
Rayalseema, 76
Reagan, Ronald, 186; Reagan administration, 108
Refineries, foreign, 102; public, 101-102
Regional structure, 1
Remote Sensing Satellite (RSS), 146
Resources, national, 2, 4
Rio Grande, 51
Rivers, 46; interstate, 52-53; river water international disputes, 50-52
River Board Act (1956), 54
Road Transport, 142, 139-142
Rockfeller, David, 152
Rudrasagar, 96
Rohtak, 22
Romania, 96, 102
Rourkela steel plant, 129

Index

SAARC (South Asian Association for Regional Cooperation), 187
SAIL (Steel Authority of India Limited), 116, 126, 127, 129
SALT II, 108
SHAR, 145
Sagar, 89
Salal Dam, 79
Salem, 86
Sampattidan, 27
Sansad, 96
Sarda Sahayak, 78
Satara, 20
Satellite Instructional Television Experiment (SITE), 144
Satellites, 145, 146
Saudi Arabia, 100, 138
Saurashtra, 22, 105
Scheduled Castes and Scheduled Tribes, 24
Sectional structure, 1
Sesagir, Dr., 108
Sethi, P.C., 178
Sethna, Homi, 105
Sharma, Cosmonaut Rakesh, 146
Shastri, Lal Bahadur, 37, 148
Sholapur, 20
Shramdan, 27
Sierra, 87
Sikhs, 18; Sikh extremists, 20; Sikh youths, 183
Sikkim, 180
Sind, 53
Singareni Collieries Company Limited, 92
Singh, C.P.M., 110
Singh, V.P., 179, 181
Singrauli Super Thermal Power Station, Uttar Pradesh, 117
Slum clearance programme in New Delhi, 162
Solar energy, 110-111
Somasila Dam, 76
South Africa, 86, 87, 94
South Asia, 79, 110, 125, 151, 176, 186, 187
Southeast Asia, 125, 176
Southwest Asia, 2
Soviet Union (*see also* USSR), 82, 87, 89, 91, 96, 100, 102, 108, 109, 118, 127, 128, 146, 148, 153, 156, 161, 186

Spate, Prof. O.F.K., 23
Sri Lanka, 79, 94, 138, 187; tension existing between Tamils and Sinhalese in, 187
Srisailam reservoir, 76
State Industrial Development Corporation, 121
State Reorganisation Commission, 93
States Reorganisation Act (1956), 59, 63
Stretched Rohini Series Satellite (SROSS), 145
Subarnarekha, 74-75
Subramaniam, 37
Sudan, 51
Surma Valley, 96
Sutlej river, 48, 54, 75
Suvarnavati, 56
Suzuki Motor Company of Japan, 152
Sweden, 87, 102
Switzerland, 152
Syria, 138
20-Point Economic Programme, 10-11, 14, 26

TISCO (Tata Iron and Steel Company), 93, 126
Taiwan, 94
Talcher, 92, 105
Tamil Nadu, 1, 22, 24, 27, 30, 31, 35, 36, 45, 49, 56-75, 76, 78, 86, 89, 104, 115, 116, 128, 129, 130, 161
Tapti, 54
Tarapur Plant, 88, 105, 107
Tawa, 78
Technology, 6
Tehri, 89
Telecommunications, 142-143, 145
Telephone department, 143-144
Television, 144-145
Tennessee Valley Authority, 78
Thailand, 79, 138
Tourism (Tourist industry), 147
Third world countries, 6, 15, 78, 113, 153, 172, 187
Transportation, 135-147
Trevelyn, Sir Charles, 44
Trade, 14; foreign trade, 147-154; international trade, 86-87; trade relations, 151-152; trade agreement, 86
Trident I, 108, 109

Trident II, 108, 109
Tripura, 27, 35
Trivedi, 107
Tungabhadra, 103; Tungabhadra Control Board, 78
Tunisia, 87
Turkey, 138
Tuticorin, 105, 142

UAE, 100
USA, 16, 23, 24, 36, 37, 41, 49, 50, 51, 52, 78, 88, 89, 91, 92, 107, 108, 109, 110, 125, 128, 135, 146, 148, 152, 153, 155, 163, 164, 186; US aid, 40; Nuclear Regulatory Agency of, 88
USSR (*see also* Soviet Union), 2, 16, 23, 36, 40, 86, 107
Ukai, 78
Unemployment, 133, 160
Unit Trust of India, 121
United Kingdom, 16, 148, 153
United Nations, 30, 50, 51, 107, 110, 148, 164, 186; UN Agencies, 79
Upper Gangetic Valley, 18
Upper Krishna, 78
Uttar Pradesh, 17, 22, 24, 27, 30, 35, 54, 71-74, 76, 78, 84, 86, 89, 94, 104, 105, 115, 130, 136, 141

Vajpayee, A.B., 179
Valeo, Francis, 13
Venezuela, 87
Venkataraman, V.S., 14, 178
Vietnam, 40, 79
Vindhyas, 97
Vinoba Bhave (*see* Bhave)
Vishakhapatnam, 22, 122, 127, 131, 142, 173

Visvesvaraya Iron and Steel Limited (VISL), 126
Vijayawada, 60

Wadia, 17
Ward, Barbara, 5
Water and Power Commission, 103
Water disputes; interstate river water disputes, 53-79
Water suppy, 28-30
West, 109, 176
West Asia, 96, 99
West Bengal, 17, 18, 20, 22, 27, 28, 33, 35, 41, 45, 78, 84, 86, 89, 96, 97, 100, 104, 115-116, 126, 128, 129, 130, 161, 174, 175, 179, 185
West Coast, 112
West Deccan, 23
West Europe, 163
West Germany, 125, 152, 156
World Bank, 50, 51, 153. 179; World Bank Report, 13
World Food Conference, Rome (1974), 42
World War, second, 163

Yamaha of Japan, 117
Yamuna river, 46, 54, 71-73
Yanaon, 35

Zambia, 138
Zamindari system, 24-25, 26; Zamindari abolition of, 25; Zamindari Abolition Act, 25
Zhiyang, Zhao, 186
Zia-ul-Haq, President Mohammad, 186, 187

DATE DUE